Byron's Heroines

Byron's Heroines

CAROLINE FRANKLIN

CLARENDON PRESS · OXFORD
1992

Oxford University Press, Walton Street, Oxford OX2 6DP

Oxford New York Toronto
Delhi Bombay Calcutta Madras Karachi
Petaling Jaya Singapore Hong Kong Tokyo
Nairobi Dar es Salaam Cape Town
Melbourne Auckland

and associated companies in
Berlin Ibadan

Oxford is a trade mark of Oxford University Press

Published in the United States
by Oxford University Press, New York

British Library Cataloguing in Publication Data
Data available

Library of Congress Cataloging in Publication Data
Franklin, Caroline.
Byron's heroines / Caroline Franklin.
Includes bibliographical references and index.
1. Byron, George Gordon Byron, Baron, 1788–1824—Characters—Heroines. 2. Feminism and literature—England—History—19th century. 3. Women and literature—England—History—19th century. 4. Heroines in literature. I. Title.
PR4392.H47F7 1992 821'.7—dc20 92—7873
ISBN 0 19 811230 0

Typeset by Pentacor PLC, High Wycombe, Bucks.
Printed and bound in
Great Britain by Biddles Ltd,
Guildford and King's Lynn

For
Geraint, Ieuan, and Mike

Acknowledgements

My first thanks are due to the English department at University of Wales College of Cardiff, and especially Professor Malcolm Kelsall who first suggested to me this area of research, and whose unfailing encouragement and interest have been a continual source of support. I must also thank the British Academy for funding my research, and the library staff at University of Wales College of Cardiff; City of Cardiff Reference Library; St David's College, Lampeter; Trinity College, Carmarthen; and Aberdare Library. Next, my gratitude is due to the editor of *The Modern Language Review*, for permission to include as part of Chapter 1 material published as '"At once above—beneath her sex": The Heroine in Regency Verse Romance' in that journal (84. 2 (April, 1989), 273–88); to the editor of *Studies in Romanticism* for allowing me to include in a different form in Chapters 4 and 5 material from an article '"Quiet cruising o'er the ocean woman": Byron and the Woman Question' (Winter, 1991); and to the editor of *The Byron Journal* for permission to include in Chapters 3 and 5 portions of an essay 'Haidée and Neuha: Byron's Heroines of the South' which appeared in the 1990 edition, pp. 37–49. Among those who have taken an interest in my work, I should like especially to thank Professor Anne Barton for her constructive criticism and encouragement, and Professor Susan Wolfson for reading and commenting on part of the manuscript. My deepest debt is to my husband, Mike.

Contents

Abbreviations

PRIMARY SOURCE MATERIALS

CPW	*Lord Byron: The Complete Poetical Works*, ed. Jerome J. McGann, 7 vols. (Oxford, 1980–91). All quotations from Byron's poetry are taken from this edition.
L&J	*Byron's Letters and Journals*, ed. Leslie A. Marchand, 12 vols. (Cambridge, Mass., 1973–82).
Works	*The Works of Lord Byron: Poetry*, ed. Ernest Hartley Coleridge, 7 vols. (London, 1898–1904).
Medwin	*Medwin's Conversations of Lord Byron*, ed. Ernest J. Lovell, Jr. (Princeton, 1966).
Blessington	*Lady Blessington's Conversations of Lord Byron*, ed. Ernest J. Lovell, Jr. (Princeton, 1969).

PERIODICALS

AUMLA	*Journal of Australasian Universities Language and Literature*
BJ	*Byron Journal*
ELH	*Journal of English Literary History*
JEGP	*Journal of English and Germanic Philology*
JMH	*Journal of Modern History*
K-SJ	*The Keats-Shelley Journal*
K-SMB	*The Keats-Shelley Memorial Bulletin*
MLN	*Modern Language Notes*
MLQ	*Modern Language Quarterly*
MLR	*Modern Language Review*
NM	*Neuphilologische Mitteilungen*
PMLA	*Publications of the Modern Language Association*
PQ	*Philological Quarterly*
SEL	*Studies in English Literature*
SiR	*Studies in Romanticism*
SP	*Studies in Philology*
SSEL	*Salzburg Studies in English Literature*
TSLL	*Texas Studies in Literature and Language*

Introduction

BYRON is often cited as an archetypal male predator: exploiter of his sister, wife, and countless other, often lower-class, women. His *master*piece, *Don Juan*, may be seen as a self-justificatory celebration of artistocratic libertinism. However, in writing on Byron's heroines, my concern is not to produce a classic feminist critique proclaiming the poet's patriarchalism, but to contextualize it. Byron's representations of women will be investigated, neither as the product of the author's possible experience of sexual abuse in childhood, troubled relationship with his mother and wife, incestuous affair with his half-sister or alleged bisexuality, nor in the light of his reported pronouncements on women and marriage, but as cultural constructs, emanating from the heart of the current debate in Regency Britain on the role of woman.

My study will show that, whereas the various manifestations of the famous 'Byronic hero' remain fairly consistent in outline, Byron's female characters range from the eroticized passive victim of patriarchal force to the masculinized woman-warrior, from the romantic heroine of sentiment to the sexually voracious virago or the chaste republican matron, and so the list goes on. Byron was constantly experimenting with the representation of women. His female characters cannot be reduced to one single prototype or 'Byronic heroine'. (The word 'heroine' is not used in this book to denote a favourable portrayal, but merely in the sense of a female protagonist.) My purpose in studying these heroines is not to exonerate Byron from charges of sexism, but to relate this male writer's ongoing experimentation with the depiction of women to contemporary ideologies of sexual difference, and to indicate the political significance of this early nineteenth-century dialectic on the nature of woman, as it relates to class and gender.

This project is relevant to contemporary feminism, in that I would argue that historicism is central to feminist literary and cultural analysis, in charting the processes of gender formation. My intention is not to privilege the present by using it as the source of authority in my readings, but to take on the otherness, the cultural specificity of past feminisms and misogynies. The ideology of gender is viewed as a dialectical process, in which stereotypes of femininity are being produced, adapted, interrogated, rejected, in a complex process of interaction between the permutations of female writer/male writer/male reader/female reader. The term 'ideology' is used here in the sense made familiar by Althusser and other Marxist theorists, as a representation of the imaginary relationship of individuals to their real conditions of existence. It is not enough merely to unmask the way male-authored canonical texts legitimize patriarchal power structures, by perpetuating ideology in the narrow sense of an imposed or false consciousness. As Fredric Jameson comments, any Marxist analysis of culture 'must also seek, through and beyond this demonstration of the instrumental function of a given cultural object, to project its simultaneously Utopian power as the symbolic affirmation of a specific historical and class form of collective unity.'[1]

At issue, then, in the case of Byron, is the male aristocratic liberal and libertarian poet who frequently offers the Utopian vision of the primacy of romantic love and liberated female sexuality, yoked to representations of woman as inevitably and sublimely self-sacrificial victims. The ideology of female self-determination which he counters is propounded by contemporary male theorists, but most widely disseminated in polite literature by bourgeois women writers. Rational, Christian, politically conservative: its own Utopian vision of woman as endowed with the important social role of guardian of society's morals is based to some extent on an internalization of such patriarchal 'feminine' norms as female chastity, submission, and propriety. This (admittedly oversimplified) formulation illustrates that it is not possible to assume that women's experience necessarily generates an oppositional politics, either straightforwardly progressive or indeed recognizably feminist in the modern sense of the word.

The historian of the politics of gender, Denise Riley, usefully draws our attention to the fact that 'woman' itself, as a category, has its own fluctuating history, shaped by various philosophical and political frameworks, rather than arising out of a given transhistorical sexual difference.[2] We should also view patriarchy

[1] Fredric Jameson, *The Political Unconscious: Narrative as a Socially Symbolic Act* (London, 1981), p. 291.

[2] Denise Riley, '*Am I That Name?' Feminism and the Category of 'Women' in History* (Minneapolis, 1988).

not as a universal term for the oppression of women, but as a concept subject to change in political discourse. In evaluating the male radical Romantic poet's contribution to the contemporary debate on differentiation of sexual role, it is therefore first essential to sketch briefly the significance of 'the woman question' to the development of political thought from the Enlightenment to the early nineteenth century.

The question of woman's role in modern society was one which had vexed the formulators of liberal ideology ever since the late seventeenth century, when it emerged as a by-product of a wider political controversy. A debate developed between Royalist pamphleteers, who were elaborating patriarchal political theory, and Parliamentarians who argued instead for a contractual concept of government. The Royalist Sir Robert Filmer, in *Patriarcha* (1680), made an analogy between the divine right of the king in ruling the nation and a father's sovereignty over his family. Biblical history was cited to endorse the patriarchal family as the basic, universal unit on which all organized society was based. Monarchy was to be perceived likewise as both a natural and divinely-sanctioned institution. The contractualists were forced to consider the aptness of this analogy. John Locke therefore countered by re-defining marriage as a secular legal contract, which should be entered into voluntarily by both parties, and which should be revocable. Locke and later Enlightenment thinkers such as Diderot, Montesquieu, Helvétius, and Voltaire all favoured the right of divorce. However, Locke could not go so far in the direction of individualism as to advocate sexual equality. He therefore declared the analogy to be a false one, conceding that the family was a natural association which predated organized society. Male authority in the family was therefore 'natural', though limited by the terms of the marriage contract.[3]

This analogy of the marriage contract and the social contract was not only significant for the status of woman, and her role in society, but also formed the basis of a general debate, extended and elaborated throughout the eighteenth century, in which distinctions

[3] See Mary L. Shanley, 'Marriage Contract and Social Contract in Seventeenth Century English Political Thought', in Jean B. Elshtain (ed.), *The Family in Political Thought* (Brighton, 1982), pp. 80–95; and Melissa A. Butler, 'Early Liberal Roots of Feminism: John Locke and the Attack on Patriarchy', in Mary L. Shanley and Carole Pateman (eds.), *Feminist Interpretations and Political Theory* (Cambridge, 1991), pp. 74–94.

are made between property-holding politically participating citizens, and mere subjects, with no stake in the well-being of the state. Locke's characterization of the patriarchal family as a private, natural institution, differentiated from the public, political sphere continued to prevail. It was not until the nineteenth-century materialist analysis of Engels that the two spheres of production were viewed on equal terms:

> According to the materialistic conception, the determining factor in history is, in the final instance, the production and reproduction of immediate life. This, again, is of a twofold character: on the one side, the production of the means of existence, of food, clothing, and shelter and the tools necessary for that production; on the other side, the production of human beings themselves, the propagation of the species. The social organization under which the people of a particular historical epoch live is determined by both kinds of production . . . [4]

Katherine B. Clinton, in her account of the Enlightenment origins of feminism, has pointed out that throughout the eighteenth century many *philosophes* urged changes in the law which would secularize marriage and limit paternal power, as well as highlighting the disparity between the legal assumption of a woman's inability to function in the public sphere and the actual power and influence wielded by contemporary women like Catherine II of Russia, Mme du Châtelet, and Mme de Tencin.[5] Montesquieu and Voltaire attacked Salic law, and the French and Scots empiricists all called for educational opportunities for women. A century of criticism of the legal and cultural restraints which prevented women taking an active part in public affairs culminated in d'Holbach's defence of women's rights in his *Système Social* (1773), followed by Condorcet's *Lettres d'un bourgeois de Newhaven à un citoyen de la Virginie* (1787), which called for a programme of the immediate advancement of women to equal rights.

Nevertheless, we should not oversimplify the *philosophes*' view of women by ignoring the implications of the nature/culture dichotomy which formed the background of the debate. The traditional Christian emphasis on a genderless soul was declining in importance with the increased secularization of philosophical

[4] Frederick Engels, *The Origin of the Family, Private Property, and the State*, ed. Eleanor Burke Leacock (New York, 1972), pp. 71–2.

[5] Katherine B. Clinton, 'Femme et Philosophe: Enlightenment Origins of Feminism', *Eighteenth Century Studies*, 3 (1975), 283–99.

thought. Simultaneously, the Enlightenment became imbued with the Cartesian sharp dualism between mind and matter. Human passions were rejected as irrational, the imagination viewed as the source of delusions. The new rationalism was accompanied by an increasingly feminized representation of nature, so that intuition and sentiment became increasingly viewed as 'feminine' qualities. The coexistence of these developments in eighteenth-century thought was crucial in the formation of sexual stereotyping. For gender difference became much more sharply defined, as masculine/feminine became aligned both with soul/body and culture/nature, and then with reason/passion.[6] This is the logocentric binary system against which Hélène Cixous protests.[7] But we see here how much the polarized gender implications of this dualism specifically appertain to French Enlightenment rationalism.

Moira Gatens has outlined the philosophical, and Sylvana Tomaselli the historical basis of the paradoxical eighteenth-century symbolic view of woman as on the one hand closer to nature than man, yet also a civilizing influence, in that she cultivates, refines, and even adulterates and corrupts.[8] Sherry B. Ortner has convincingly speculated that such a polarized ambiguity is a result of woman's mediating role.[9] She is the representative of the domestic unit, the crucial agency for the conversion of nature into culture, particularly through the socialization of children. Because of woman's mediating role she is viewed ambivalently when considered as a political subject by political theorists.

For example, the culture/nature dichotomy comes into play in Montesquieu's consideration of the role of women. In his epistolary novel *The Persian Letters* (1721), he used a variation of the original marriage contract/social contract analogy: a foreigner's view of French government is ironically juxtaposed with a corresponding

[6] See Denise Riley, '*Am I That Name?*', pp. 18–40.

[7] Hélène Cixous, 'Sorties: Out and Out: Attacks/Ways out/Forays', in David Lodge (ed.), *Modern Criticism and Theory: A Reader* (London and New York, 1988), pp. 286–93.

[8] See Moira Gatens, 'Rousseau and Wollstonecraft: Nature vs. Reason', *Australian Journal of Philosophy* supplement to vol. 64 (1986), 1–15, and Sylvana Tomaselli, 'The Enlightenment Debate on Women', *History Workshop Journal*, 20 (1985), 100–24.

[9] Sherry B. Ortner, 'Is Female to Male as Nature is to Culture?', in Michelle Z. Rosaldo and Louise Lamphere (eds.), *Woman, Culture, and Society* (Stanford, 1974), pp. 67–88.

account of the tyrannical enslavement of women in an Eastern harem. In *Spirit of the Laws* (1748) the political systems of various cultures, historically and geographically remote, are examined in order to ascertain why despotism is so near-universal, and to analyse the difficulty of establishing and maintaining a moderate government. There follows an overt examination of the relationship between the role of women in society and the strategies of government. For example, in Book VII, Chapter 9, 'The Condition of Women Under Diverse Governments', Montesquieu looks at women as subjects first under monarchies, then despotisms, and finally republics.[10] Woman is in her element under monarchy: self-seeking and luxury-loving, she can make her fortune through exploiting factionalism. In a despotism, she must be entirely enslaved: in order to maximize the ruler's power, there must be no opportunity for female petty intrigue and indiscretions. In the classical republics, women were controlled, not by force but by custom, by being segregated into the domestic sphere, which had correspondingly low status—thus minimizing their influence, and enabling male citizens to effect disinterested government, uncorrupted by luxury and dynastic ambition.

In Book XVI, Chapter 9, 'The Liaison Between Domestic and Political Government', he comments that female frivolity, indiscretions, and passions are so subversive that if they were allowed free reign in an Oriental despotism: 'What father of a family could rest tranquil for a moment? . . . the state would totter, one would see flowing rivers of blood.' It can be seen that Montesquieu hives off on to women all the negative aspects of individualism: materialism, personal ambition, scheming for influence, private passions. Elsewhere he characterizes them as particularly inclined to irrational subjectivity, both from external stimuli like climate, and from their own passions.

Rousseau went further. He specifies in *Émile* that the state comprises male-headed families, rather than a collection of individuals. Political participation is based on the capacity to bear arms; women are not citizens but should exercise influence only privately, through their conjugal relationships. In Books I and II of *The Social Contract* he outlines an ideal republic based on the General Will, but in the section on Sparta he makes it clear that, in

[10] Montesquieu, *Œuvres Complètes*, ed. Roger Caillois (Dijon, 1951), vii. 341, 514. My translation.

practice, even the participation in government of a small number of noble citizens could only be achieved at the necessary cost of relegating women to the domestic sphere, and keeping the lower classes as slaves. Rousseau identifies republican virtue with masculinity. In his *Lettre à d'Alembert* he asserts that as women become more active, using their seductive power to influence public attitudes, men submit to their 'empire' and lose all sense of initiative. It can be seen that Rousseau's view that the function of a woman's life is to please man, outlined in the education of Sophie (*Émile*, Book V), is not mere thoughtless prejudice but a concomitant of his political philosophy. It is 'reasonable' for a highly developed society to separate private particularist interests from public universal concerns, and to use sexual difference to achieve this: this will diffuse any possible subversive effects of the former on the latter. Moira Gatens summarizes Rousseau's view of the importance of the family in providing the individual male citizen with access to both private and public spheres and facilitating his transcendence of the natural: 'The world of the family, infant education, morality and sensuality is private, domestic, whereas the world of work, citizenship, legality and rationality is public. Man's possibilities in culture are predicated on woman remaining as close as possible to nature.'[11] Rousseau saw the subjection of women as a tragic yet necessary sacrifice for the greater good of society. He also used the marriage of convenience as a metaphor for the social contract in his novel of sentiment, *Julie, ou La Nouvelle Héloïse*, where the heroine's sacrifice of autonomy represents that of the subject to the General Will.

We are beginning to see that liberal ideology developed as a dialectic which challenged hierarchical authority on the one hand, yet created a series of exceptions and exclusions on the other, in order to minimize the dangers of rampant individualism. Liberal ideology rested on the premise that the basis of power could be extended, yet its limits had to be defined to forestall incipient

[11] See Gatens, 'Rousseau and Wollstonecraft', p. 2. On Rousseau's view of woman's role in society, see Joel Schwartz, *The Sexual Politics of Jean-Jacques Rousseau* (Chicago and London, 1984); Susan M. Okin, *Women in Western Political Thought* (Princeton, 1979), pp. 99 ff.; Margaret Canovan, 'Rousseau's Two Concepts of Citizenship', in Ellen Kennedy and Susan Mendus (eds.), *Women in Western Political Philosophy: Kant to Nietzsche* (London, 1987), pp. 78–105. On Rousseau's comments on sexual difference in *Lettre à d'Alembert*, see Patrick Coleman, *Rousseau's Political Imagination* (Geneva, 1984), pp. 113 ff.

egalitarianism and preserve for its beneficiaries the traditional structures of authority. The culture/nature and reason/passion dichotomies came into play here, so that some revolutionary ideas could be construed as reasonable and relevant to the development of civilization (the attack on the church and absolute monarchy), whilst some traditional power relationships (the family, the class system, European world domination) could be portrayed as determined by nature. Those groups of subjects who mediated between the citizens and nature, providing their material needs—women, the working classes, and colonized races—were therefore characterized ambivalently: as innocently unsophisticated yet dangerously volatile.

Much eighteenth-century bourgeois literature therefore features the sentimental portrayal of oppressed females, peasants, and natives, paternalistically evoking sympathy on their behalf, yet also simultaneously suggesting their potentially dangerous subjectivity, which justifies the existing authority structure. Also, the late eighteenth-century novel concentrated to an extraordinary extent on the theme of the education and courtship of an individual young girl: her successful socialization could result in a possible rise through the ranks through a wealthy marriage; her transgression, however, meant social ostracism. It seems possible that these novels displaced and expressed metaphorically the universal preoccupation of the age with the possibility of the socialization of the individual subject in general.

By the end of the eighteenth century some female political writers were beginning to question liberal ideology's marginalization of women on the basis of their supposedly passionate and subjective natures. Mary Wollstonecraft, in her *Vindication of the Rights of Woman* (1792), attacks, not the conservatives who believed women were created inferior to man in the chain of being, but Rousseau, supposedly the apostle of the French Revolution. In her previous *Vindication of the Rights of Man* (1790), written to refute Burke's *Reflections on the French Revolution*, she had criticized another liberal writer's attempt simultaneously to support a constitutional rather than absolute government, yet also to perpetuate exclusions from power of large sections of the population, by mythologizing, through the use of sentimentalism, the traditional structures of authority. Now she attempted to expose Rousseau's comparable attempt to relegate women to a purely private role. She selects again the 'masculine' genre of political polemic, and writes in a deliberately abrasive 'masculine' style. Her strategy is to deny that the split between reason and passion accords with that of public/private and masculine/feminine, by asserting reason as the guiding principle of both sexual spheres.[12]

The demand for women's civil rights by the *philosophes*, which we have seen as a sporadic but never central issue in the eighteenth century, was taken up in a coherent way by women themselves in France. An organized, vocal, and specifically political 'feminism' arose in the early years of the French Revolution. Founders of women's clubs like Théroigne de Mericourt, Pauline Léon, and Claire Lacombe caused a sensation with their comprehensive programme for equal rights. At first they were listened to, for women had played a prominent part in the revolution. In 1792 divorce was introduced into France, for both sexes. However, the demise of sexual egalitarianism came in 1793 with the guillotining of Olympe de Gouges, author of *Déclaration des droits de la femme et de la citoyenne*. From henceforth the Jacobins reverted to regarding the state as a collection of male-headed families. Women were declared not to be citizens; the women's clubs were suppressed. Nevertheless, as Jane Abray has commented: 'While it lasted it was a very real phenomenon with a comprehensive programme for social change, perhaps the most far-reaching such programme of the Revolution.'[13]

Of course, the perceived collapse into slaughter and anarchy of France, the foremost centre of Enlightenment rationalism, threw liberalism into crisis in Britain. It is significant that the Tories were in government for almost all of Byron's lifetime. In the post-revolutionary period, the memory of the Terror cast a long shadow, and one which was intimately bound up with sexual role differentiation. Both aristocratic and proletarian French women were implicated in the cause and course of the French Revolution in bourgeois nineteenth-century discourse: the former had weakened monarchical authority by their dynastic string-pulling and influential

[12] For a detailed consideration of Wollstonecraft, see Moira Gatens, '"The Oppressed State of My Sex": Wollstonecraft on Reason, Feeling, and Equality', in Shanley and Pateman (eds.), *Feminist Interpretations and Political Theory*, pp. 112–28; Diana H. Coole, *Women in Political Theory from Ancient Misogyny to Contemporary Feminism* (Brighton, 1988), pp. 103–32.

[13] Jane Abray, 'Feminism in the French Revolution', *American Historical Review*, 80 (1975), 43–62 (62).

salons; the latter had exhibited an unnatural propensity for revolutionary street politics.

As the European monarchies of the *ancien régime* were transformed into bourgeois nation-states in the nineteenth century, the extension of the citizen's prerogatives was therefore made conditional on the exclusion of women, as well as the lower classes and colonized races, from the public arena. The idealized bourgeois cult of the wife and mother is the Utopian vision contingent on the denial of civil rights to women. Byron, as the fashionable poet of erotic love in the years of fame, and the liberal scourge of the establishment in his self-imposed exile, will be shown to be explicitly and increasingly concerned with the issue of sexual role differentiation, both as an aristocratic critic of bourgeois ideology, and as a Romantic writer who projects the feminine as the repressed lost self of an idealized masculinity.

In a historicist study of this kind, the question of genre is a useful starting point for textual criticism, in that a tension may be set up between expectations engendered by the history of the form, and the reactive nature of the individual text. Of course, it must be recognized that as a genre itself consists of the coexistence of overlapping modes, a rigidly schematic approach is not appropriate, but the value of broadly indicating the generic parameters of groupings of Byron's narrative and dramatic poetry has a mediatory function, allowing a diachronic perspective both on the literary forms themselves and the specific historical context of the texts under consideration. My study of Byron's heroines therefore opens with an indication of the generic horizon of the poetic tales, and the considerations of *Don Juan* and the closet drama which follow also begin with a literary-historical perspective. The first three chapters consider the oriental tales as a group, together with Byron's last narrative romance, *The Island*. Chapters 4 and 5 deal with *Don Juan*; and the drama is divided into the political plays and the mythological dramas (Chapters 7 and 8). Although written much earlier, *Manfred* has been grouped with the biblical plays, *Cain* and *Heaven and Earth*, because of its similarity of theme and poetic style, to which Byron himself drew attention.

This study will show that as Byron tested the parameters of a genre and moved from one genre to another, and as the nature of his readership changed, he experimented with many different representations of women. In any genre or subgenre, Byron often begins by dramatizing primitive patriarchal oppression within power structures like feudal despotism, or emanating from Judaeo-Christian ethics, and he frequently uses his heroines as passive victims of force or repression. In subsequent poems in the series, the heroine may be portrayed more fully and also positively: actively emancipating herself, and perhaps the hero as well, in the name of love and freedom. However, it will be shown that both Byron's Utopian republicanism and his idealization of romantic love are inextricably connected to modern developments in patriarchal political theory, the Rousseauistic notion of separate gendered spheres. Whilst the Romantic poet also interrogates this new patriarchal ideology, in so far as it circumscribes the freedom of individuals of either sex, his consideration of the role of women in society is nevertheless ultimately bound by it.

1

'At Once Above—Beneath Her Sex': The Heroine in Male-authored Regency Verse Romance

THE heroines of the verse tales either of Byron or of his contemporaries have not been the object of much critical attention, having been eclipsed, both at the time of publication and ever since, by the overriding interest in the Romantic phenomenon, the Byronic hero. In Peter Thorslev's analysis of the types and prototypes of this hero, the only reference to Byronic heroines is, appropriately enough, in parenthesis. After quoting Samuel Chew on the Byronic pairing of the daemonic male with the *femme fatale*, Thorslev comments: '(And the *femmes* in Byron, so far as I can see, are sometimes spaniel-like, but never fatal.)'[1]

Later critics have elevated the importance of the Oriental tales as complete poems, rather than as mere vehicles for the Byronic hero, but they have usually seen the heroine as merely his counterpart, or even a Blakean emanation of his soul.[2] However, considering that Byron's finest poem, *Don Juan*, consists of a gallery of largely female characters, novelistic in its diversity, it is appropriate that his earlier poetry should be reviewed in the light of his portrayal of women.

Male-authored Regency verse romances, published in the first fifteen years of the century, will be examined initially as a group with regard to their ideology of gender. Irene Tayler and Gina Luria have suggested that genre itself may be a function of gender in this period, because the novel was dominated by female authors, readers, and protagonists, while the canon of Romantic poets is entirely male.[3] However, this period actually abounded in popular,

[1] Peter L. Thorslev, Jr., *The Byronic Hero: Types and Prototypes* (Minneapolis, 1962), p. 10.

[2] See e.g. Jerome J. McGann, *Fiery Dust: Byron's Poetic Development* (Chicago, 1968), p. 189.

[3] Irene Tayler and Gina Luria, 'Gender and Genre: Women in British Romantic Literature', in Marlene Springer (ed.), *What Manner of Woman: Essays on English and American Life and Literature* (Oxford, 1978), pp. 98–124.

productive, and highly-regarded female poets such as Joanna Baillie, Margaret Hodson, Mary Russell Mitford, Amelia Opie, Sydney Owenson Morgan, Caroline Bowles Southey, Jane West, Felicia Hemans, and Letitia Landon.[4] These writers were carrying on a tradition of women's poetry begun in the eighteenth century by Anna Barbauld, Hannah More, Anna Seward, Charlotte Smith, Helen Maria Williams, and Mary Robinson, and their work retained vestiges of its Augustan heritage well into the nineteenth century. Yet the poetry of Hemans and Landon also remained popular into and throughout the Victorian era. It was self-consciously feminine both in its polished crafsmanship and in its sentimental celebration of domesticity. The relationship between female-authored poetry and male Romanticism is therefore problematic for literary historians. In *The Contours of Masculine Desire* Marlon Ross puts forward the thesis that British Romantic ideology was forged partly in reaction to the very success of literary women. The Romantics' inflation of the poetic vocation arose to proclaim the superiority of the lofty male bard over the popular female scribbler: 'Resorting to the myth of the masculine poet's unrivalled power over culture, the Romantic plants the seeds for his own self-canonization, for his victory over popular woman poets.'[5]

Male Romantic poets also sought to incorporate the 'feminine' qualities of sympathy and sensibility into poetic projections of their subjectivity, making self-possession a masculine Romantic quest. The fact that critical discussion of both Keats and Shelley has so often centred around charges of softness and effeminacy shows how literary criticism reflects Romantic ideology itself, which incorporated assumptions of gender in the notion of the poet's mastery and control of the inchoate realm of nature and feeling. Alan Richardson, in his phrase 'the colonization of the feminine', like Ross, suggests the unconscious identification of the male Romantic poet with the 'masculine' quest for scientific and capitalistic self-aggrandizement which appertained in the age of British imperialism, and which entailed repression of 'feminine' qualities.[6]

[4] Stuart Curran, 'The I Altered', in Anne K. Mellor (ed.), *Romanticism and Feminism* (Bloomington, Ill., and Indianapolis, 1988), pp. 185–207, p. 188.

[5] *The Contours of Masculine Desire: Romanticism and the Rise of Woman's Poetry* (Oxford, 1989), p. 12, pp. 270–1. See also his 'Scott's Chivalric Pose: The Function of Metrical Romance in the Romantic Period', *Genre*, 18 (1986), 267–97.

[6] Alan Richardson, 'Romanticism and the Colonization of the Feminine', in Mellor (ed.), *Romanticism and Feminism*, pp. 13–25.

As the original meaning of the word indicates, the Romantic was perceived at the time as the influence of narrative on poetry—and specifically the incorporation into serious art of elements associated with exotic tales of heroic adventure: sentimental medievalism, pathos, sensationalism, imagination. By writing metrical tales the male authors considered here were appropriating and masculinizing what they perceived as a particularly 'feminine' and therefore debased genre. In this chapter it will be suggested that male Regency poets therefore compensated by emphasizing historical or mythic active adventure, minimizing the theme of romantic love, and suffusing the issue of female chastity with the ideology of patriotism. Chapters 2 and 3 will show that Byron, however, pares down the narrative complexity of the Scott and Southey types of adventurous quests, brings back the 'feminine' focus on romantic love, and uses the genre to do something new—to present sexual relationships in an overtly political light.

In undertaking a feminist critique of this nature, one must take into account the split in feminist criticism, analysed by Elaine Showalter, in its attitude to the male-dominated literary canon on the one hand and women's literature on the other. This has produced either feminist critiques of male writers (dedicated to chronicling stereotypes of women) or a self-contained 'gynocritics'.[7] To avoid the pitfalls of the former, the automatic berating of the male author's sexism, or the obsessive chronicling of women's oppression, the heroines of Byron's tales will be considered in the context of the ideology of gender of the genre. The study of Byron's heroines is also not without interest to gynocritics. For while it is well known that these poems influenced the Brontës, once again it is the Byronic heroes Rochester and Heathcliff who have received most attention. But Byron's use of the passionate heroine to endorse an anti-authoritarian stance in these poems was a crucial factor in the genesis of the feminism of *Jane Eyre*.

In order to examine the cultural production of gender, it is necessary, as Michèle Barrett has suggested, to move away from the present convention of making the text itself the only basis for analysis, and to adopt a materialist approach in which the literary

[7] See Elaine Showalter, 'Towards a Feminist Poetics', in *The New Feminist Criticism* (London, 1986), pp. 125–43.

and historical context is also considered.[8] Consider the circumstances of the literary production of the genre of the Regency verse tale. First, it stands in interesting relation to the development of the novel. Scott and Southey, Byron's predecessors, were experimenting with the relationship between history and romance; both later turned to prose, one inventing the historical novel and the other the historical biography. Secondly, this poetry may be seen as an attempt by the male poets to capitalize on the popularity of novels by attracting the same sort of readership. At first a feature of periodical literature, the poems began to be published in expensive quarto editions, to cater for the demand for fashionable literature by an expanding, middle-class, leisured, and literate public. This readership was largely female. In his first verse tale Scott tailors his narrative method to a female readership by having the minstrel sing to the Duchess of Buccleuch and her ladies. Byron frankly admitted he wrote 'to please the women'.[9]

Thirdly, because romances were considered feminine, Scott and Byron openly disparaged the genre as mere entertainments carelessly dashed off, in comparison with their more manly pursuits of law or writing *Hints From Horace*. These poets prided themselves, however, on the accuracy of the setting and backgrounds of their exotic or chivalric tales, where the authority of the author as traveller or man of the world was at stake.[10] A notable feature of the genre is the paraphernalia of prose dedications and notes that envelop the texts, directed not at the female readership but at a small circle of predominantly male friends and literati. In *Marmion* Scott actually prefaced each canto with a verse epistle to a separate antiquarian friend. Southey's notes became so voluminous that they rivalled the texts themselves in length. (The notes to Byron's *Childe Harold* IV even took on a life of their own with a separate author and publication.) This division between 'feminine' romance and

[8] See Michèle Barrett, 'Ideology and the Cultural Production of Gender', in Judith Lowder Newton and Deborah Rosenfelt (eds.), *Feminist Criticism and Social Change* (New York and London, 1985), pp. 65–85.

[9] Medwin (206) quotes Byron as saying: 'I am sure I was more pleased with the fame my *Corsair* had than with that of any other of my books. Why? For the very reason because it did shine, and in boudoirs. Who does not write to please the women?'

[10] Byron wrote to Murray over a query on his accuracy in describing Muslim customs: 'I don't care one lump of sugar for my *poetry*; but for my *costume* and my correctness on those points (of which I think the funeral was a proof), I will combat lustily', *L&J* iii. 165.

'masculine' historical comment reflects the male authors' ambivalent desire to capitalize on the new middle-class and largely female readership, yet also to be recognized as literati, addressing a mainly male, classically-educated, and aristocratic élite (as in the eighteenth century). But it is also indicative of the use made of an escapist genre of romance or pseudo-myth to re-examine the concept of history itself. Written in the period following the French Revolution, when a Napoleonic invasion was a possibility, the romances released from the confinement of rationality fears and desires directly relevant to the present, while also endowing them with the credentials of a conscious antiquarianism. This is a characteristic feature of the romance genre. Paradoxically, its escapist nature makes it all the more revealing of the preoccupations of its age. Lastly, under the influence of *Sturm und Drang* ballads and gothic novels, the narrative mode of this poetry stimulated experimentation in metre, and facilitated the development of a freer poetic form working more directly on the emotions of the reader than polished Augustan verse had done.

The literary-historical context of the verse tales having been briefly indicated, their ideology in regard to gender will now be considered. Ideology has been defined dialectically by Terry Eagleton as 'a set of discourses which wrestle over interests which are in some way relevant to the maintenance or interrogation of power structures central to a whole form of social and historical life.'[11] Ideology of gender is not an authoritarian formula imposed from above, as Barrett reminds us, but a continuous and evolutionary process of the production and transformation of meaning. Thus, we must take into account the collusion of women themselves in the formation of these feminine stereotypes (especially as these poems were particularly popular with female readers) as well as the subsequent reaction to them of women writers.

A brief survey of the tales of those (exclusively male) poets Byron admitted to the pyramidal *Gradus ad Parnassum* in his journal of 1813—Scott, Rogers, Moore, Campbell, Southey, Wordsworth, and Coleridge—shows a repetition of themes, despite the plethora of exotic backgrounds. The ideology implicit in the thematics of the tales of Byron's contemporaries will first be considered, in order to ascertain the nature of his difference of emphasis.

[11] See Terry Eagleton, 'Ideology and Scholarship', in Jerome J. McGann (ed.), *Historical Studies and Literary Criticism* (Wisconsin, 1985), pp. 114–25.

In many cases the heroine is the daughter of a family threatened by invasion, or by a change in political circumstances: for example, Scott's Margaret in *Lay of The Last Minstrel* (1805), Ellen Douglas in *The Lady of the Lake* (1810), Matilda in *Rokeby* (1813); Southey's Florinda in *Roderick* (1814), Kailyal in *The Curse of Kehama* (1810); and Gertrude in Campbell's *Gertrude of Wyoming* (1809). Her plight, therefore, is often tied to that of her father, usually a representative of traditional loyalties or ideals, now in the process of being superseded. It is notable how frequently the heroine is the only child of her widower father. This is true, for example, of Scott's Ellen Douglas and Matilda; Southey's Florinda and Kailyal, and Oneiza of *Thalaba the Destroyer* (1801); Hinda in 'The Fire-Worshippers' in Moore's *Lalla Rookh* (1817); Campbell's Gertrude; Rogers's *Jacqueline* (1814); Coleridge's Christabel; and the heroine of Wordsworth's 'The Female Vagrant'. Nearly all the fathers in these tales are involved in some sort of armed struggle, often a rebellion or civil war. Most are depicted sympathetically, as venerable but vulnerable patriarchs. The patriarch is sometimes portrayed as powerless in the crisis; for example, the imprisoned Rokeby; or the cursed Ladurlad in Southey's *Curse of Kehama*. Father and daughter together are imperilled, representing both the heritage and the future fertility of the dynasty. The nature of the threat varies with the political sympathies of the authors, yet a concern with the possible extinction of a dynastic tradition, identified in the plot with a historical struggle for preservation of nationhood, is common to almost all.

The relationship between the heroine and her father is of central importance. Thematically it outweighs the sub-plot of thwarted romantic love, which tends to exist only to emphasize the greater priority of duty and to provide an ending of social reconciliation. In other words, the romance genre is put to the use of quashing its own romance elements, in order to inculcate all the more strongly the ideology of loyalty and obedience to the patriarchal leaders of society.

The lovers of the dutiful daughters in these tales are sometimes, therefore, their foster-brothers; the sibling relationship ensures a domestic rather than a romantic love, and a doubling of filial piety for the patriarch. This is the case with Gertrude and Waldegrave in Campbell's *Gertrude*, and with Oneiza and Thalaba in Southey's *Thalaba*. Even when romantic love does play its part, it is the pathos and sentiment of filial love that is often the emotional heart of these poems. This is shown clearly in Scott's *Lady of the Lake*, where Ellen's quest is to save her father. Even when she has the ear of the king, it is first for her father, and later even for Roderick Dhu, that she pleads, not for Graeme. This is foreshadowed by the stanza in which Graeme is first introduced:

> Some feelings are to mortals given,
> With less of earth in them than heaven:
> And if there be a human tear
> From passion's dross refined and clear,
> A tear so limpid and so meek,
> It would not stain an angel's cheek,
> 'Tis that which pious fathers shed
> Upon a duteous daughter's head!
> And so the Douglas to his breast
> His darling Ellen closely press'd,
> Such holy drops her tresses steep'd,
> Though 'twas a hero's eye that weep'd.
> Nor while on Ellen's faltering tongue
> Her filial welcomes crowded hung,
> Mark'd she, that fear (affection's proof)
> Still held a graceful youth aloof;
> No! not till Douglas named his name,
> Although the youth was Malcolm Graeme. (II, xxii)[12]

The 'hero' of this passage is the patriarch, whose authority is sanctified by his age: 'passion's dross' is set in opposition to his 'pious' and 'holy' paternal sentiments. His tears are sacramental, anointing the head of his daughter, consecrating her purity. His embrace of the heroine—conditional only on her being 'duteous'—monopolizes her feelings, excluding the young man from notice. The reverence and modesty of the young people is evidenced by her 'faltering' endearments (to her father) and Graeme's 'fear' of intrusion. Their circumspect 'affection' contrasts with the emotional intimacy of the parent–child relationship.

In the vein of the Richardsonian novel of sentiment, Southey's Kailyal, in *The Curse of Kehama*, is under constant threat of attempted rape from Arvalan, but when she is taken to heaven (presumably having died) she implores the gods to restore her to

[12] All quotations are taken from *The Poetical Works of Sir Walter Scott*, ed. J. Logie Robertson (London, 1926).

earth, in order that she can look after her father (VII, xi).[13] When the father and daughter are borne aloft by the Ship of Heaven, the poet exclaims:

> Rich is the freight, O vessel, that thou bearest!
> Beauty and Virtue,
> Fatherly cares and filial veneration . . . (X, i)

In a touching scene in Canto XIII, 'The Retreat', Ladurlad grants Kailyal her dearest wish, that they will never again be parted:

> O best beloved, and to be loved the best . . .
> Be thou in all my wanderings, still my guide;
> Be thou, in all my sufferings, at my side. (XIII, iii)

It is made clear that her sexuality is a burden to such a heroine: the idealization of a purely filial, yet nurturing, young and virginal girl reflects the puritanical basis of the cult of domestic piety. The frequent absence of a mother-figure shows the preference for depicting a young, even pre-pubescent, girl in the maternal role, instead of a potentially-threatening sexually active older woman. When a heroine is depicted as a wife and mother, she is frequently shown alone, deserted, or dying; a figure of pathos in her vulnerability. Wordsworth's 'The Mad Mother', 'The Thorn', 'The Female Vagrant', 'The Forsaken Indian Woman', and 'The Ruined Cottage' provide well-known examples of these heroines, who were also popular in the periodicals of the day. His choice of peasant or vagrant life reflects the democratic spirit of the 1790s; a decade later it is the beleaguered aristocratic lady who is more likely to be depicted.

Even when the heroine is depicted as a wife and mother, as in Campbell's *Gertrude of Wyoming*, her relationship with her father may still be paramount. Gertrude is portrayed as an infant praying for her father, whilst held in his arms (I, xii). As she grows up: 'To soothe a father's couch her only care, | And keep his reverend head from all annoy' (II, viii).[14] When Waldegrave returns to claim his bride, he is quick to reassure her: 'I will not part thee from thy father's shore; | But we shall cherish him with mutual arms' (II, xxii). The War of Independence breaks out, but he refuses

[13] All quotations are taken from *The Poetical Works of Robert Southey*, 10 vols. (London, 1837–8).

[14] All quotations are taken from *The Poetical Works of Thomas Campbell*, 2 vols. (London, 1836).

Gertrude's suggestion of escaping to England; their duty to defend Freedom is identified with their duty to stay and protect her father (III, ix). When hostilities begin, father and daughter are portrayed in a tableau, as in a historical painting, representing America under attack:

> Calm, opposite the Christian father rose,
> Pale on his venerable brow its rays
> Of martyr light the conflagration throws;
> One hand upon his lovely child he lays, (III, xxiii)

Just as they deem themselves safe in the fort, father and daughter are tragically felled by the same sniper, and fall, clasped in a last embrace:

> And tranced in giddy horror Gertrude swoon'd;
> Yet while she clasps him lifeless to her zone,
> Say, burst they, borrow'd from her father's wound,
> These drops?—Oh God! the life-blood is her own! (III, xxviii)

The father–daughter configuration is obviously consciously used here as a political allegory. Gertrude is a symbol of the young republic, America; the patriarch, Albert, represents the tradition of British liberalism from which she was born. Their murder by the British and their allies is mourned by Waldegrave, representative of British republican sympathies. Similarly, in Moore's 'The Fire-Worshippers', in *Lalla Rookh*, Hafed and Hinda's love is intended to recall that of the Irish patriot Robert Emmet for Sarah Curran; Hinda's father, the Emir, tyrannically subjugates Iran in the name of his religion, and the reader is meant to draw his own parallel with the British government, against whom the United Irishmen rebelled in 1803. Though Moore uses a Byronic theme of romantic love, he protects his heroine from suspicion of disloyalty to her father (rather unrealistically) by making her fail to realize that Hafed is a Persian. When she finds out she makes clear her horror at her father's danger: 'Holy Alla save | His grey head from that lightning glance!'[15]

It is significant that Landor, Scott, and Southey all wrote metrical tales featuring the story of the sixth-century King Roderick who defended Spain from an invasion by the Moors. The context is, of

[15] *The Poetical Works of Thomas Moore: Collected by Himself*, 10 vols. (London, 1841), VI, 219. All quotations are taken from this edition.

course, the contemporary invasion of the peninsula by Napoleon. Consider Southey's *Roderick, the Last of the Goths*. The rape of the heroine, Florinda, by the king, is emblematic of the Spanish monarchy's tyrannical rule, but the fact that Roderick is eventually exonerated of much of the blame, both by Florinda and by her father, demonstrates that the invasion brought about in revenge, by Count Julian, proved a greater evil than the original injustice. Whilst it is implied that Florinda's chastity was out of place (she should have accommodated the king's desires), the sexual appetite of three renegade Spanish women for their Moorish lovers is severely castigated. An urgent and reactionary moral is clearly meant to be drawn by Southey's British readers, particularly those inclined to criticize the (Tory) government. Evidently, a message of political quietism (reinforced by fear of invasion) is being inculcated here, through the metaphor of the necessity for female sexual obedience to the will of the male leaders of their society.

It will be noted that despite the range of political sympathies of these poets, from republican to reactionary, the sexual ideology remains fairly constant. Whatever the party-political differences, the father–daughter relationship is inevitably a simplified and desexualized vehicle for the highest ideal in these tales—that of the family. Even in its Hindu tribal dress the bourgeois values portrayed in *Thalaba* are evident: the father, content with his middling station of life; the obedient daughter providing him with his domestic comforts, and demonstrating the moral value of work sanctified by long tradition.

> Nor rich, nor poor, was Moath; God had given
> Enough, and blest him with a mind content.
> No hoarded gold disquieted his dreams;
> But ever round his station he beheld
> Camels that knew his voice,
> And home-birds, grouping at Oneiza's call,
> And goats that, morn and eve,
> Came with full udders to the Damsel's hand.
> Dear child! the tent beneath whose shade they dwelt
> It was her work; and she had twined
> His girdle's many hues;
> And he had seen his robe
> Grow in Oneiza's loom.
> How often, with a memory-mingled joy

Which made her mother live before his sight,
He watched her nimble fingers thread the woof!
Or at the hand-mill, when she knelt and toil'd,
Toss'd the thin cake on spreading palm
Or fix'd it on the glowing oven's side
With bare wet arm, and safe dexterity. (III, xxi)

The anxious stress, in these tales, on a father and his only daughter reveals a preoccupation with heredity, and the passing on of such traditional values. Scott, however, is keen to stress his heroine's heritage in terms of blood: she is always an aristocrat.

And ne'er in cottage-maid was seen
The easy dignity of mien,
Claiming respect, yet waiving state,
That marks the daughters of the great.
(*Rokeby*, V, xxv)[16]

Scott's heroines are ladies in distress. They appeal to the reader's sentiment as symbols of the call for chivalric defence of traditional aristocratic values against the forces of change. This could be compared with Burke's use of the Richardsonian sentimental heroine in his famous rhetoric on Queen Marie Antoinette besieged in her bedroom by the mob in *Reflections on the French Revolution*. Thus in *Rokeby*, when Scott wants to underline the horror of the burning down of the Rokeby ancestral mansion by the Parliamentarians, it is with the loss of 'Matilda's bower', scene of her 'duteous orisons', that he begins Canto VI, before detailing the loss to the peasant of the 'weekly dole' which doubtless she had been used to distribute. Later, within the church itself, the villainous Roundhead erects a scaffold on which he proposes to hang Matilda's father, supported by the violent and aristocracy-hating mob, unless she agrees to marry his son.

The fate of the heroine in *Rokeby*, as in Scott's other tales, is crucial because she represents, as sole child and heir, the only hope the beleaguered patriarch has of passing on his values and sphere of influence in society to a future generation. Generation is the key word here. The heroine is of noble lineage but as a mere woman she cannot carry on the family name. Her value lies in her capacity, through her future fertility, to revitalize the endangered nobility by a dynastic alliance with an ally and possible successor to her father.

[16] Cf. *The Lady of the Lake*, I, xxx; II, x; *Marmion*, VI, iv.

The Scott heroine is therefore seen entirely in terms of nubility. Her attributes are her stock, her beauty (signifying health), virginity (guaranteeing legitimate paternity of offspring), and the obedience to her father which will be transferred to her husband.[17] Because her worth is of a purely sexual nature, she cannot be sharply individualized, as can the male characters, whose assertions of will are played out in the public arena of history and politics.

The satisfactory outcome of a Scott tale hinges therefore on the successful marriage of the heroine to her father's ally. At the least, the pollution of his blood by a foreign enemy, dissident, or social inferior must be avoided. The tales thus tacitly endorse the idea of the arranged marriage, for the plot is manipulated so that the daughter's wishes and her father's neatly coincide. In *The Lady of The Lake*, Douglas's decision on where to bestow his daughter's hand is made purely on the basis of political allegiance. Roderick Dhu asks for Ellen as surety for her father's support in an uprising against the king.

> Grant me this maid
> To wife, thy counsel to mine aid;
> To Douglas, leagued with Roderick Dhu,
> Will friends and allies flock enow. (II, xxx)

Douglas does not consult Ellen, but refuses the pact on account of his friendship with the king, who is as dear to him as his daughter is. Her blush is the only response attributed to the heroine herself—and it betokens agreement with her father. For Scott never uses fathers as blocks to romantic love as is the case in Shakespearian comedy. When he does introduce a theme of forbidden love, in *Marmion*, he avoids a father/daughter confrontation, by making Clare an orphan, rightly repudiating a marriage arranged by mercenary relatives, and by depicting Margaret as oppressed by the overweening pride of her widowed mother in *The Lay of the Last Minstrel*. But fathers and daughters never come into conflict.

The ultimate in arranged marriages (between young Asians who have never met) forms the narrative framework of Thomas Moore's excursion into this genre, *Lalla Rookh*. When Lalla Rookh is taken

[17] We could compare Burke, who in order to demonstrate the primary importance of heredity in monarchical government, gives as an example the Princess Sophia who was chosen as a 'stock and root of inheritance to our kings and not for her merits', *Reflections on the French Revolution* (London, 1790), p. 33.

on a journey to marry Aliris, King of Bucharia, whom her father has chosen, she unfortunately falls in love with his court poet who entertains her on the journey. But again Moore manages to pre-empt a clash of wills between father and daughter, since the poet Feramorz turns out to be the bridegroom in disguise.

It can be seen that the sub-plot of romantic love, the only ethos articulated in these tales which apparently allows the heroine any form of self-determination, is blatantly manipulated by these poets. A happy outcome of the love story in Scott's verse tales is always linked to the defeat and death of the rebel-villain and, as in Shakespearian comedy, the further strengthening of traditional society by a marriage approved by its patriarchal leaders. A sub-plot of fulfilled romantic love, in Scott's tales, in Moore's *Lalla Rookh*, and in Rogers's *Jacqueline*, only reinforces the role of the heroine as conservative in nature, by making acceptable to her a function in life determined by her sex (that of wife and mother) and by idealizing the family as a necessary bulwark against the evils of revolt.

In fact, romantic love is regarded ambivalently in these tales. Fulfilled love is portrayed as domestic and conjugal rather than romantic in nature in Campbell's *Gertrude*, Wordsworth's 'The Female Vagrant' and 'Margaret, or The Ruined Cottage'. Even when it is portrayed, it is always overshadowed by the higher good of duty or morality. In *Marmion* and *The Lay of the Last Minstrel* sexual love is plainly opposed to that of the spiritual. The romantic love of the heroine must therefore be associated with religion, so Clare's love for Wilton is literally overseen by the church. It begins under the aegis of the beadsman (VI, vi) and is protected by Clare's sojourn in the convent. When she is taken to Tantallon Castle and is musing on the battlements, Scott has her sighing—not for her lover—but to be back in the convent, ' . . . where Duty, free, | Walks hand in hand with Charity' (VI, iv).

Scott frankly admitted that he did not excel in writing of young love.[18] It was necessary to his scheme of values that the heroine's lover be of suitable rank and political allegiance to be acceptable to

[18] 'But the Devil is, that your true lover, notwithstanding the high and aristocratic rank he inherits in romance and poetry, is in my opinion the dullest of human mortals, unless to his mistress—I know nothing I dread more in poetry than a love scene . . . ', *The Letters of Sir Walter Scott*, ed. H. J. C. Grierson, 11 vols. (London, 1932), iii. 185–6.

her father, yet subordinate to his authority, since her love for him was only the prelude to conformity with society in perpetuating her almost-extinct dynasty. As Scott humorously acknowledged, such a conventional creature was bound to be dull.

Southey went even further, voicing his detestation of romantic love, and declaring that he 'would like to see the tales which Jean-Pierre Camus, Bishop of Belley, wrote to inspire horror and disgust for the passion'.[19] He obviously tried to emulate the bishop's example. For sexuality is a snare in Southey's poetry, and is always associated with violence, evil, and subversion of the kingdom. His heroic protagonists, who embody a martial ethos validated by religious rectitude, are usually depicted as being too high-minded even to be tempted by sensuality. Thus Thalaba easily withstands the ploys of the siren voluptuaries to inveigle him with wanton dancing in the Paradise of Sin. The real dilemma is not between sin and morality but between two forms of Duty, domestic and patriotic, as when Joan, in *Joan of Arc*, reluctantly sacrifices her family life to go to war.[20]

Thalaba, however, falls prey to the temptation of romantic love and earthly marriage, instead of putting his quest first. Oneiza is unwilling to marry, as she would prefer to become a nun, but when he persuades her she dies just as the marriage is about to be consummated, and is transformed into a vampire. Her spirit tells Thalaba that he has now been abandoned by God. But her father instructs his son-in-law to thrust his lance through her body to reveal it as an evil fiend. When this is accomplished, the true spirit of Oneiza appears to tell him to go on with his quest as he should have done originally, and be reunited with her in Paradise. In this Freudian nightmare, it is evident that father and husband must unite to desecrate the heroine's body as repugnant snare, and deem romantic love no more than lust if it should interfere with Duty. The heroine herself is made to endorse this view. Southey is giving the traditional Dido and Aeneas theme a newly puritanical emphasis.

[19] Geoffrey Carnall, *Robert Southey* (London, 1944), p. 22. On the influence of Southey upon his contemporaries, see Marilyn Butler, 'Repossessing the Past: The Case for an Open Literary History', in Marjorie Levinson *et al.* (eds.), *Rethinking Historicism: Critical Readings in Romantic History* (Oxford, 1989), pp. 64–84.

[20] The puritan conflict between two kinds of righteousness in *Joan of Arc* is discussed by Brian Wilkie, *Romantic Poets and Epic Tradition* (Madison and Milwaukee, 1965), p. 39.

Sexual or romantic love for a woman is constantly portrayed in *Thalaba* as inimical to either the moral good of an individual man or the nation at large. The hero discovers a failed champion chained, Prometheus-like, to a rock for succumbing to romantic love for a maiden who herself is condemned eternally to steer the boat of Death. The angels Haruth and Maruth also fell from grace through lust for an earthly woman. Significantly, in order to release these lovers from the snare of sexuality into death, and destroy the power of the subversive sorcerers, Thalaba has to kill a virgin who has been sequestered in the land of eternal snows.

Southey's heroines demonstrate their purity by their willingness to embrace death and renounce earthly love. Florinda's death is typical:

> My Roderick! mine in heaven!
> Groaning, he claspt her close, and in that act
> And agony her happy spirit fled.
> (*Roderick*, xxiv, p. 231)

In *The Curse of Kehama* the heroine, Kailyal, loves a spirit (Ereena) from the start, never succumbing to earthly love at all. Like Southey's other heroines, she is happy to die to be united with him. Kailyal spends the whole poem warding off the attacks of the rapist Arvalon or caring for her aged father, Ladurlad. Her repudiation of human sexual attraction is shown in her welcoming of an attack of leprosy that will destroy her beauty.[21]

Although Southey's poetry suggests that yielding to romantic love is to risk overthrow by sin, it also concedes the power of sexuality, the fertility necessary to further the aims of nationalism and the necessary control of it. In *Roderick* and *Madoc* particularly, both the sexual continence of the women and their fertility must be regulated for the sake of racial purity and the preservation of European civilization. The possible marriage of Florinda to a Moor, and the attempted rape of Goerfyl by an American Indian, are averted only by orgies of violent warfare. Florinda's name indicates her potential fertility as her only value both to her father

[21] Cf. Julie's attack of smallpox in *La Nouvelle Héloïse* and Esther's in *Bleak House*. This device emphatically asserts the spirituality and denies the physical in the attraction of the heroine, by stressing the unchanged love of the young lover for the disfigured beloved. Nevertheless her loyalty to the father or father-figure is her first priority. In other words duty comes before romantic love, even at its most spiritual. The physical attractiveness of the female is doubly repudiated.

and to her king. She declares that the reason for her father's pact with the Moor, Orpas, is his 'heart's desire | To see his ancient line by me preserved' (*Roderick*, ix, p. 85). It was only the infertility of his wife, Egilona, that led to King Roderick's desire for Florinda, as 'A fruitful wife and crown of earthly joys' (x, p. 96). In all other respects, as she herself explains, Florinda was Roderick's spiritual inferior. Florinda's obstinate refusal of his advances, like the defection of his wife, sister, and aunt, for sexual relationships with the Moors, is an example of female sexual disobedience, which leads the way to the invasion of Spain.

> Woman, woman,
> Still to the Goths art thou the instrument
> Of overthrow, thy virtue and thy vice
> Fatal alike to them. (xxii)

The ideological paradox that is beginning to emerge in the characterizations of the heroines of these verse tales is that they must embody their fertility (in beauty), which constitutes their value in perpetuating their noble blood, but that they themselves must not be tainted with sexual desire, which is linked thematically with subversion and demonic energy in the character of the villain. Virginity enhances their value both as commodity in dynastic marriage and as spiritual symbol. Nubile, yet virginal, such a heroine is prey to constant attacks of rape and abduction. None of Southey's romances is complete without at least one scene of rape or attempted rape. Scott's heroines are luckier, but Matilda, in *Rokeby*, is imprisoned and threatened with a forced marriage; and Clare, in *Marmion*, has to take refuge in a nunnery to escape the attentions of the villain, and is eventually abducted by him before the Battle of Flodden decides his fate.

When the threat of rape or abduction of the heroine (a frequent subject of the eighteenth-century novel) is combined with the sentimental idealization of her father as vulnerable and venerable patriarch, and set against a background of political crisis, a powerful sexual myth is evoked. The deepest fears for sexual, domestic, and national security are tapped, calling forth a patriarchal view of society and sexuality that is perceived by these writers as rooted in ancient and universal truths. The importance of the family is central to the ideology of these tales. First, it is a necessary curb on the sexual appetite of man (and more particularly woman). Secondly, it is the transmitter of traditional values, enabling civilization to progress both morally and materially. The nation is the family writ large, the king its father. The defence of maidenly virtue is therefore endowed with the fervour of nationalism. Edward Meachen comments on Southey's *Roderick*: 'Each level of interpretation depicts a threat to the family unit, and therefore a threat to moral progress. In *Roderick*, Southey asserts the family's right to use violence to defend itself for the good of humanity.'[22] The invasion of Spain by Napoleon is imaged in the rape or pagan marriage of its daughters and wives.

Sexuality is always portrayed in these romances as a source of power. It is potentially disruptive when associated with forces of revolt in characters such as Marmion, Arvalon, and the Moors in *Roderick*. The supernatural may be used to symbolize its hidden power, as in *The Lay of the Last Minstrel*, *Thalaba*, Moore's 'The Veiled Prophet of Khorassan' in *Lalla Rookh*, *Christabel*, and *The Curse of Kehama*. Virility is an essential component of a villain such as Marmion. On the other hand, Roderick, Thalaba, and Madoc, by sexual abstinence, convert the power of sexuality into the martial prowess of the superhero.

In his antiquarian revival of the romance genre Scott was plainly changing the role of the heroines to accord with these puritanical preoccupations. Gone is the medieval troubadour's romantic (and often adulterous) passion for a lady, which equals exalted spirituality in its fervour. Scott censures the impure love of Lancelot and Guinevere in the first verse epistle of *Marmion*. Extreme modesty is the new ideal: 'Pure love who scarce his passion tells'. The censuring of women's sexuality is accompanied by the idealization of the pre-sexual innocence of childhood. (Scott views the onset of puberty for the Pringle boys with dread, in the second epistle.) The affection of Scott for his male friends is instead celebrated in these epistles, mingled with the patriotic love of his country, now threatened with invasion. In these introductory epistles fear of the force of sexual passion is therefore associated with the French threat, just as it brings about the shameful defeat of Scotland in the text, through the three sexually active women characters.

[22] Edward Meachen, 'History and Transcendence in Robert Southey's Epic Poems', *SEL* 19 (1979), 589–608.

This preoccupation in these poems with the regulation of sexuality and control of legitimacy brings to mind Michel Foucault's suggestion in *The History of Sexuality* that an improvement in life-expectancy in the eighteenth century brought the mechanisms of the life of the species into the sphere of man's political existence, so that the heredity of the race began for the first time to take over from the prestige of blood in the concerns of power:

> The mechanisms of power are addressed to the body, to life, to what causes it to proliferate, to what reinforces the species, its stamina, its ability to dominate, or its capacity for being used. Through the themes of progeny, race, the future of the species, the vitality of the social body, power spoke of sexuality and to sexuality.[23]

Significantly, this period saw Godwin's anarchist rejection of marriage in *Enquiry Concerning Political Justice* (1793), refuted by Malthus's *Essay on Population* (1808), which considers the subject of human reproduction from the point of view of the political economist, advocating late marriage and sexual restraint in the name of national prosperity.

The literature I have been considering certainly combines the twin themes of the preservation of the heroine's virginity with the retention of power in the hands of the traditional rulers, evidencing a concern with the transferral of hereditary power through blood (particularly in Scott), and with maintaining the purity of the race (in Southey). Control of female ability to contaminate legitimacy is common to both, in the newly-puritanical, anti-revolutionary, patriotic revival of the concept of chivalry.[24]

The heroines idealized in these poems therefore enshrine in their beauty the worth of their sexuality, but in their characterization—passive and fragile—its desired regulation and control. Clare is 'Lovely, and gentle, and distress'd' (*Marmion*, II, vii). Blushes, sighs, and swoons characterize all of Scott's heroines, perhaps most noticeably Edith of *The Lord of the Isles* (1815). These are

[23] Michel Foucault, *The History of Sexuality*, trans. R. Hurley (London, 1976), pp. 143–7.

[24] The intense interest in the age of chivalry which arose during the period of the Napoleonic wars produced numerous translations of medieval romances and chronicles. These are documented by Mark Girouard, *The Return to Camelot: Chivalry and the English Gentleman* (New Haven, Conn. and London, 1981), pp. 42–3. Girouard notes that the dominant painter and illustrator of medieval subjects in the period was Thomas Stothard, the illustrator of Byron's Tales.

simultaneously signs of a passionate nature and its repression. Matilda of *Rokeby* has 'a soft and pensive grace', and 'a downcast eye', signifying modesty and submission. 'The mild expression spoke a mind | In duty firm, composed, resign'd' (IV, v).

The obverse of the passive, gentle virgin is the creature she becomes through diabolic transformation once she is sexually active. For the sexuality of the female characters is also portrayed as a secret power: dangerous, predatory, and to be regulated strictly. It is often identified with the demonic forces of revolt. For example, Constance, in *Marmion*, is changed physically as well as spiritually by her adulterous affair: she becomes 'fierce and unfeminine' (III, xvii), dresses in men's clothing, develops into an intriguer and poisoner, and is condemned to be walled up alive (II, xxv; III, xv). Lady Heron and the Queen of France are siren temptresses, who use their sexual hold over King James to gain power over him, ultimately causing him to dismiss the English ambassador and prepare for a disastrous war. The sexual temptation of women is also responsible for the corruption of Marmion. J. H. Alexander suggests that Scott's chief concern in depicting a chivalric society in decline is with the corrupting effects of impure passion, chiefly lust.[25]

An even more extreme example is Moore's Zelica in 'The Veiled Prophet of Khorassan'. The force of her passion for Azim and her sorrow at his absence lead to her madness, which paves the way for her seduction by the prophet through misguided idealism. She encapsulates within her person the capacity for extreme spirituality and extreme sensuality, which make up the face and obverse of the contemporary stereotype of woman. Common to both is her subjectivity, not amenable to rational control. Female sexuality is thus portrayed as diabolic: Zelica's union with the prophet is consummated in a charnel house, with attendant Gothic horrors. She then becomes animated with an alien force of energy: 'A loathsome thing, all pestilence, all flame!' (VI, 56). Powerful women are also portrayed as in touch with the powers of darkness:

[25] J. H. Alexander, *'Marmion': Studies in Interpretation and Composition* (*SSEL*: Salzburg, 1981), p. 25. Alexander quotes from Scott's *Essay on Chivalry*, in which he declares that the modern system of manners derives fron chivalry, in comparison with 'classic times, when women were slaves and men coarse and vulgar or overbearing and brutal, as suited their own humour, without respect to that of the rest of society'.

for example, the Lady of Branksome Hall, who speaks to the spirits from her tower, in the opening of *The Lay of the Last Minstrel*.

This threatening obverse of the chaste, obedient heroine, however, is glimpsed only occasionally. For the most part, the sexual ideology of these poems is given over to what Marlene LeGates calls 'the cult of womanhood'. LeGates has shown that the chastity of women, while always inculcated in the past, had become the subject of a dramatic new apotheosis in the eighteenth-century novel: 'The image of chaste Womanhood represents a fantasy about what could be done with women in terms of social conditioning, testifying to the faith in the infinite malleability of human nature.'[26]

In the intense idealization of meek, suffering feminine virtues, the virtuous heroine of these tales has become a Christ-like figure. She exemplifies the virtues of meekness and stoicism, often, like Him, on behalf of or in support of a patriarchal leader or father. As LeGates comments: 'The family, religion, and the state are now identified with woman rather than seen as being threatened by her.' She is sometimes a spiritual inspiration to others (Southey's Joan, or Adosinda in *Roderick*) or demonstrates the necessity for sexual morality to the leaders of society (Ellen to King James, in *Lady of the Lake*). The spiritual purity combined with weakness in this heroine justifies a martial ethos in her defence, in the call for a return to chivalry in these tales. This sentimentalized Christianity, by implication, characterized the Napoleonic wars as a Christian crusade. In Southey's *Madoc*, Celtic Christianity and culture is imposed by force on the South American Indians (for their own good), in the way missionary activity was currently being used to justify the extension of the British Empire.

The most famous vignette of one of these heroines is that of Clare proffering water to her wounded oppressor, Marmion, like a female Sir Philip Sidney.

> O Woman! in our hours of ease,
> Uncertain, coy and hard to please,
> And variable as the shade
> By the light quivering aspen made;
> When pain and anguish wring the brow,
> A ministering angel thou!
>
> (*Marmion*, VI, xxx)

[26] See Marlene LeGates, 'The Cult of Womanhood in Eighteenth-Century Thought', *Eighteenth-Century Studies*, 10 (1976), 21–39.

It is interesting that in the midst of this eulogy Scott should turn aside to depict woman as 'uncertain' and unreliable, although he has given no such characterization to Clare herself in the course of the poem. This reflects, in fact, the poet's own insecurity and fear at the subversive potential of the obverse of the stereotype: the hidden sexual power that could threaten the stability of the family, duty, and hereditary authority, if not strictly regulated. Scott smoothes over the uneasy paradox, by assigning the contradictions to her female 'mystique' and reassuring himself of woman's 'natural' role as nurse, tending the man of action.

When we compare Byron's Oriental tales with the romances of his male contemporaries we find similar narrative themes. Typically, the self-seeking leader of a failed or futile rebellion in a feudal state attempts to elope with the wife or daughter of one of the patriarchal leaders of society. This is true of *The Giaour* (1813), *The Bride of Abydos* (1813), *The Corsair* (1814), and *The Siege of Corinth* (1816). Zuleika and Francesca are the only daughters of their widower fathers, and are conventionally pious. All the heroines seem to be motherless, and are young and nubile. Most are pawns in the furtherance of dynastic power.

Critics traditionally focus on Byron's innovation in creating the famous 'Byronic hero', but this lay less in the characterization as such (compare Scott's Marmion, Radcliffe's Schedoni, Schiller's Karl Moor) than in presenting him as a lover, not a threat to the heroine. The heroine is still a damsel in distress, but now at the hands of established authority—her own father or husband—while the Napoleonic anti-hero (renegade, rebel, criminal as he is admitted to be) becomes the potential liberator of the heroine. For Thorslev, who sees the tales merely as vehicles for these anti-heroes, this development is seen as no more than a cynical manœuvre on Byron's part to obtain the reader's sympathy for a morally reprehensible character: 'Make your protagonist a Hero of Sensibility in his regard for women, and this characteristic alone will mitigate all his other crimes, no matter how Gothic.'[27]

But this is to ignore the significance of Byron's creation of an 'anti-heroine' complementary to the Gothic anti-hero. The love of Leila and Gulnare is adulterous; that of Zuleika and Parisina appears to be incestuous. Leila, Gulnare, and Kaled put earthly love

[27] Thorslev, *The Byronic Hero*, p. 55.

before the spiritual by choosing a 'giaour' or pagan as lover. Harem slaves engaged in a forbidden love could not be made to exemplify domestic piety as Southey's heroines were, or to dispense grace and favour as Scott's aristocratic ladies did. Her repudiation of her arranged marriage means that the Byronic heroine—far from symbolizing the continued fertility of the ruling dynasty—articulates a cry for individual freedom. Byron's heroines are alienated from society by their love, not integrated through a suitable marriage at the conclusion. In the following chapter I shall examine the tales as a series of poems which interrogate the nineteenth-century bourgeois identification of romantic love with marriage, and the idealization of woman as the guardian of morals within the family.

Consider also the significance of Byron's Orientalism. Edward Said's *Orientalism* points out that the Orient functioned as a passive object of Eurocentric study; that nineteenth-century Orientalism was a projection both of the romance and yet also the will to govern the Otherness of the East. Such scholarly and literary Orientalism underpins the ideology of imperialism. Said points out that the British exploitation of India made this connection clear to British writers: 'Romantic writers like Byron and Scott consequently had a political vision of the Near Orient and a very combative awareness of how relations between the Orient and Europe would have to be conducted.'[28]

The narrative romances of Byron's contemporaries written in the period of the Napoleonic wars often expressed the call for a return to Christian chivalry, imbued with an appeal to patriotism and sexual purity, in stories set in the middle ages. Byron's use of settings in the contemporary feudalism of the Turkish Empire challenged this implied encoding of the counter-revolutionary Holy Alliance, as a new Christian crusade. Scott's and Southey's idealization of the medieval past as the high point of Christian culture is undercut by Byron's recasting of courtly love as violent forbidden passion, and of feudalism as a brutal despotism based on militarism, the oppression of women, and a slave economy. Byron's own aristocratic birth gave credence to his ironic rebuttal of the Burkean sentimentalization of chivalry, as did his claims to realism, asserted in the notes, by reference to his personal experience of a country still living in the age of feudalism. Through the medium of

[28] Edward Said, *Orientalism* (London, 1978), p. 192.

romance Byron unmasks the patriarchalism of the calls to religious, patriotic, and filial duty made at the time of the Napoleonic wars, and bolstered by the Evangelical Movement.

By substituting contemporary Eastern feudalism for mediaeval Britain, Byron himself is enabled to utilize the sentimentalism of chivalry, but on behalf of the people, not the rulers, in a correspondingly Utopian liberal project: to justify Western intervention in the Orient, to emancipate colonized nations. For while the otherness of Islamic culture is a fascination in the tales, Byron's stress on its brutality can also be seen as endorsing its overthrow by European powers in the name of the chivalric rescue of subjugated Greece. Turkey was a byword for tyranny, in Whiggish political jargon. (The Tory administration had been compared to Turkish tyranny in Byron's House of Lords speech against capital punishment for Luddism in 1812.[29])

Sexual politics had always been of primary interest in the genre of the Oriental tale. Both the *Arabian Nights* and the *Persian Tales*, translated into English and French at the beginning of the eighteenth century, were given a framework based on the war of the sexes.[30] In travel books on the East, too, so well-represented in Byron's library, the treatment of women was a fascination. Tavernier's and Chardin's descriptions of Persia, published in 1676 and 1686, provided information on the severity of the restrictions on wives and concubines, details of marriage customs, and the treatment of women in harems. The earliest European Eastern tales, purporting to be true stories or translations, often centre around female slavery or suttee. Just as the Turks became a byword for despotism in eighteenth-century political rhetoric, their sexual tyranny also drew attention to the existence of power relations between the sexes.[31] The Turkish harem is the constant referent of Mary Wollstonecraft's rhetoric in *Vindication of the Rights of Woman*.

Sexual politics was the basis of Montesquieu's epistolary novel

[29] 'I have been in some of the most oppressed provinces of Turkey; but never, under the most despotic of infidel governments, did I behold such squalid wretchedness as I have seen since my return, in the very heart of a Christian country', 27 February 1812.

[30] My account of the 18th-cent. Oriental tale is derived from Martha Pike Conant, *The Oriental Tale in England in the Eighteenth Century* (Columbia, NY, 1908; repr. London, 1966), pp. 13–25.

[31] Conant, loc. cit.

Lettres Persanes (1721) which Shanley and Stillman describe as 'a sustained and profound meditation on the interrelationships of familial and political life'.[32] The Eastern visitor to the West, Usbek, corresponds with his wives and eunuchs, both giving his impressions of French government and society, and reacting harshly to reports from home of disorder in the harem. Montesquieu thus ironically parallels control of the seraglio with strategies of monarchical tyranny—comparing France with Turkey. Under Usbek's rhetoric of love lies an absolutism based on mutual fear: he is both husband and prince; the eunuchs are both harem guards and political ministers. The denouement is shocking: his favourite wife writes defiantly that she has taken poison, her lover having been executed, and that she dies proclaiming her joy at release through death from Usbek's tyranny.

Byron had read *Esprit Des Lois*,[33] and the story of brother and sister love in Letter 67 of *Lettres Persanes* may have given him the name Astarte for *Manfred*. Like Montesquieu, Byron identified the sexual self-determination of his odalisques with the liberty of the subject. It is significant that Byron begins *The Giaour* where Montesquieu's novel finishes—with the shocking death of the heroine. In the early tales, comparison of East and West is simplified into the juxtaposition of the two antagonists' attitudes to the heroine, and post-revolutionary pessimism, rather than questioning irony, makes the plot an impasse. The essentially negative quality of Byron's liberalism is demonstrated by the image of freedom in these tales as a few snatched moments of romantic love in a garden: the impossible desire for a private enclave where authority cannot penetrate.

Byron's tales resemble those of contemporary women poets in their frequent portrayal of the heroine's tragic death. (All the heroines of the Oriental tales die except Gulnare and Kaled.) Antagonistic male critics were wont to point out that such pathetic victimized heroines abounded in Regency periodicals catering specifically for female readers.[34] As a Greek harem slave, the

[32] Mary Lyndon Shanley and Peter G. Stillman, 'Political and Marital Despotism: Montesquieu's *Persian Letters*', in Jean Bethke Elshtain (ed.), *The Family in Political Thought* (Brighton, 1982), pp. 66–80.

[33] *L&J* i. 148.

[34] For example in the January 1814 issue of the *Female Preceptor*, which was published from 1813–15, and whose list of contributors include Byron, Scott, Hannah More, Maria Edgeworth, and others, are to be found a poetic tale entitled

Byronic heroine is triply oppressed: by her class, race, and sex. I shall argue in Chapter 3 that at the heart of this series of poems is an ambivalent view of the representative dispossessed political subject—the heroine.

The extreme polarization of sexual roles is the best-known feature of Byron's Oriental tales. Even his contemporaries found it exceptional. Francis Jeffrey, in a review of Byron's *Bride of Abydos* and *The Corsair* for the *Edinburgh Review* in 1814, commented: 'At present, he will let us admire nothing but adventurous courage in men and devoted gentleness in women.'[35] Jeffrey discusses the verse tales of Byron, Scott, Southey, and Campbell as studies of primitive societies: 'The savages and barbarians that are in the world, are no doubt, very exact likenesses of those whom civilization has driven out of it; and they may be used accordingly for most of the purposes for which their ancient prototypes are found serviceable.'[36] The extreme differentiation of sexual role and oppression of women emphasized in Byron's portrayals of the Turkish Empire could be perceived by the contemporary Western believer in progress simply as a barbarous system appropriate to a less civilized society where power derives simply from physical force. On the other hand, those subscribing to the nineteenth-century cult of womanhood would identify with such representations of extreme sexual difference. Jeffrey singles out Byron's heroines for praise: 'He has also made a fine use of the gentleness and submission of the females . . . There is something so true to female nature in general, in his representations of this sort . . . '. The exaggerated fragility of Byron's early heroines (Zuleika and Medora expire through mere excess of grief) is construed as 'natural' by contemporary readers like Jeffrey, because it justifies and excuses the hero's complementary male self-aggrandizement on her behalf as equally fundamental to human nature. The commitment of Byron's middle-class readership to the ethos of individualism

'Seduction', which ended with the death of mother and baby in a snowstorm, 'The Deserted Female' by Oliver Goldsmith, another narrative poem, 'The Prostitute', as well as prose tales on similar subjects. This magazine advertised itself as containing 'Essays chiefly on The Duties of the Female Sex: with a variety of Useful and Polite Literature'. See Alison Adburgham, *Women in Print: Writing Women and Women's Magazines from the Restoration to the Accession of Victoria* (London, 1972), pp. 198–200.

[35] *The Romantics Reviewed*, ed. Donald H. Reiman, part B, 5 vols. (New York and London, 1972), i. 863.

[36] Ibid. ii. 848.

made his adventurers attractive; the hero's pretensions to chivalry paralleled theirs to nobility, but, most of all, the deaths of his heroines purged the liberal's guilt for the plight of the oppressed, through a sentimentalism comparable with that of Dickens's death-bed scenes later in the century.

I have been talking about the Byronic heroine as if she were a fixed entity. However, as the series of tales unfolds, the role of the heroine develops. Leila is dead at the beginning of the poem, and her story and death must be pieced together from the scattered recollections and viewpoints of various men: her master, her lover, a fisherman. Zuleika exists in the 'present time' of the story and is given dialogue, but is unable to choose her own destiny. Medora invests her whole being in wifelike devotion, but finds Conrad puts his individual aggrandisement in the world of men before his commitment to her. Gulnare, however, speaks passionately of her sexual humiliation as a harem slave, and finding the Byronic hero ineffectual, she stabs her oppressor herself, and effects the rescue of them both (despite her knowledge that her love for him is unrequited). Kaled dresses and acts the part of a male comrade-in-arms to Lara. She is his constant companion, accompanies him into battle, and tends him when he is wounded. It is not made clear whether Lara even knows that Kaled is a woman. It is hinted that she may have murdered his enemy. Gradually the heroine, once the fragile victim, becomes more and more resourceful and independent. The defiant repudiation of conventional femininity and female sexual mores is perhaps even more subversive a subject than the hero's insurrection, because control of woman's sexuality was fundamental to ensure the legitimacy of heirs, essential to the patriarchal system of hereditary property and power. The following two chapters will show that the erotic charge of these poems lies in the paradoxical project of eulogizing sexual difference, yet counter-pointing and interrogating this with a daring exploration of sexual role-reversal.

2

'A Soulless Toy for Tyrant's Lust?': The Heroine as Passive Victim

IN the verse tales of Byron's contemporaries, romantic love was minimized or manipulated by the plot to accord with social duty to the heroine's father, the venerable patriarch of beleaguered traditional values. In Byron's tales, however, the heroine has to choose between love and conformity. To her father or husband she is seen as an object of value in the exchange of women by men in a patriarchal social system based on dynastic alliance and male primogeniture. To her Western lover she is the unattainable ideal in his internalized individualistic quest for self-completion.

> My good, my guilt, my weal, my woe,
> My hope on high—my all below.
> (*The Giaour*, 1182–3)

Traditionally, critics have seen the latter view as that of the poet himself. But it will be shown that Byron deconstructs the romantic love of man for woman as the uneasy conjunction of these two impulses, by his ironic comparison of the Eastern and Western male view of women.[1] The series of tales evolves through creative ongoing experimentation with the presentation of sexual relationships, rather than (as is sometimes assumed) the repetition of a static dualism resulting either from the poet's own sexual obsessions or from his cynical cashing-in on a successful formula.

Byron's earliest heroines—Leila, Zuleika, Francesca, Medora, and Parisina—are characterized chiefly by their passivity, sensibility, and tragic deaths. Like the muses of Byron's lyric poetry, these heroines are objects of the male gaze—the feminine Other. Examples of the beauty of nature, they are compared to their native land of Greece. The function of such a heroine is to be, not do. Her

[1] Byron originally intended to portray Hassan and the Giaour with equal emphasis, but his additions gave the latter more weight. See Michael G. Sundell, 'The Development of *The Giaour*', *SEL* 9 (1969), 587–99 (590).

power lies in her capacity to inspire men to action. The first of these passive heroines functions as an object of differing value to the male characters, and thus is an absence, even a lacuna in the poem.

LEILA

The Giaour best illustrates the reification of the heroine, though all the early tales focus her through the male point of view. Like Astarte in *Manfred* and Francesca in *The Siege of Corinth*, Leila is viewed entirely from the vantage point of her death—which is therefore simultaneously the starting-point and climax of the story, and fixes her as an icon. *The Giaour* is presented as a series of fragments to be pieced together, with varying degrees of success, by its readers. Critics interested in Byron's experimentation with point of view have compared the earlier and later texts to elucidate the poem's development.[2] The questions which concern us here are why Byron decided this narrative technique (derived from Rogers's *The Voyage of Columbus* (1812)) to be particularly appropriate to his subject-matter and why he did not use a similar technique in any of the other tales.

The clue is to be found where the 'manuscript' is most dramatically ruptured in the middle of line 373. It is at the very point at which the ceremonial drowning of Leila is being related that the Emir's voice is lost, and the poem resumes with the fisherman's description of the sinking body. The execution of Leila for adultery is the most shocking of any of the heroines' deaths—the manner of the disposal of the live human parcel demonstrates her status as a chattel. Both the fragmentation of the text and the multiple narration are devices to distance the reader from this central event of the poem, and to bring out the mystery and the full horror of the murder as gradually as possible.

Drowning for adultery

Chattel.

The autonomous feminine voice is totally suppressed in *The Giaour*. The heroine's story has to be reconstructed by the reader from various male viewpoints: those of her master, her lover, and the Turkish fisherman who assisted in her execution, as relayed by a

[2] On the accretive composition of *The Giaour* see Sundell; William H. Marshall, 'The Accretive Structure of Byron's *The Giaour*', *MLN* 76 (1961), 502–9; Robert Gleckner, *Byron and the Ruins of Paradise* (Baltimore, 1967), pp. 96–117; Jerome McGann, *Fiery Dust*, pp. 141–8; and David Seed, '"Disjointed Fragments": Concealment and Revelation in *The Giaour*', *BJ* 18 (1990), 14–27.

Turkish oral bard, and imperfectly pieced together by the modern European poet/editor. Her silent presence vanishes from view like her sinking body, as it recedes from the fisherman's gaze. She dies without protest, hardly moving enough to show she is alive as she drowns (375–9).

The gap in the narrative invites a horrified response from the reader, an eroticized mix of pathos and excitement at this dramatization of male power of life or death over woman. But the sentimental Gothicism of the poetry is ironically juxtaposed with the caustic tone of the prose Advertisement and the notes, in which the poet assures us that the drowning of alleged adulteresses is still practised by the Turkish Empire, and describes the recent drowning without trial of twelve women on the word of a wronged wife, though the husband apparently went unpunished.[3] Furthermore, Byron toyed with the idea of publishing an account of the personally-experienced event on which the poem was based. As he had returned from swimming in the Piraeus, he had met a procession, and on enquiring found that they were about to throw into the sea, for infidelity, a girl sewn into a sack. Byron interfered, but had to draw his pistol to halt the proceedings. He managed to procure her pardon and helped her to escape to Thebes. The device of quoting Lord Sligo's account of the incident would of course have raised in the reader's mind the very suspicion which it was intended to refute: that Byron himself had been the girl's lover. The evidence for this is inconclusive.[4] The salient fact, however, is that Byron identified his own sexual guilt with the barbarity towards women which he had witnessed. The impression it made on him is evident from his journal:

> L.[Lewis] wondered I did not introduce the situation into *The Giaour*. He may wonder;—he might wonder more at that production being written at all. But to describe the *feelings* of *that situation* were impossible—it is *icy* even to recollect them.[5]

Like Francesca in *The Siege of Corinth* and Astarte in *Manfred*, Leila exists only as a ghostly presence in the consciousness of the hero, her death a riddle only partially solved by the narrative. In

[3] *CPW* iii. 39; 422–3.

[4] The inconclusive evidence as to this is summed up by M. K. Joseph, *Byron the Poet* (London, 1964), p. 65 n. 16.

[5] *L&J* iii. 230.

these poems, which all had their origin in 1812, even if completed and published later,[6] the male speakers construct the feminine in terms of natural beauty, passivity, and vulnerability. Nostalgia is engendered by the act of projecting these qualities from the self, and defining them as 'feminine' and Other. They are therefore by definition 'lost' to the masculine men of action doomed to an ethos of action and violence.

Anthony Vital has commented how a power relationship between the sexes informed the rhetorical structure of the sentimentalism of the early lyrics, determining how the poems are read: '. . . in the speaker's mind the woman's potential for action is doubly suppressed: not only is she mute, and her powers of expression made over to her body, but her body is there simply to be made over to the language of the feminine for any male to read.'[7]

The bodies of the heroines of the earliest tales are used as mute objects of male reverence in exactly the same way as the subjects of the amorous lyrics. Thus in the account of Leila's beauty (473–518), the poet guides the subjective reader via the Turkish fisherman, who advises him to 'gaze' on a gazelle to assist him in imagining her eyes. Though the fisherman's religion postulates woman as 'nought but breathing clay', the gazer is promised spiritual inspiration from reading her glance:

Oh! who young Leila's glance could read
And keep that portion of his creed
Which saith, that woman is but dust,
A soulless toy for tyrant's lust?
On her might Muftis gaze, and own
That through her eye the Immortal shone. (487–92)

Compared with examples of earthly physical beauty and purity—blossoms, mountain sleet, and swan—Leila is endowed with a natural nobility in spite of her lowly sexual and social status. Even the Turkish fisherman concedes that, like the swan, she remains

[6] McGann suggests that *The Siege of Corinth* and *Parisina* developed out of an original MS tale begun in 1812 (*CPW* iii. 479–80). *Manfred* 'was based on an unfinished Witch drama', parts of which were written from 1812–13 (*CPW* iv. 464).

[7] Anthony Vital, 'Lord Byron's Embarrassment: Poesy and the Feminine', *Bulletin of Research in the Humanities*, 86:3 (1983–5), 269–90. On the attitudes to women in the early lyrics see also ch. 2 of Gloria T. Hull's unpublished Ph.D. thesis, 'Women in Byron's Poetry: A Biographical and Critical Study', Purdue University, 1972.

loyal to her chosen mate—but she did not choose Hassan (515–18). Her stature is such that by the end of the encomium she has come to assume a dominant role over the now-subservient gazer:

> Thus armed with beauty would she check
> Intrusion's glance, till Folly's gaze
> Shrunk from the charms it meant to praise.

She is now 'armed' like a warrior whilst he shows 'feminine' embarrassment and must withdraw his gaze. The half-naked posed body of Leila in Thomas Stothard's illustration of these lines also invites the reader's gaze, which her accusatory eyes simultaneously repel.

The passage brings into ironic juxtaposition the 'Turkish' language of courtly love with the belief of ordinary Muslim men that women have no soul: their only function is to please men on earth as the houris do in the afterlife. Byron's sarcastic note draws attention to the fact that officially Islam does not deny *all* women immortality: 'The Koran allots at least a third of Paradise to well-behaved women.'[8] Here—as in the poem as a whole—the theoretical idealization of women in the Eastern code of chivalry is shown to be conditional on their actual subordination in religio-societal structures. Byron goes on to emphasize in a later note that it is an emir, whose claim to holiness is via male primogeniture as he is a supposed descendant of the prophet, who superintends the drowning of Leila.[9] Byron's irony, of course, depends on his Western reader's Christian belief in the sexual equality of the soul.

The civilization destroyed by Leila's avenger is seen through Turkish eyes in lines 288–351. Hassan's 'deserted bower' is a symbol of 'the fortress of his power' with which it is made to rhyme. The slavery of women is concomitant with this hierarchical society, evoked by references to 'serf' and 'vassal', and to the military life of 'fortress' and 'steed'. Hassan has acted, not sadistically but logically, in his relations to Leila, in complete

[8] Byron continues: 'but by far the greater number of Mussulmans interpret the text their own way, and exclude their moieties from heaven. Being enemies to Platonics, they cannot discern "any fitness of things" in the souls of the other sex, conceiving them to be superseded by the Houris' (*CPW* iii. 419).

[9] In his note on the Emirs Byron comments: 'they are the worst of a very indifferent brood', and that, basing their power on their lineage from the prophet, they enforce strict religious legalism (*CPW* iii. 418).

accordance with the mores of his civilization. This is emphasized by the acceptance by his mother of his treatment of women, the disposal and immediate replacement of Leila (689–722). He dies, as he had lived, showing no remorse for her death (1092), and secure in the belief that even the most impressive earthly woman is inconsiderable in comparison with the attainment of a warrior's paradise and the service of the Houris (737–46).

> There sleeps as true an Osmanlie
> As e'er at Mecca bent the knee. (729–30)

The Turkish view of Leila is patriarchal in the anthropological rather than the generalized feminist sense of the word. Kate Millett quotes the definition of Sir Henry Maine, the nineteenth-century historian of ancient jurisprudence, on the archaic patriarchal family: 'The eldest male parent is absolutely supreme in his household. His dominion extends to life and death and is as unqualified over his children and their houses as over his slaves.'[10] In much of his poetry, Byron's liberal rhetoric is framed by the background of a patriarchal power system of the present or past. Apart from representations of the Turkish Empire in the tales and *Don Juan*, *Parisina*, *Sardanapalus*, and *Heaven and Earth* all depict a male ruler or leader exercising the power of life and death over his household.

Turkish patriarchy, polygamy, and Muslim doubt as to whether women have souls are not contrasted with a specifically Christian alternative view of woman in *The Giaour*, for the eponymous hero is an infidel to both Muslims and Christians (807). While the traditional Christian dogma of an ungendered soul was still available to nineteenth-century 'feminist' discourse asserting sexual equality,[11] the Giaour's depiction of Leila reflects instead the contemporary ideology of a specifically womanly sanctity comprising the quintessence of femininity. Thus while Leila is treated as merely an object of physical lust by Hassan, she has become for the Giaour the complete opposite of this—his sole source of spiritual meaning in earthly life: 'My life's unerring light' (1144).

[10] Kate Millett, *Sexual Politics* (London, 1969; repr. 1981), p. 76.

[11] e.g. 'It is my spirit that addresses your spirit; just as if both had passed through the grave, and we stood at God's feet, equal,—as we are!' (*Jane Eyre*, ch. 23).

Byron's poem thus contributes to the cult of womanhood, while at the same time, by combining the roles of adulteress and spiritual icon in the same heroine, he focuses attention on the very contradictions that his male contemporaries sought to minimize. The reader endeavours to piece together not just the story but the versions of Leila offered by the various voices in the poem. At every point the construct of woman is exaggerated in order to interrogate its contradictions. Thus Leila's identification with the beauty of nature both sanctifies her and yet intensifies the traditional association of woman with sinful sexuality, which drives men to destructive violence. As a harem slave she is a fallen woman in Western eyes, yet her complete separation from men and the tainted public arena endows her with an aura of unworldly purity.

However, whereas the heroines of the verse tales of his male contemporaries, like those of the female novelists, were given specifically social roles as inspirers of familial morality in the cult of womanhood, Byron's Leila functions only as the personal inspiration of an individual. For if most Muslims think woman soulless, the title of *The Giaour* draws attention to the relationship between the Westerner's abandonment of religion and his substitution of an extremely idealized individualistic romantic love. Love of woman becomes a secular form of Grace and a means of restoring the lost paradise on earth:

> Yes, Love indeed is light from heaven—
> A spark of that immortal fire
> With angels shar'd—by Alla given,
> To lift from earth our low desire. (1131–4)

As Frederick Beaty has shown, the definition of love as 'light from heaven' is a characteristic Romantic metaphor for endowing earthly emotions with a halo of celestial light.[12] 'A ray of him who formed the whole—| A glory circling round the soul!' (1140)

Byron rejects Scott's and Southey's puritanical concept of love as chaste friendship leading to matrimony. On the other hand, the Giaour despises courtly gallantry: 'I cannot prate in puling strain | Of ladye-love and beauty's chain' (1103–4). This is true, for we notice that in the Giaour's long speech to the Friar he is concerned

[12] Frederick L. Beaty, *Light from Heaven: Love in British Romantic Literature* (Illinois, 1971).

only with the changes love has wrought in himself, rather than in imaginatively recreating Leila and her situation, or in perceiving her as an autonomous being. For the Giaour, Leila has become part of his way of perceiving the world: '. . . a form of life and light | That seen—became a part of sight' (1127–8). She is part of his consciousness: 'The Morning-star of Memory!' (1130).

Lesley Rabine, writing on the novelistic romantic heroine, compares the use of a heroine as an intermediary between the hero and his self-knowledge with Hegel's 'circle of the self'. For Hegel, the feminine principle is 'eternal love that merely feels', while only the masculine principle is the 'self-driving force of self-conscious existence'.[13] Similarly, McGann sees Byron's heroines as Platonic emanations of the hero's soul:

> The female counterparts of the heroes . . . correspond exactly to the state of the hero's soul which they inhabit. They objectify the passionate impulses in the man whose imagination made them what they are. This is as much to say that none of them are truly 'persons' . . . These women are allegorical figures set in an allegorical framework. Blake's females are of the same order . . .[14]

Irene Tayler and Gina Luria, in their essay on women in Romantic literature, extend the point to all male Romantic poets. Whilst women novelists of the Regency period stress the community and its shared moral values, the aesthetic of the male Romantic poet sanctified the uniquely individual experience. Consequently, his female muse-figure exists as merely the objectified impulse of his ego. This study will show that the heroine's role develops from that of a mere emanation in this series of poems. But certainly the hero's romantic love for the dead heroine in *The Giaour*, *The Siege of Corinth* and *Manfred* can thus be interpreted as a displaced form of male narcissism.

Byron's tales were not written in Romantic literary isolation, but specifically to challenge the consensus on female propriety—the shared moral values—that Tayler and Luria point out were paramount in the female-authored Regency novel. The Western

[13] See Lesley Rabine, *Reading the Romantic Heroine: Text, History, Ideology* (Ann Arbor, Mich., 1985), ch.1.

[14] McGann, *Fiery Dust*, p. 189. See also Irene Tayler and Gina Luria, 'Gender and Genre', p. 118.

hero's creed of passionate romantic love is preferenced in the hierarchy of discourses within the poem by the adoption of direct speech and by endowing his retrospective view with the closure of the poem. However, it is insistently questioned as well as dramatized. Byron's strong sense of irony asks us to compare and judge Hassan and the Giaour in their attitude to Leila. We find the egotistical nature of the latter's internalized quest underlined in the lines which shocked the reviewers:

> 'Tis true, I could not whine nor sigh,
> I knew but to obtain or die.
> I die—but first I have possest. (1112–14)

The Giaour values love freely given, not extorted: 'To me she gave her heart, that all | Which tyranny can ne'er enthrall' (1068–9).

Yet he can still judge Leila as 'faithless', and refer to her 'treachery' to Hassan, thus endorsing the Turkish patriarchal rule of women. The Giaour respects Hassan: they share the same military ethos. Moreover, both believe in punishing female adultery with death: 'Yet did he but what I had done | Had she been false to more than one' (1062–3). The Giaour is a fervent believer in monogamous love, even after the death of his lover, whereas Hassan practises polygamy: 'The swan that swims upon the lake, | One mate, and one alone, will take' (1170–1). Though the adulterous hero and heroine have both broken society's moral laws, the Giaour's delineation of the heroine's guilt in his confession to the Friar reinforces conventional values with regard to female chastity, while reserving for himself a heroic posture of defiance. Like Manfred, he worries for the consequences of the woman's 'guilt' (1141–4) more than his own. He even regrets—for her sake—that she ever returned his love: 'Yet sometimes with remorse in vain | I wish she had not loved again' (1054–5). However much her doom haunts him, he sees it as 'deserv'd' (1066).

He recognizes and castigates society's double standard in judging female adultery more harshly than male (see lines 1172–9), and deplores heartless seducers. However, rather than postulating a changed attitude towards female sexuality, he advocates strict monogamy for both sexes. Like the other heroes of the tales, he prides himself on his own monogamy for life.

Finally, the Giaour's attitude to women is also comparable to Hassan's in the way he sees the possession of women as a measure of success. As Hassan's harem is a visible sign of his power, so the Venetian equates Leila with the lure of booty or property:

> But place again before my eyes
> Aught that I deem a worthy prize;
> The maid I love—the man I hate,
> And I will hunt the steps of fate. (1016–19)

His passions are forged by the thought of her defence and revenge into an inflexible weapon in the competitive warfare of men (922–36).

By this deeply ironic point-by-point comparison of the attitudes of Hassan and the Giaour towards Leila (and their joint guilt for her death), we see that the Venetian's romantic love retains many of the basic ideological assumptions of primitive patriarchy. The poem thus is paradoxically both a strongly charged plea for female sexual autonomy, and an acknowledgment that as the fabric of society is built on the foundation of female chastity, woman will always be the chief victim of illegitimate love.

ZULEIKA

The unresolved ambivalence upon which *The Giaour* had turned was the poet's sensationalizing of Turkish patriarchal oppression of woman, set against his Western hero's simultaneous condemnation of female sexuality as sinful unless under male control. Each of the Oriental tales which followed evidences a strategy for exploring, yet failing to resolve this contradictory stance. Just as in his politics Byron unsuccessfully sought to synthesize radicalism with belief in the leadership of the aristocracy, as a love poet he sought simultaneously to subvert the post-revolutionary inculcation of female virtue and to retain the traditional authority of the male sex.

Either the plot unravels to provide mitigating circumstances which render the heroine's forbidden love relatively innocent (Zuleika, Parisina), or this love is unrequited by the hero (Gulnare, Kaled). For good measure, Leila, Zuleika, Medora, Francesca, and Parisina all die the death conventional in literature of the period for heroines evincing sexual passion.

Byron's first attempt at fully characterizing the heroine of a narrative poem is Zuleika. He writes of his aims in the new poem:

'... I also wished to try my hand on a female character in Zuleika—and have endeavoured as far as ye. grossness of our masculine ideas will allow—to preserve her purity without impairing the ardour of her attachment.'[15] Byron here demonstrates surprising critical self-consciousness in analysing his aims. He set himself the task of portraying a woman as both sexually passionate and yet innocent, to combat the nineteenth-century bifurcation of the female stereotype into Mary and Magdalen.

The title of *The Bride of Abydos* is ambiguous, as Byron acknowledged,[16] for Zuleika has been promised by her father to his ally Osman, but also plights her troth to her cousin Selim. She makes no decision between the arranged marriage and that based on romantic love. She stands frozen in impasse, 'mute and motionless' (II, 491), her heart literally bursts under the strain of conflicting loyalties. Had she lived long enough to choose between her suitors then it would have been Byron's attempt to wed passion and purity in the characterization of the heroine that would have split asunder!

Zuleika, in true verse tale heroine fashion, is the only child of a widower father who is a feudal ruler: she is 'last of Giaffir's race' (II, 623). The poem opens with a portrayal of their genuine and mutual father and daughter love, and closes with her death as an unsullied virgin. Her loyalty to her father (and adherence to traditional values) remain unimpugned. As in the tales of Scott and Southey, this guarantees the heroine's true femininity and purity, which, as we have seen, Byron appeared anxious to preserve.

Yet Byron subverts the nineteenth-century medievalism of the Regency verse tales of Tories like Scott and Southey, by drawing attention to the brutality of the feudal military ethos as practised in contemporary times in Turkey. The Pacha is a despot (I, 45), 'begirt with many a gallant slave' (I, 120), whose only pastime is 'the game of mimic slaughter' (I, 247). Though he represents lawful authority in the present time of the story, and thus seems sanctioned to put down the revolt of Selim and his band of patriots, it emerges that he had himself usurped the rightful ruler. The issue is further complicated by the fact that he only contracts to marry Zuleika to Osman to cement their agreement to embark on rebellion against their own feudal overlord. The link between feudal tenure of land

[15] *L&J* iii. 199.
[16] Ibid. 232–3.

and militarism in Turkey is explained by the poet in his note to line 201. The feudal hierarchy is not a Burkean static naturally-ordained order guaranteeing peaceful government, but involves a perpetual struggle for power. This is made clear in the note to line 213, where Byron implies that such a Pacha's 'loyalty' to the Sultan would merely indicate his relative military weakness.[17]

When Giaffir summons Zuleika, his language is reminiscent of punishment or even execution rather than marriage:

> Hence, lead my daughter from her tower—
> Her fate is fixed this very hour . . .
> By me alone be duty taught. (I, 40–2)

Zuleika's father is specifically referred to throughout the poem as a 'despot' (I, 45; II, 326), as 'haughty' (I, 439; II, 268), and as a 'tyrant' (II, 298). The marriage with Osman is arranged for a purely political purpose (I, 192, 210–15), and is imposed on Zuleika by Giaffir's patriarchal authority. It his right 'to bid thee with another dwell' (I, 197). His absolute authority over her will be transferred to her husband:

> And now thou know thy father's will—
> All that thy sex hath need to know—
> 'Twas mine to teach obedience still,
> The way to love, thy lord may shew. (I, 215–18)

Her husband will replicate her father in authority. He is of high lineage (I, 201–2) and advanced years:

> His years need scarce a thought employ—
> I would not have thee wed a boy. (I, 208–9)

Through the portrayal of the relationship of Turkish father and daughter in this scene Byron demonstrates the simultaneous extreme idealization and utter subjection of women in Islamic culture, whose courtly love poetry had been an important influence on that of the West in the Middle Ages.[18] The poem sees the Orient

[17] *CPW* iii. 437.

[18] It seems likely that Islamic culture influenced Western mediaeval art through mercantile and cultural exchanges, particularly via Sicily and Mozarabic Spain. See Peter Dronke, *Mediaeval Latin and the Rise of the European Love Lyric* (Oxford, 1965), pp. 26ff.

as frozen in time, and a contemporary European writer on women in the Ottoman Empire makes exactly the same point that the organization of the world of women had remained static from the Middle Ages, with a nineteenth-century unmarried woman being of a status little better than a chattel.[19]

There is no doubt that Giaffir idolizes his daughter, but we see, in the juxtaposition of his sneers to his 'son' and his encomium on his daughter in Stanza 5 of Canto I, that the very attributes despised in a male are prized in a daughter only as they represent his domination of her. Female beauty is, like the dowry, a currency of exchange between two feudal aristocrats, to be locked in a tower and jealously guarded by Giaffir and subsequently Osman: 'Woe to the head whose eye beheld | My child Zuleika's face unveiled!' (I, 38–9).

Idleness and cultivation of literature are despised by the Pacha in his son (I, 99–100) but cherished in his daughter, because a wealthy Turk demonstrates his power by the number of women he maintains in idleness—their sole function being to cater for male sexual needs. Thus Zuleika's room in the zealously guarded 'women's tower' (I, 80) symbolizes her femininity: it is described as a refuge from the world and a treasure-house for the life of the senses. Yet because it is separate from public life even the gorgeousness of its concentrated essence cannot dissipate its 'air of gloom', for it is also an artificial prison from which she yearns to escape to the cypress grove and the natural equality of the sibling relationship. Symbols of the arts of civilization—religious artefacts (II, 66, 71), poetry, a lute, together with the urns, flowers, rich carpets, and perfume, 'all that can eye or sense delight' (II, 82)—are, like the room's occupant, 'feminine' material luxuries irrelevant to 'masculine' warfare, yet amassed to testify to the Pacha's status.

Byron ironically juxtaposes Zuleika's devoutness with a reminder of the anti-feminism institutionalized in her religion. Zuleika

> . . . oft her Koran conned apart;
> And oft in youthful reverie
> She dream'd what Paradise might be—
> Where woman's parted soul shall go
> Her Prophet had disdained to show;
> But Selim's mansion was secure . . . (II, 103–8)

[19] Ian C. Dengler, 'Turkish Women in the Ottoman Empire', in Lois Beck and Nikki Keddie (eds.), *Women in the Moslem World* (Cambridge, Mass., 1978), pp. 229–44.

Though her father idealizes her purity—her voice is 'like Houris' hymn' (I, 146), she is magical as a Peri (I, 151)—she is not accorded spiritual equality with her father and brother by Islam. When she is about to swear her oath of loyalty to Selim by Mecca's shrine, she again wonders about her lack of status: 'If shrines that ne'er approach allow | To woman's step, admit her vow' (I, 313–14).

Giaffir's love for Zuleika is based on her obedience: she is a 'child of gentleness' (I, 193), described meekly awaiting 'one kind word' to permit her to embrace her father affectionately (I, 182–6). Moreover, it is her virginity which endows her with especial value, so much so that she is dearer to him than her mother was (I, 149). The sexually experienced older woman was a source of anxiety, for, once aroused, her desires might lead to infidelity and even the tainted paternity of her children. But the virgin Zuleika is prized as an untouched commodity 'with all to hope and none to fear' (I, 150).

The narrator's description of Zuleika's beauty is dangerously charged with the ambivalence of her potential sexuality. Compared both to the vision of an angel and the purity of a child's prayer (I, 162–7), Zuleika is also as fair as Eve but as beguiling as the serpent (I, 158–61). Though her passivity is stressed in her 'changing cheek' and 'softness', her beauty is also awe-inspiring in its 'might' and 'majesty' (I, 174–81). As 'last of Giaffir's race' (II, 623), Zuleika represents female sexuality's disturbing potentiality either to perpetuate her father's power after his death through her obedient furthering of his line in the dynastic alliance he has forged or to dissipate it by wilful transgression. She appears to accept her fate odediently: 'In silence bowed the virgin head' (I, 219), with 'stifled feeling'. But, even in the harem where she has seen no man but her 'brother' 'from simple childhood's earliest hour' (I, 420–4), her subversive capacity for passion has been aroused, and it is this same excessive feminine subjectivity that brings about her fatal seizure. The masculine narrator directly addresses her father in describing how her early death robs him of a stake in the future. She had been 'Hope of thine age—thy twilight's lonely beam' (II, 659). The significance of her death for Giaffir is expressed in terms of the loss of a valuable means of exchange of power with other men in the feudal system: as 'thy bride for Osman's bed' (II, 656), or 'she—whom thy Sultan had but seen to wed' (II, 657).

The love of an heiress like Zuleika for a man of (apparently) low birth challenges the whole basis of such feudal power in its system of dynastic alliances. The courtly love theme is clearly indicated by the use of the Persian name for Potiphar's wife for the heroine. Harold Wiener points out that it is uncommon[20], being mentioned only in *The Works of Sir William Jones*, and Herbelot's *Bibliothèque Orientale*. Herbelot's entry is cross-referenced with the comparable story of Megnoun and Leila by the Persian poet Sa'dī, which Selim and Zuleika have been reading together in the poem's opening scene (I, 71–2).

As in Rousseau's *Julie, ou La Nouvelle Héloïse*, an analogy is therefore established between a medieval heroine of tragic courtly love literature and the modern poem's heiress who must choose between allegiance to her father by accepting an arranged marriage with his ally from the ruling class, and her purely personal romantic love for someone of a lower class, in this case, the 'son of a slave . . . from unbelieving mother bred' (I, 81–2). Rousseau had embodied the political theory of his Social Contract in the form of a novel. The heroine symbolized the subject, whose voluntary sacrifice of 'natural law' for social duty is deemed tragic but at the same time a form of chivalric selflessness which marks the highest form of civilization. Women readers empathized with Julie as society's martyr. Madame de Staël commented: 'Son ouvrage est pour les femmes; c'est pour elles qu'il est fait; c'est à elles qu'il peut nuire ou servir.'[21]

Byron and Shelley led a revival of enthusiasm for this novel of sentiment in the early nineteenth century.[22] But because Byron saw Rousseau as a Romantic rebel, the attraction of the novel for him lay particularly in its subversive subtext—the portrayal of consummated forbidden love—rather than its orthodox resolution in a detailed account of how a social marriage ensured the ideal management of a country estate.

[20] Barthelemi D'Herbelot comments that the story of Zuleika and that of Megnoun and Leila are treated similarly in Moslem literature: ' . . . lorsqu'ils parlent non-seulement de l'amour naturel et humain, mais aussi lorsqu'ils s'élèvent jusqu'à celui qui est surnaturel et divin' (*Bibliothèque Orientale* (Maestricht, 1776), p. 926, quoted by Harold Weiner, 'Byron and the East: Literary Sources of the "Turkish Tales"', in Herbert Davis, *et al.* (eds.), *Nineteenth Century Studies* (New York, 1940), pp. 89–129 (104)).

[21] Quoted by Ellen Moers, *Literary Women: The Great Writers* (New York, 1977), p. 150.

[22] See Edward Duffy, *Rousseau in England* (Berkeley, 1979), pp. 71–5.

Byron overtly politicized the romance theme of forbidden love by setting his tale in patriarchal Turkey. The two proposed marriage contracts take the reader back to the dawn of liberal ideology, when the Royalist propagandist, Filmer, argued in *Patriarcha* (1680) that both absolute monarchy and patriarchy in the family were divinely ordained, and Locke responded by his formulation of both government and marriage as contracts by mutual agreement. Because Regency verse tales identified a return to chivalry as sexual propriety and sentimental loyalty to the patriarchal leaders of society, Byron countered by reinstituting courtly love as forbidden passion in the context of brutal Turkish patriarchy.

Most contemporary readers would endorse Zuleika's preference for a voluntary monogamous contractual marriage over Turkish polygamy, of course. But Byron rendered Zuleika's forbidden love more shocking still, by invading the incest taboo—thus giving the poem a decidedly antinomian edge. The use of courtly love to invest disruptive passion with a subversive desire to transgress the laws of society has been current in Western literature ever since the archetypal eternal triangle of Tristan, Isolde, and King Mark.[23] Many critics minimize the significance of incest in *The Bride* because Zuleika and Selim are later revealed to be only cousins. Robert Gleckner asserts that: 'Byron himself finally saw the theme of incest to be really irrelevant to the dramatic development he had in mind.'[24] But this is to ignore Zuleika's viewpoint entirely. For Zuleika's speeches declaring and describing her love are all based on their supposed sibling relationship. When she hears that they are cousins and that Giaffir has murdered Selim's father, she still thinks only in terms of their familial relationship and imagines he has lured her away to revenge himself by stabbing her. Apart from trying to save herself by beseeching him to accept her loyalty as his slave (II, 183), she only utters one further line of speech urging him to escape the Pacha (II, 502).

It is before she knows their true relationship, and in order to retain the sexual equality of their sibling relationship, that Zuleika decides to risk the anger of her father by rejecting the marriage contract he has arranged: 'His wrath would not revoke my word'

[23] Denis de Rougemont, *The Myths of Love*, trans. Richard Howard (London, 1963), pp. 30–75.

[24] Gleckner, *Byron and the Ruins of Paradise*, p. 129.

(II, 416). Afraid of the unknown (I, 225) and of losing her brother's friendship (I, 309–16), Zuleika rejects not just marriage with Osman, but marriage itself. The reader is aware of the eroticism of which Zuleika is innocently unconscious. Her refusal to marry is based on a potentially incestuous love of siblings (I, 394–9), which is intrinsically a fundamental rejection of the concept of marriage as the instrument of forging a network of social and property alliances.

As a Turkish woman, Zuleika is inherently classless: her caste is conferred only by her husband or father. As a female she represents the laws of nature rather than those of society. Because she is without power she is paradoxically free to live entirely in her emotions. The sibling love she offers Selim is seen to be proscribed because it is a re-enactment of that total freedom of the individual which Byron visualized in a pre-lapsarian world: 'We to the cypress groves had flown | And made earth, main and heaven our own!' (I, 169–70). Their love is a rejection of the tyrant's law, but because it is potentially incestuous, it is a rejection also of 'natural law'. This shows the antinomian tendency in Byron's depiction of romantic love.

Alan Richardson stresses the origins of the theme of sibling incest in eighteenth-century associationist psychology and the cult of sentiment.[25] Certainly Byron stresses the naturalness and friendship of a relationship between the sexes founded on common experiences in childhood and shared interests, in comparison with the artificiality of the rigid divisions and sexual stereotyping which appertains in a climate of mercenary matchmaking. *The Bride* echoes the idealization of the childhood pseudo-sibling relationhips in Beckford's *Vathek* and Bernadin de Saint-Pierre's Rousseauistic fable, *Paul et Virginie*. This theme can also be found in the female-authored novel of the Regency period. In Austen's *Mansfield Park*, for example, a love based on the companionship of cousins in childhood (and proscribed by the father of the household, Sir Thomas Bertram) is similarly preferenced both to a marriage of convenience and the dangers of superficial physical attraction for a stranger. But of course Byron differs from such novels by specifically making romantic love anti-social in linking it with armed revolt against the patriarch, and by temporarily actually raising the spectre of incest

[25] Alan Richardson, 'The Dangers of Sympathy: Sibling Incest in English Romantic Poetry', *SEL* 25 (1985), 737–54.

itself. This set his depiction of romantic love apart, not only from that of the female novelists and the tales of Tory writers like Scott and Southey, but also from Whigs like Campbell, Rogers, and Moore, who eulogized marriage and domesticity.

The sibling relationship of Zuleika and Selim also challenges—as socially induced—the polarization of the sexes itself. For their intimacy in upbringing results in a transference of 'feminine' qualities of sensibility to the hero,[26] and a corresponding liveliness and spontaneity in the heroine. Giaffir is contemptuous of Selim's love of natural beauty and literature (I, 71–2). His 'listless eyes . . . pore where babbling waters flow, | And watch unfolding roses blow' (I, 88–9); he is 'pale', 'mute', and 'mournful' (I, 256). While he stands before his 'father' with downcast eyes and gentle voice (I, 49) the Pacha taunts the younger man with his lack of beard (I, 122), poor hunting ability (I, 136), and effeminacy: 'Vain were a father's hope to see | Aught that beseems a man in thee' (I, 83–4). 'Greek in soul', Selim has no aptitude for war, and is thus so unnatural to his sex that he is even below a woman in Giaffir's estimation: 'Go—let thy less than woman's hand | Assume the distaff—not the brand' (I, 99–100).

The very fact that he is allowed into the harem (I, 67) shows that, like Gulchenrouz in *Vathek*, he is an androgynous figure, regarded as sexually immature or impotent. Zuleika, on the other hand, displays her 'unfeminine' capacity for liveliness in the equality of the sibling relationship. She shows disobedience in leaving the harem without permission, and uninhibited playfulness in taking the initiative with the sulky Selim, as well as lack of modesty in showering him with affectionate caresses.

The ritualistic sensuality of the rose scene in Canto I is obviously symbolic of the change in their relationship brought about by Selim's sexual maturation. This is unintentionally initiated by Zuleika's playful attempts to gain his attention. Knowing he is sad at their imminent parting, she eventually pledges her undying love and promises not to marry without her 'brother''s consent:

> Ah! Were I severed from thy side,
> Where thy friend—and who my guide?

[26] Richardson discusses this transference of feminine sensibility to the male protagonist in the portrayal of the poet and his sister in the poetry of Wordsworth, see pp. 747–8.

Years have not seen—time shall not see
The hour that tears my soul from thee. (I, 319–22)

Unwittingly, by her declaration of loyal love, she rouses Selim out of the 'trance' of adolescence into manhood:

Thy cheek, thine eyes, thy lips to kiss,
Like this—and this—no more then this,
For, Alla! sure thy lips are flame,
What fever in thy veins is flushing?
My own have nearly caught the same,
At least I feel my cheek too blushing. (I, 393–401)

This portrayal of a heroine taking the sexual initiative was so innovative that it shocked Byron's contemporaries—liberals and conservatives alike—more than the incest theme itself. The *Anti-Jacobin* censured her language 'which would be indecent even in the mouth of her lover'; the *British Critic* compared her to Scott's and Southey's heroines as 'foreign to the general description of poetical heroines' in the rose scene; *The Champion* found her 'indelicate', as did *The Monthly Museum*, in speeches 'not wholly compatible with the purity of the virgin character'. A later *Anti-Jacobin* review castigated Byron's principal female characters—Zuleika, Medora, and Gulnare—because they 'make strong love to the man, which is not very decorous, nor yet very natural'.[27] For female sexual desire was always portrayed as unnatural in the literature of the period. Zuleika's sexuality is sympathetically portrayed as autonomous, developing spontaneously out of her demonstrative and loving nature. The androgyny of the lovers, and the role-reversal of the sentimental passive hero and lively heroine who takes the sexual initiative, would beome a recurring feature not only of Byron's later tales—particularly *The Corsair*, *Lara*, *The Island*, and *Beppo*, but also would determine the structure of *Don Juan*, and the plays *Sardanapalus* and *Heaven and Earth*.

Peter Manning relates sexual role-reversal in Byron's poetry to his supposed psychological orientation. The poet's conflicting desire for autonomy, yet dependence upon a nurturing female presence in life, leads him to depict women in his poetry in a hostile way. 'If women are sought for their nurturance, they are also shunned lest that very nurturance stifle freedom.'[28] Byron's stormy

[27] Reiman, *Romantics Reviewed*, part B, i. 36, 240; ii. 251; iv. 1715; i. 46.
[28] Peter J. Manning, *Byron and his Fictions* (Detroit, 1978), p. 42.

relationship with his mother, sexual abuse in childhood, lameness, bisexuality, and possible incest with his half-sister Augusta certainly provide plenty of scope for a psychoanalytical approach to his work. But we should also remember that in his letters and journals Byron perpetually described himself and others in terms of the literary roles they appeared to be acting out in life. Byron acted the part of the Gothic villain with a guilty secret (often incest) in life as well as in literature. As for his portrayal of women, Moore commented: 'While persuading himself that they [his women friends] furnished the models of his heroines, he was, on the contrary, but fancying that he beheld his heroines in them.'[29]

One of the most interesting aspects of Byron's poetry is both his use of sexual stereotypes, and his experimentation with role-reversal. Challenging the stereotypes of gender was not merely a personal Byronic trope, but an important feature of the depiction of love in Romanticism. (Remember Blake's idealized androgyny in his art,[30] and the sexual equality and sibling incest of the revolutionary protagonists of Shelley's *Laon and Cythna* (1817)). Peter Thorslev suggests that Romantic poets were influenced by the doctrine of Platonic love, in which the original hermaphrodite soul of man was split by Apollo into two sexes, each destined to search for the other. This idea was then 'translated' into the sibling incest theme, as a reflection of the Romantic hero's narcissistic sensibility.[31] Byron's *Manfred* illustrates this relationship between sibling incest, romantic love, and individualism. Astarte will be shown to be a projection of the hero's own feminine qualities. She functions as a masculine assimilation of the feminine.

In *The Bride*, however, Byron shows his androgynous hero seeking power by the attainment of masculinity—casting off his erstwhile effeminacy. Weiner's research into the literary sources of the tales

[29] Thomas Moore, *Letters and Journals of Lord Byron: with Notices of His Life* (London, 1892), ii. 116.

[30] On Blake and androgyny see Irene Tayler, 'The Woman Scaly', *Midwestern Modern Language Association*, 6 (Spring 1973), 82–98; and Anne K. Mellor, 'Blake's Portrayal of Women', *Blake: An Illustrated Quarterly*, 16: 3 (1982–3), 148–55.

[31] Peter L. Thorslev Jr., 'Incest as Romantic Symbol', *Comparative Literature Studies*, 2 (1965), 41–58. Joanna E. Rapf ('The Byronic Heroine: Incest and the Creative Process', *SEL* 21 (1981), 637–45) suggests that sibling incest in the depiction of the Byronic heroine may be a result of the poet personifying his own creative unconscious as his feminine anima in Jungian terms.

provides evidence of Byron's careful detailing of the way gender roles were strictly determined by education and social custom in Turkish society.[32] The incident of Zuleika's escape to the cypress grove brings the reader's attention to the extent of the restriction on women's freedom of movement, which Byron would have found in Rycaut. His description of the opulent interior of the harem is comparable to that in the letters of Lady Mary Montagu. The contents of Zuleika's room indicate that she was literate and musical, and Byron's note explains that 'many of the Turkish girls are highly accomplished, though not actually qualified for a Christian coterie', though 'Greek females are kept in utter ignorance'.[33] Giaffir's contemptuous criticism of Selim's inadequacy reflects the fact that male education was emphatically military. In his edition of Scott's *Introduction to the Arabian Nights*, Byron would have found a lengthy explanation of the perfunctory education for females and militaristic education for males in Turkey.

In the description of Zuleika's funeral, on which he prided himself as to 'correctness' of detail,[34] Byron's emphasis is on how sentiment is assumed to be a feminine preserve. He describes the 'Wul-wulleh' or death song of the Turkish women, and his note points out, should the reader have missed the point, that the 'silent slaves' of the text 'are the men whose notions of decorum forbid complaint in *public*' (Byron's italics).[35] As Scott commented, in a funeral 'the men take no share, but assume a resigned silence, and retire to sorrow in private'.[36] Even the tombstones of the Turks were sexually differentiated. The woman's is in the shape of a pillar like Zuleika's (II, 720). Byron's note on Selim's headstone (II, 618) makes clear: 'A turban is carved in stone above the graves of *men* only' (Byron's italics).[37]

Byron's classical allusions also show his concern with the differentiation of sexual roles. The allusion to Hero and Leander in the opening of Canto II recalls the *Heroides*, where Ovid rewrites the stories of famous lovers in epistolary form, from the heroine's point of view. As the bride of Abydos, Zuleika is a modern Hero. Robert Ogle has commented that, like Ovid's Hero, Zuleika demonstrates the circumscription of the heroine by her feminine role in society, in her inability

[32] Weiner, 'Byron and the East', *passim*.
[33] *CPW* iii. 439.
[34] *L&J* iii. 165.
[35] *CPW* iii. 442.
[36] Quoted by Weiner, 'Byron and the East', p. 166.
[37] *CPW* iii. 442.

to comprehend the hard realities of the male external world from which she is rigorously separated.[38]

In this feudal society where power is based on the capacity for physical violence, sexual polarities are at their most extreme. When Zuleika's declaration of love transforms the boy into a man, Selim's dramatic transformation from epicene youth to warrior denotes male puberty as a fall into both sexuality and martial aggression. The multiple simile which describes the process (I, 327–46) moves from natural images of the concealed stream of his sexuality, through animal and martial similes, until by line 342 he is likened to 'a tyrant', and will indeed henceforth be all too comparable to the Pacha himself.

Female sexuality, however, makes no such change in the childlike disposition of Zuleika. Femininity for Byron represented the extension into adult life of the unworldliness, subjectivity, and sentiment of childhood, which the male child must perforce reject when entering into adulthood and public life. Lady Blessington recalls Byron commenting:

> To describe woman, the pen should be dipped . . . in the heart of man, ere eighteen summers have passed over his head, and to dry the paper, I would allow only the sighs of adolescence . . . When I attempted to describe Haidée and Zuleika, I endeavoured to forget all that friction with the world had taught me; and if I at all succeeded, it was because I was, and am, penetrated with the conviction that women only know evil from having experienced it through men; whereas men have no criterion to judge of purity of goodness but woman.[39]

The 'purity' of woman is therefore a condition of her separation from public life. After the wearisome masculine business of 'firmans, imposts, levies, state' (I, 455) Zuleika is a refreshing sight to her father: 'Sweet, as the desart-fountain's wave | To lips just cooled in time to save' (I, 151–2). Yet, as Daniel Watkins argues:

> What is projected in the narrative as an example of nonsocial and nonpolitical purity is at every turn politically and socially operative, serving the ends of state power . . . Through the ideological processes of this culture, she is manipulated, deprived of control over her will and her body, and then is given to understand that her powerlessness is in fact virtue, more laudable than the

[38] Robert B. Ogle, 'The Metamorphosis of Selim: Ovidian Myth in *The Bride of Abydos II*', *SiR* 20 (1981), 21–31.

[39] *Blessington*, p. 196. Cf. 'I feel with an Italian woman as if she was a full-grown child, possessing the buoyancy and playfulness of infancy with the deep feeling of womanhood' (ibid. pp. 112–13).

ugly business of politics . . . The very act of idealization, of elevating Zuleika above experience, is seriously political, an act of repression and deprivation . . . [40]

Zuleika's offer of lifelong sisterly devotion parallels the *fraternité* of Selim's band of patriots. Her desire is:

> To soothe thy sickness, watch thy health,
> Partake, but never waste thy wealth,
> Or stand with smiles unmurmuring by,
> And lighten half thy poverty. (I, 400–3)

But Selim transforms the equality of sibling loyalty into a binding marriage contract based on masculine possession, as is emphasized in the thrice-iterated 'mine':

> Now thou art mine, for ever mine
> With life to keep, and scarce with life resign;—
> Now thou art mine, that sacred oath,
> Though sworn by one, has bound us both. (I, 347–50)

When he reveals his concealed masculinity and martial identity, Selim assumes authority by right of gender in his relationship with Zuleika. Likewise, he assumes leadership of the patriots through his newly-discovered aristocratic birth—they are the 'vulgar rank', while he is 'like the ocean-Patriarch' (I, 376; 388). In fact, the new Selim speaks with the same contempt of the capacity of Zuleika's 'softness' to endear him to tyranny and simultaneously to 'unman him' (II, 333–4) as he does of his band's 'visionary schemes' (II, 383).

As an androgynous youth, Selim had been subject to the same patriarchal authority as Zuleika. But when he takes on the attributes of manhood enjoined by Giaffir, he attains a higher status in the patriarchal hierarchy than his sister. He not only adopts a comparably martial ethos to that of the Pacha in rebelling against his rule, but also proposes to take possession of his heiress daughter, along with his rightful inheritance of property and power. His attitude to her becomes proprietary, yet simultaneously reverential: he now adopts the elevated language of the Pacha in speaking of his erstwhile childhood friend in celestial and Biblical imagery:

> But be the star that guides the wanderer—Thou!
> Thou, my Zuleika, share and bless my bark—

[40] See Daniel P. Watkins, *Social Relations in Byron's Eastern Tales* (London and Toronto, 1987), pp. 62–3.

> The Dove of peace and promise to mine ark!
> Or since that hope denied in worlds of strife—
> Be thou the rainbow to the storms of life!
> The evening beam that smiles the clouds away,
> And tints to-morrow with prophetic ray! (II, 395–401)

He even echoes Burke's famous image of Marie Antoinette as queen of chivalry, in citing the defence of Zuleika's purity as sanctioning warfare: 'A thousand swords—with Selim's heart and hand | Wait—wave—defend—destroy—at thy command!' (II, 409–11). It does not surprise us to find that Selim has built his own island 'bower' for Zuleika, where she will be kept away from contamination by the world (II, 408).

In place of the polygamous arranged marriage with Osman, Selim offers a union based on Western monogamous romantic love: 'Unnumber'd perils—but one only love!' (II, 417). It would be a marriage contract voluntarily entered into, like Rousseau's Social Contract. But Selim would be the dominant partner, by virtue of his sex, as his rank gives him leadership over the 'patriots' or subjects (II, 363–8) who 'prate | Of equal rights' (II, 385–6).

The arranged marriage was aristocratic, but the marriage proposed by Selim is bourgeois in character. Zuleika will have to forgo the 'languid years of listless ease' she would enjoy as Osman's wife (II, 414). Her role will be nurture (II, 415), repaid by her husband's 'toils' on her behalf (II, 418). His firmness will be tempered by her tenderness (II, 422–3). The union is specifically linked to masculine individualism: it will inspire the landless (II, 432–3) adventurer in his bid for wealth and power. Her hair is now compared in worth to buried treasure (I, 353–8). He promises: 'The spoil of nations shall bedeck my bride' (II, 413). The match will cement his political alliance with some of Giaffir's followers (II, 269–75), and assist his rise to power:

> Thy name in which thy heart hath prided
> Must change—but, my Zuleika, know,
> That tie is widened—not divided
> Although thy Sire's my deadliest foe. (II, 193–6)

The marriage contract which Selim proposes is based as much on the exchange of protection for power as the social contract defined by Locke and Rousseau. The weaker vessel will benefit by being protected by military strength:

So may the Koran verse displayed
Upon its steel direct my blade,
In danger's hour to guard us both
As I preserve that awful oath! (II, 189–92)

Furthermore, Selim endorses his self-seeking, anti-social ethos as an adventurer by elevating his personal idealization of Zuleika above the values of society. The language of the Covenant (II, 395–9) he uses indicates his wife will be the keeper of his conscience, freeing him from social responsibility. Their marriage will not be part of the traditional ordering of society through its ruling dynasties, but as a bonding together of two individuals in resistance to that society:

To soothe each sorrow—share in each delight—
Blend every thought—do all but disunite!
Once free—'tis mine our horde again to guide—
Friends to each other, foes to aught beside. (II, 424–7)

The nuclear family, by its nurturing of the individualist male, is perceived as fostering a subversive independence in opposition to institutional authority: 'Power sways but by division . . . | Ours be the last' (II, 434–5).

Selim's discourse endows the role of bourgeois wife with the romance of helpmate to a buccaneer. Modern sociologists like Michael Anderson have speculated that domesticity in the nineteenth century 'became associated with a new set of sex-role ideologies involving the strict segregation of work (performed by men away from home) from domestic concerns . . . The home came to be seen as a haven, a retreat from the pressures of a capitalistically-orientated competitive world.'[41] Lawrence Stone, too, believes that the individualistic ideology of an expanding and educated middle class, enjoying sufficient affluence to support a life-style based on privacy and leisure, changed the character of marital relationships.[42] This class, of course, provided Byron with his huge readership for the tales.

The sexual politics of the marriage contract were also the focus of controversy in the early nineteenth century. The cult of

[41] Michael Anderson, *Approaches to the History of the Western Family 1500–1914* (London, 1980), p. 47.

[42] Lawrence Stone, *The Family, Sex, and Marriage in England 1500–1800* (London, 1977), p. 661.

womanhood eulogized the home, and elevated the importance of the status of the wife and mother as performing a socially useful task. Yet the Evangelical movement advocated stricter patriarchal authority. As late as 1846, the anonymous author of *The English Matron* was using the analogy between government and marriage which had originated with the pamphlet battles of Filmer and Locke: 'The government of a household, for the sake of all its inmates, should be a monarchy, but a limited monarchy. Of all forms, a democracy is most uncomfortable in domestic life.'[43]

Obviously, in *The Bride* marriage as a voluntary contract is preferred to the patriarchal arranged marriage, although the heroine's loyalty to her father is given its full weight. But even the proposed marriage by mutual consent does not sufficiently answer the questions the poem has raised on society's circumscription of the individual, through its strict apportioning of sexual roles. The idyllic equality of sibling love would be lost in the transformation to a conjugal relationship, for the Western marriage is seen to retain a modified form of patriarchalism. Selim echoes Giaffir's words on Zulkeika's mother when he envisages that even Zuleika would, when sexually experienced, be tempted to adultery if allowed to live in society:

> . . . in time deceit may come
> When cities cage us in a social home:
> There even thy soul might err—how oft the heart
> Corruption shakes—which Peril could not part!—
> And woman, more than man, when death or woe
> Or even Disgrace would lay her lover low—
> Sunk in the lap of Luxury will shame—
> Away suspicion!—*not* Zuleika's name!
> But life is hazard at the best—and here
> No more remains to win and much to fear. (II, 436–45)

We see that Selim expresses the same proprietary attitude in outlining a monogamous modern marriage as had Giaffir with regard to a polygamous marriage of convenience. Both feel insecure with regard to a woman's sexuality. Whilst her virginity is prized, her much-vaunted purity is revealed as only conditional on her control by men, not deriving from her own moral fortitude. Even a

[43] Quoted by Stone, p. 667.

marriage based on romantic love would be riddled with fear of infidelity and the consequent tainting of offspring.

The putative marriage separates the 'masculine' and 'feminine' values of life: Selim now projects his own former sentiment on to the ethereal image of a saintly wife. Yet he would be the dominant partner, rejecting the equality of their sibling relationship. Selim claims power to challenge the father-figure, through both class and gender heredity, by his pretention to aristocracy and male prerogative over Zuleika. The heroine barely speaks after his transformation to manhood; her death marks Selim's transcendence of his own feminine qualities.

Zuleika's female passion was simultaneously portrayed as both 'natural', in developing out of innocent affection, and having subversive potential, in that it is incompatible with organized society, which is based on the exchange of women by men and the principle of dynastic male primogeniture. While patriarchy is seen to oppress the heroine, Western marriage is eulogized by the hero. Nevertheless, the poet ironically shows how such a marriage might lack sufficient male authority to control female sexuality, even whilst replicating some of the features of a patriarchal sexual relationship.

MEDORA

The relationship between Conrad and Medora in *The Corsair* (1814) is thematically a sequel to that of Selim and Zuleika. It is clear that this is conjugal in nature although, as the reviewer of the *Anti-Jacobin* irritably complained, one is not to know whether Medora is wife or concubine![44] The assertions made by the Giaour and Selim of a romantic love of spiritual dimensions and monogamous unto death had been abstracted from the context of social life: the love affair of *The Giaour* was imaginatively re-created in retrospect by the hero; and in *The Bride* Selim sketches a possible relationship for the future when Zuleika has fled from her father. Medora is the first heroine who is not a victim of a Turkish patriarch, but shown in a monogamous conjugal relationship with her pirate lover. Her unhappiness (and that of Conrad)

[44] Reiman, *Romantics Reviewed*, part B, i. 44.

demonstrates that the bourgeois ideology of domesticity—recognizable even in its exotic setting—and necessity for separate masculine and feminine spheres form a constriction on individual freedom as irksome as that of external authority.

There are three acts to this tragedy: the lovers' parting, Medora learning of Conrad's capture, and his eventual return only to find that she has died of grief. These brief lachrymose scenes are interposed with the long and adventurous narrative of Conrad's capture by Seyd, and escape with the queen of his harem. The structure underlines the rejection of marriage: Conrad's conjugal relationship with Medora is juxtaposed with the scenes of his imprisonment (yet honourable refusal to free himself); her death is coterminous with his release.

Medora is an Oriental version of the 'angel of the house' ideal. Her beauty is described entirely in terms of submissiveness. Her face is 'hidden', her eyes 'downcast drooped', her long fair hair 'dishevelled' (I, 467–71), her form 'meek' (III, 95), 'fainting' (III, 120), and 'still' (III, 603). Her nubility is rendered erotic yet not threatening, by the extreme emphasis on fragility. Byron himself commented: 'I flatter myself that my Leila, Zuleika, Gulnare, Medora and Haidée will always vouch for my taste in beauty: these are the bright creations of my fancy, with rounded forms and delicacy of limbs, nearly so incompatible as to be rarely, if ever, united.'[45]

Medora's 'femininity' is also shown in the way she reacts with impotent and inarticulate emotion to crisis. She clasps Conrad 'mutely' (I, 476) and is unable to frame the word 'farewell' (I, 488). When the pirates return with news of Conrad's capture, her words are wild and irrational (III, 103–6), and, like Parisina, rather than face reality she becomes 'senseless' through emotional trauma (III, 113).

The exaggerated excess which characterizes the sexual stereotyping of the relationship of Medora and Conrad almost slips into self-parody.[46] Medora lives like a caged 'bird of beauty' (I, 346) in her island tower. The light that she keeps burning there for Conrad's ship symbolizes the 'sepulchral lamp' (I, 351) of her

[45] *Blessington*, p. 96. Compare *Medwin*, p. 73: 'My imagination has always delighted in giving them (i.e. women in his poetry) a *beau idéal* likeness.'

[46] Marina Vitale, 'The Domesticated Heroine in Byron's *Corsair* and William Hone's Prose Adaptation', *Literature and History*, 10 (1984), 72–94.

eternal love for him. From the moment he first mentions her, she is associated with Conrad's 'sinking heart' (I, 323). Next he hears her song of unrequited or deserted love, in which the female is characterized in images of darkness, silence, and non-existence in the absence of her lover. She abjectly beseeches just a single tear at her grave: 'The first—last—sole reward of so much love!' (I, 362).

In contrast, the song of the pirates celebrates the freedom of travel, change, danger, and excitement which characterizes a man's life of action: a Hobbesian picture of ruthless individualism and materialistic endeavour. Whereas woman is so fragile that even to hear of her lover's impending departure causes Medora's heart momentarily to cease beating, so that she must be carried to her lone couch, where she will later die of grief (I, 478), the pirates despise the effeminacy of both sickness and death by natural causes: 'Ours the fresh turf, and not the feverish bed' (I, 30).

Both Conrad and Medora are unhappy in their separation and the roles assigned to them through gender. Conrad is a lone figure in the all-male society of the ship; he does not share in the masculine camaraderie and is tortured by the capacity for sentiment he attempts to deny. Medora's feminine destiny is love, yet she is fated always to be left behind by the male adventurer, like Ariadne (I, 444) deserted by Theseus, and Ariosto's Olympia 'loved and left of old' (I, 440). Compare Julia's letter: 'Man's love is of man's life a thing apart, | 'Tis woman's whole existence (*Don Juan*, I, 194).

The death of Medora at the moment he kisses Gulnare in gratitude for her rescue of him from prison implies that the basis of the Byronic hero's guilt is his inadequacy either to fulfil the traditional male role of heroic warrior or to satisfy the virtuous heroine's desire for a lifelong monogamous romantic love.

The poem opens when Conrad eventually returns from sea after a long absence, but it is only to tell Medora he must set out again, doubly emphasizing the continual separation of their lives. Refusing to listen to his explanation (I, 412–20), she eagerly proffers the comforts of home, urging him to partake in the 'feast', and telling him of her 'toil' in selecting the 'best' and 'fairest' fruits, and how she has three times climbed the hill to search out snow to cool his sherbet (I, 425–6)—'Think not I mean to chide'. She proffers, too, civilized entertainment: singing, music, dancing, and literature (I, 433–40). Conrad's rejection, like Selim's, of a 'feminine' domestic existence is underlined by the fact that even if he had been able to stay for the meal he would have taken little pleasure in it, for he is sternly ascetic in his tastes, even compared to the pirates:

> Ne'er for his lip the purpling cup they fill,
> That goblet passes him untasted still—
> And for his fare . . .
> Earth's coarsest bread, the garden's homeliest roots,
> And scarce the summer luxury of fruits,
> His short repast. (I, 67–73)

The point is repeatedly emphasized (I, 422, 429–31; II, 123–4). Medora's desire to nurture him is thus rendered doubly superfluous.

The island society is firmly divided by sex. Whilst the men are away the women must support each other, as Conrad reminds Medora (I, 461). But since woman exists only for love, Conrad's absence is a continual source of reproach:

> . . . wilt thou ne'er,
> My Conrad! learn the joys of peace to share?
> Sure thou hast more than wealth; and many a home
> As bright as this invites us not to roam. (I, 388–91)

Conrad rejects the quietism which underpins the appeal to domesticity. His pride will not rest content until he has stormed the very citadel of Seyd's power. The men's piratical enterprises are fuelled by the desire to defy Turkish authority (I, 399); to amass wealth (I, 390–1); and to fend off any attack by Seyd of the island settlement of wives and dependants (I, 457–9). The helplessness of women—evidenced in the text by the portrayal of Medora perpetually in a state of collapse—is perceived as necessitating male aggression on their behalf. Yet romantic love also brings into being male chivalry: Conrad's love for Medora inspires him to save Seyd's harem, even though it entails losing the battle: 'Oh! burst the Haram—wrong not on your lives | One female form—remember—*we* have wives' (II, 202–3).

However, the vacuous passivity of the woman's role is pushed to such an extreme in the depiction of Medora that the feminine ideal which she represents is questioned in the tale, even while its pathos is idealized. Gulnare, the slave Conrad rescued from the blazing harem, rejects both Eastern patriarchal oppression of women and the Western notion of wifely domesticity. She compares herself to Medora:

Though fond as mine her bosom, form more fair,
I rush through peril which she would not dare.
If that thy heart to hers were truly dear,
Were I thine own—thou wert not lonely here:
An outlaw's spouse—and leave her lord to roam!
What hath such gentle dame to do with home? (III, 298–303)

Gulnare demonstrates the possibility of a heroine who retains the beauty, romantic love, and selflessness of Medora, but who chooses the role of companion in the 'masculine' sphere of action, rather than the separate domestic role assigned to her by her femininity. When Medora dies, she is replaced by the active but masculinized Gulnare and Kaled: the first Byronic heroines who survive their adventures and are not a source of sentimental pathos.

The renegade heroes of the Oriental tales have transferred the idealism they once had for their religion, class, and country to a personal commitment to one woman. Their romantic love proclaims their sexual freedom from both social and natural law as the ultimate expression of their individualism. But the moment that such a love ceases to be in conflict with tyrannical authority, becoming institutionalized in marriage and a source of social conformity, then it ceases to be true romantic love, which for Byron was always subversive and antinomian. Conrad makes this clear to Medora:

My very love to thee is hate to them,
So closely mingling here, that disentwined,
I cease to love thee when I love mankind. (I, 403–5)

In *The Siege of Cornith*, however, the identification of a virtuous domestic heroine with the trap of social conformity would be treated not with pathos, but with savage irony.

FRANCESCA

In *The Siege*, Byron creates a heroine whose character and situation at first appear to conform most closely to those of the verse tales of his contemporaries. Francesca is the only child and heir of the Venetian Minotti, the Christian city-father of Corinth, besieged by the Turks. In his attempt to marry Francesca against her father's will the renegade Alp joins the Turks. His attack on the city combines the military and the sexual in an act of conquest, a veiled violence on the virgin herself:

> Alone, did Alp, the renegade,
> The Moslem warriors sternly teach
> His skill to pierce the promised breach:
> Within these walls a maid was pent . . . (133–55)

As in Southey's *Roderick*, the theme of pagan incursion is a product of the British fears of invasion current at the time of the Peninsular War. The fate of the Christian virgin focuses fear of the Napoleonic anti-hero.

Like Leila and Astarte, Francesca is dead before the opening of the poem, confirming the hero's guilt by the paradox that his very love for her has prompted her demise. Like them she appears to him as a spirit, and thus functions as an abstract symbol in the poem. Byron was influenced in *The Siege* by Goethe's *Die Braut von Korinth* ironically to frame his hero's perception of the heroine, suggesting that her image could be read in an alternative way.[47]

The reader is alerted to Francesca's allegorical significance by the highly-charged tableau of her appearance, sitting motionless with upraised arm and flowing hair in a ruined Greek temple (501–57) and dressed in Grecian style: 'Around her form a thin robe twining, | Nought concealed her bosom shining' (509–10).

Alp's vision of Francesca thus combines the appeal of the erotic with the visual imagery of the Goddess of Liberty. In his study of revolutionary imagery, Ronald Paulson points out that when the masculine icons of Church and monarchy were supplanted by female allegorical figures in Republican France, the Goddess of Liberty combined attributes of Venus and the Virgin Mary or a Caritas figure: 'The act of love, the quintessential act of rebellion in a patriarchal society, was perhaps more significant than the Roman shape of the woman Liberty, which replaced the symbol of the unruly crowd but embodied the underlying symbolism of sexual release and fulfillment beyond the bounds of primogeniture and hierarchy.'[48] Francesca is depicted as a Liberty figure here because

[47] See my note 'The Influence of Madame de Staël's Account of Goethe's *Die Braut von Korinth* in *De l'Allemagne* on the Heroine of Byron's *Siege of Corinth*', *N&Q* NS 35, no. 3 (Sept. 1988), 307–10.

[48] Ronald Paulson, *Representations of Revolution (1789–1820)* (New Haven, Conn., and London, 1983), p. 22.

she appears to Alp as he perceives her: the object of his quest for both freedom and love.

But Alp notices that Francesca is unnaturally still and cold. The reader becomes aware, unlike the hero, that she is a cipher and the speech urging him to do his duty as a Christian is merely projected through her image: 'And her motionless lips lay still as death, | And her words came forth without her breath' (567–8). As in Goethe's poem, the idea of a *femme fatale* is turned on its head. Instead of tempting a male mortal with pagan female sexuality, the shade articulates the constricting ideology of Christianity which has killed her *doppelgänger*—the live girl. While she was alive and reciprocating Alp's love, Francesca was the oppressed victim of her 'inexorable sire' (138) who forbade her marriage to Lanciotto/Alp and caused her broken heart (149–66), and who prefers her death to Alp's victory (817–19). But now she is dead, her image demands his loyalty to 'thy father's creed' (530), threatening him with hell-fire if he does not spare 'thine injured country's sons' (587).

The reader (but not the hero) is thus made aware that the image of Francesca has dual significance. To Alp she is the Marianne of his individualistic quest for freedom, worth attaining by any means, even the Turkish army. But the image of the patriarch's daughter is also a sign used by the Christian powers to try to secure the potential revolutionary's sentimental assent to patriotic, religious, and imperial orthodoxy. The ambivalence of the spirit is shown in the discrepancy between the message its appearance conveys to Alp (love and freedom) and that of its speech (obedience and death).

Alp refuses to desist, and it is Francesca who causes his death, albeit indirectly. During the siege, he pauses in amazement when Minotti tells him she is dead, thus enabling a sniper to take aim (822–33). Significantly, the shot comes from the church porch. The devout Francesca, 'constant at confessional' (157), 'with downcast eyes' (159), recalls the image of the Virgin Mary, who 'with eyes of light and looks of love' (906), presides over the altar of the church, where Minotti stands when he makes the sign of the cross before igniting the gunpowder which is stored in the vaults. Daniel Watkins has commented on the sledgehammer irony here, in that the Christian church is resting upon foundations stored with the weapons of destruction.[49] The father of Francesca is here plainly

[49] Watkins, *Byron's Eastern Tales*, p. 115.

associated with the vengeful God of the Old Testament who, it is threatened, will punish Alp in Hell. As the icon of the Madonna smiles on, Minotti is prepared to exterminate real mothers and babies in its name: 'Still she smiled; even now she smiles, | Though slaughter streams along her aisles' (913–14).

In *The Siege*, Byron has written a verse tale in which the heroine's vulnerability focuses the appeal to the readership's sentiment on behalf of endangered patriarchal, national, and religious orthodoxy. Yet the conventional formula is simultaneously undermined by the ambivalence of this image of pure womanhood. Francesca, like Leila and Astarte, has no independent existence in the poem. Her transparency in the moonlight (516–17) almost cynically indicates her image as an arbitrary sign, whose meaning may be determined by rival ideologies.

3

'The Firmness of a Female Hand': The Active Heroines of the Tales

As in the tales of his contemporaries, the heroines of Byron's Oriental romances are a vehicle for the pathos of beleaguered nationalism. But not for Britain under Napoleonic threat: Byron's fear is that European and Eastern movements for national liberation would be stillborn. For the younger poet was writing his Oriental tales to counter the conservative nostalgia for feudalism of Scott's romances, and particularly to rebut Southey's imperialist ethic. Marilyn Butler has drawn attention to Southey's participation in the successful campaign of the Clapham Sect, which resulted in the Charter Act of 1813, which allowed Christian missionaries into India.[1] *Madoc*, once idealizing the young radical's dream of pantisocracy, was turned about and put to use by the now militant Evangelical and Tory poet, to propagandize the necessity for wholesale conversion of native peoples to the religion and, by implication, the culture of their conquerors. *The Curse of Kehama* portrays Hinduism as a barbaric religion, which it would be a kindness to extirpate. As Butler comments, Byron's response is to create his own Oriental tales, in which the subjugation of the country we now know as Greece is portrayed in the context of two warring monotheistic religions. Both Islam and Christianity are portrayed with equal distaste, as instruments of personal, political, and imperialist control over individuals.

It was a natural development for the poet of *Childe Harold's Pilgrimage*, who took the spirit of place as his muse, to progress to the characterization of narrative heroines who embody both the subjugation and the beauty of Greece. The famous comparison of Greece to a recently dead girl in *The Giaour* (66–102) relates the fate of the drowned female odalisque, Leila, with the poem's

[1] Marilyn Butler, 'The Orientalism of Byron's *Giaour*', in Bernard Beatty and Vincent Newey (eds.), *Byron and the Limits of Fiction* (Liverpool, 1988), pp. 78–96 (81).

opening meditation on her country's decline into slavery. Just as the Muslim fisherman asks us to gaze on the live Leila's soulless body (472–518), here we must contemplate a girl's corpse: 'So coldly sweet, so deadly fair, | We start—for soul is wanting there' (92–3). The necrophiliac imagery simultaneously invokes a feminine Greece and foregrounds the Turkish association of the female with mere carnality: Eden as cadaver. With no male animating spirit of nationalism, its beauty is but 'A gilded halo hovering round decay' (99).

As a harem slave, Leila typifies the Greek subject of the Turkish Empire. Lest the reader should miss the point, Byron explains in a note: 'Athens is the property of the Kislar Aga (the slave of the seraglio and guardian of the women) who appoints the Waywode. A pandar and a eunuch—these are not polite yet true appellations—now *governs* the *governor* of Athens.'[2]

Byron's oriental heroine is the fought-over focus of the eternal triangle, situated between a Turkish tyrant and a debased would-be Western liberator. The obvious political allegory is a commonplace of modern criticism,[3] and could be compared with a political cartoon, like Seymour's *Mrs Greece and her Rough Lovers* (1828) on the later Greek Revolution. Whereas the Sultan holds her by a noose and openly wields his scimitar, the Czar holds a pistol to the Turk's head as if to rescue her, but conceals his scourge behind his back, ready to abuse her himself. Greece's bid for independence is symbolized by Mrs Greece's cry for sexual autonomy.

The association between the rights of woman and political freedom was forged in the revolutionary decade of the 1790s, when the concept of natural law was cited to challenge hierarchical authority. Compare Byron's use of the eternal triangle with that of Blake in *Visions of the Daughters of Albion* (1793). Blake's central character is the heroine Oothoon, a female negro slave, who, having been raped by her owner, is therefore devalued in the eyes of her righteous lover Theotormon and rejected by him. Almost certainly influenced by the ideas and the life of Mary Wollstonecraft, whose children's stories Blake illustrated, the poem is a

[2] *CPW* iii. 416–17.

[3] On the political significance of the eternal triangle see Gleckner, *Byron and the Ruins of Paradise*, pp. 105–6, and McGann, *Fiery Dust*, p. 156.

1. R. Seymour, *Mrs Greece and her Rough Lovers* (1828)
Reproduced from MS 15554 by permission of the Trustees of the British Museum

vehicle for Oothoon's articulation of female sexual freedom.[4] Both Blake and Byron used the concept of romantic love to stress sexual autonomy as the primordial freedom of the individual and the source (not result) of political freedom. For Oothoon's secondary significance is as a symbol of the land of America, justified in tearing off the imperial manacles of Bromion (both patriarchal slave-owner and symbol of British law) in revolutionary fervour. Byron, as a second generation Romantic, had the history of the Terror to contend with, and is therefore far more ambivalent in his portrayal of the Greek slave, Gulnare, who wields the assassin's knife to free herself from Turkish tyranny.

As an odalisque, the female slave was regarded by Byron's readership as tainted by both her servitude and the sexual experience which constitute her oppression.[5] Likewise, the ideal purity of her country when free—in the past or in the future—is extolled by the poet in comparison with the degradation of the present inhabitants. Hellas is hailed in *The Giaour*: 'Clime of the unforgotten brave! . . . / Shrine of the mighty' (103–6). But the present-day Greek subjects of the Ottoman Empire are 'slaves' who 'crawl from cradle to the grave' (149–51). 'Stained with each evil that pollutes mankind' (153–4), they are hardly human, 'least above the brutes'. The fate of the harem odalisque in *The Corsair* is treated with the same mixture of morbid fascination and genuine indignation as is the casual use of the Greeks as target practice by Seyd's soldiers (II, 16–28).

The heroine is not merely conventionally used as the genius of her country in these poems of Blake and Byron, for the concept of femininity is central to the relationship between Romanticism and revolution. Blake's and Byron's female slaves are quintessential subjects, inferior in sex, class, and colonized race. Traditionally, those subject to authority had been conventionally perceived as also subject to emotion, in the sense of matter worked upon. Children, peasants, natives, and women were conventionally characterized as both innocently close to nature and dangerously prone to subversive passions, thus justifying the necessity for their subordination.

[4] On *Visions of the Daughters of Albion* see D. V. Erdman, *Blake: Prophet against Empire* (Princeton, 1954; repr., 1977), p. 228.

[5] For example, Ellis of *The Quarterly Review* describes Leila as 'a beautiful Circassian slave, highly seducing, and like most slaves, easily seduced' (Reiman, *Romantics Reviewed*, part B, v. 2002–12).

But with the revolutionary fervour of the '90s, Romantic poetry such as Blake's vindicated both the quintessential subject and her 'feminine' emotion. Wordsworth's *Lyrical Ballads* also expressed this democratic spirit in sympathetically portraying female peasants, as did much popular verse of the time. Significantly, by the early nineteenth century, the word 'subject' was beginning to take on, from the development of German idealist thought, the new meaning of active mind or thinking agent.[6] As theories of the imagination developed, male Romantic poets invaded the formerly despised 'feminine' domain of sensibility and made it their own.[7]

During the Napoleonic period, however, the liberal cult of sentiment was countered by a backlash of Regency women novelists influenced by the Evangelical movement, who portrayed a new notion of woman, as emphatically not subject to irrational emotion, but capable of becoming well-educated, prudent, obedient, Christian, rational members of society with an essential domestic role. Cora Kaplan speculates that the intense focus on female sexual conduct in the novel of the period suggests that the subject of female subjectivity had become 'the displaced and condensed site for the general anxiety about individual behaviour, which republican and liberal political philosophy had stirred up'.[8]

Byron's contribution to the dialectic was typically a contradictory one. He rehabilitated, and even exaggerated, the pejorative traditional characterization of woman as the essence of subjectivity, as we have already seen. On the other hand, he celebrated this subversive 'feminine' capacity for passion, as a defiant avowal of individualism at a time when there seemed to be a consensus on the need for moral rigour and social conformity.

GULNARE

Byron's *Corsair* marked the apex of his popularity as the fashionable poet of the day. Ten thousand copies were sold on the

[6] Raymond Williams, *Keywords: A Vocabulary of Culture and Society* (Glasgow, 1976), pp. 259–64.

[7] See Ross, *Contours of Masculine Desire*, ch. 1; and Richardson, 'Romanticism and the Colonization of the Feminine', in Mellor (ed.), *Romanticism and Feminism*, pp. 13–25.

[8] Cora Kaplan, 'Pandora's Box: Subjectivity, Class, and Sexuality in Socialist Feminist Criticism', in Gayle Greene and Coppélia Kahn (eds.), *Making a Difference: Feminist Literary Criticism* (London, 1985), pp. 146–76.

first day of the poem's publication, and within a month twenty-five thousand copies, comprising seven editions, had been sold.[9] In it Byron seemed to abandon poetic experiment: he returned to the heroic couplet, and adopted an almost purely narrative form, after the romantic fragments of *The Giaour* and the dramatic dialogue of *The Bride*. The glowering hero was another Giaour. The relationship between Conrad and Medora, as we have seen, is a thematic sequel to that of Selim and Zuleika, the lovers apparently now married.

Where Byron does break new ground is in introducing a second and contrasting heroine, Gulnare. Scott's contrast between Clare and Constance in *Marmion* was probably an influence, but rather than a simple dichotomy between good and evil, Medora embodies feminine passivity in the heroine as victim, whilst Gulnare enacts the active passion of the heroine as rebel. In the development of the sequence of Oriental tales, the function of the heroine has evolved from a mere memory or ghostly presence conjured up by the hero's psyche to a fully-realized characterization. In Gulnare, the heroine plays, for the first time, a more active and resourceful part in the story than the hero. This trend was to be continued in the portrayal of Haidée in *Don Juan* and Neuha in *The Island*.

The development of the heroine's role has prompted various critical responses. Bernard Blackstone comments on the 'growing importance of the feminine element' in general in *The Corsair*, seeing the poetic imagery in terms of dualistic symbolism.[10] McGann finds *The Corsair* and *Lara* most clearly illustrative of his comparison of the tales with Blake's Orc cycle, the heroines being allegorical representations of the heroes' souls.[11] This neatly schematic overview of the tales takes no account of the fact that Gulnare—supposedly a mere emanation—becomes the prime mover in the adventure. Gleckner, however, notes the development of Byron's heroines from one-dimensional symbols to the complexity and conflict of Medora and Gulnare, reading the sexual dynamics of the tale in terms of Platonic theory. Byron 'sees man as temperamentally hermaphrodite', and although he associates heart with woman and mind with man, 'the ultimate outcome of each poem proclaims clearly the mixture of these in all men and women,

9 *Life*, i. 433.
10 Bernard Blackstone, *Byron: A Survey* (London, 1975), p. 121.
11 McGann, *Fiery Dust*, p. 190.

their essential humanity residing in the former (their 'feminine' side), their inhumanity and corruption in the latter (their 'manliness').' The irony of *The Corsair* is that in order to escape Gulnare must become masculinized, but Conrad must passively submit to being rescued by feminine means.[12]

Though Gleckner's comments are apposite, he does not give sufficient weight to the ambivalence with which Gulnare is portrayed. In this ambivalence lies the popular appeal of romance to both subversive desires and the conservative fears of the reader simultaneously. Gulnare is first seen in her conventional role of maiden in distress, being rescued by Conrad from the blazing harem. But in the second part of the story she herself becomes the rescuing warrior. By attributing the assassination of the tyrant to the heroine the poet is utilizing the shock of reversing sexual stereotypes to underline the full horror of the revolutionary action.

The ambivalence of the portrayal of Gulnare lies in the power of decontextualized exotic romance to tap revolutionary fervour on behalf of Greece, which might be safely and nostalgically indulged, yet simultaneously to play with the possibility of the application of the image to Regency Britain. McGann sees *The Corsair* as 'partly a symbolic formulation of the political situation of the day, as Byron saw it, with its contest between equivocal forces of revolt and the established powers of an old and corrupt order'.[13] A Byronic hero like Conrad is first and foremost a class-traitor who allies himself with a rebel band of patriots, to proclaim his individualism and hatred for the status quo. The parallel with the poet's own ambivalent attraction to political radicalism is sufficiently obvious.[14] The Byronic hero's relationship with these commoners is always laconically admitted to be self-seeking, cynical, and seignorial (*The Giaour*, 1008–21; *The Bride*, II, 363–87; *The Corsair*, I, 169–86; *Lara*, II, 157–225).

The image of the disaffected and dispossessed nobleman allying himself Coriolanus-like with his country's enemy, either external, or internal in the shape of rebellious peasants, was a threatening political image with contemporary significance for Britain, at the

[12] Gleckner, *Byron and the Ruins of Paradise*, pp. 145–8.

[13] *CPW*, iii. 445.

[14] For a detailed discussion of Byron's ambivalence towards political radicalism see Malcolm Kelsall, *Byron's Politics* (Brighton, 1987), pp. 82–118.

time of the Napoleonic wars. Byron deliberately underlined the political significance of Conrad by giving him the name of a Ghibelline aristocrat who unsuccessfully tried to retain traditional Republican government, only to be defeated by the despotic Guelphs, in thirteenth-century Italy. Those who had read their Sismondi would also know that the House of Hanover was descended from the Guelphs.[15] The poet's insistence that *Lines to a Lady Weeping* be published with *The Corsair* shows that he wanted the readership to make the connection between the alienated noble, Conrad, and the Whig leaders abandoned by their erstwhile patron, the Regent, in 1811. The Byronic hero's leadership of a band of piratical 'patriots' indicates the poet's fears that the rejected Whigs will be driven to ally themselves with radical extremists. The symbolism of the poem's contrasting heroines makes clear that the death of the distressed lady of chivalry in her tower is accompanied by the hero's adoption of a very different companion, from the lowest section of society.

The depiction of Gulnare is therefore the heart of the poem, encapsulating both the excitement and the fear of popular revolt: the dream of Greece freeing herself from Turkish tyranny and the nightmare of the French Terror. The sexual oppression of a young girl by a Turkish tyrant was a subject certain to engage the sympathies of the widest spectrum of readers. This powerful appeal of the heroine in distress was combined with that of Philhellenism, likewise a political sentiment with which most of his readership could identify. The metamorphosis of Gulnare from compliant slave to assassin is an even more powerful image of revolution than that of the hero, because it is actually dramatized in the poem, whereas Conrad's change of heart from idealist to criminal is merely recounted by the narrator.

The relationship between Conrad and Gulnare is complementary. He gives her insight into her condition; she rescues him from the impasse of despair. The romance displaces and explores the dilemma of a Regency radical aristocrat with regard to the emancipation of the lower classes. It is not until she experiences Conrad's Western respect for women that Gulnare realizes the extent of her oppression by Seyd (II, 261–8). Conrad's aristocratic ideal of chivalry to women can thus be portrayed as enlightening in

[15] See *CPW*, iii. 445.

the context of an Oriental harem, just as Philhellenism—the product of a Western aristocratic education—was perceived as enlightening to the contemporary Romaic population, who were ignorant of the republicanism of ancient Greece. The tale thus provides a context in which aristocratic values are the inspiration behind the dawning of revolutionary consciousness of the subject, but simultaneously dramatizes the hero's impotence as he languishes in chains in the Pacha's prison.

Gratitude for her rescue and pity for the Westerner's impending execution prompt Gulnare to defy Seyd for the first time, by visiting Conrad in his dungeon to thank him, at the risk of her life: 'Ah! rather ask what will not woman dare? | Whom youth and pity lead like thee, Gulnare!' (II, 407–8). In return she learns from him of the existence of romantic love, from his account of his relationship with Medora (II, 493–6). Falteringly, she learns to distinguish between love and duty in sexual relationships.

> My love—stern Seyd's! Oh—No—No—Not my love—
> Yet much this heart, that strives no more, once strove
> To meet his passion—but it would not be.
> I felt—I feel—love dwells with—with the free.
> (II, 499–502)

The hesitations of the verse emphasize the gradual revelation she is experiencing. Only by knowing Conrad does she learn the meaning of freedom—the primary freedom of sexual autonomy.

Now her acquiescence in fulfilling Seyd's sexual needs turns to disgust:

> I am a slave, a favoured slave at best,
> To share his splendour, and seem very blest! . . .
> He takes the hand I give not—nor withold—
> Its pulse nor checked—nor quickened—calmly cold:
> And when resigned, it drops a lifeless weight
> From one I never loved enough to hate.
> No warmth these lips return by his imprest,
> And chilled remembrance shudders o'er the rest . . .
> But still—he goes unmourned—returns unsought—
> And oft when present—absent from my thought.
> Or when reflection comes, and come it must—
> I fear that henceforth 'twill but bring disgust.
> (II, 503–22)

In the midst of Oriental melodrama we are given this detailed and sensitive insight into a young bride's view of a marriage of convenience, as apposite in Regency England as in Turkey. The reviewer of the *Anti-Jacobin* condemned 'the indelicate and disgusting picture of a woman consigned to the embraces of a man she loathes'.[16]

The tableau of a 'seraph' holding a lamp aloft (II, 398) in a dungeon or dropping a single tear of pity on a prisoner's chains (II, 541) employed familiar Whiggish sentimental imagery. But Gulnare does not stop at sentiment. She now attempts to save the life of her rescuer by the use of 'feminine' cunning. She appeals to Seyd's greed by suggesting that by releasing Conrad he could obtain a large ransom, and still have the opportunity to kill Conrad in battle since his band is so depleted (III, 145–52). The Pacha is intelligent enough to see through this, but, unable to comprehend Gulnare's pity, he can only ascribe her motivation to lust (III, 178–85). She is now also threatened with death. But the violence of Seyd's reaction only confirms Gulnare's growing realization that she herself is as oppressed as Conrad: 'She was a slave—from such may captives claim | A fellow-feeling, differing but in name' (III, 202–3). The transformation of Gulnare from the proponent of feminine sympathy to avenger is achieved when the strong feelings aroused by the Corsair's plight turn to anger: 'And little deemed he what thy heart, Gulnare! | When soft could feel, and when incensed could dare' (III, 198–9).

When she visits Conrad for the second time, her demeanour has changed. Her hesitation has vanished; she no longer refers to Seyd as merely 'the Pacha' but 'That hated tyrant, Conrad—he must bleed!' (III, 319). Like Conrad, she has been stung by wrongful accusation of treachery into defence of her honour as an individual: 'Wronged—spurned—reviled—and it shall be avenged' (320). She owes Seyd no allegiance; their relationship was of power not love: 'I never loved—he bought me—somewhat high' (III, 329). When Seyd passed the death sentence on her, merely on suspicion of her motives in pleading for Conrad's life, she became fully aware of her status as little more than a chattel:

> When wearier of these fleeting charms and me,
> There yawns the sack—and yonder rolls the sea!

[16] Reiman, *Romantics Reviewed*, part B, i. 46.

What, am I then a toy for dotard's play,
To wear but till the gilding frets away? (III, 340–3)

The final indignity is that her execution has been deferred until her owner has tired of her sexually. Until then he 'Would fain reserve me for his lordly will' (III, 339). She had decided to escape and to free the prisoner, but it is revenge for her treatment as a chattel that determines her to murder Seyd (III, 346–8).

Moreover, her heart's rebellion is further fired by unrequited love for Conrad: 'With all that woman feels but should not tell . . . | It feared thee—thanked thee—pitied—maddened—loved' (III, 293–5) This revelation of the subversive, changeable passions, uncontrolled by reason and linked with madness and murder, beneath the exterior of silent, modest femininity taps two contemporary fears simultaneously. Gulnare is the image of revolutionary subversion; she also embodies male fear of explicit female sexuality. This fear is enacted by Conrad, who is so startled by her frank 'Now, I am all thine own' that she has to reassure him that only through such 'fire' will his freedom be attained:

Oh! could'st thou prove my truth, thou would'st not start,
Nor fear the fire that lights an Eastern heart,
'Tis now the beacon of the safety—now
It points within the port a Mainote prow.
(III, 352–5)

Gulnare urges: 'If thou hast courage still, and would'st be free, | Receive this poignard—rise and follow me!' (III, 306–7). But the Corsair refuses to knife a sleeping man. He recognizes the legal basis of Seyd's authority: 'Well have I earned—not here alone—the meed | Of Seyd's revenge, by many a lawless deed' (III, 286–7). He cites his aristocratic code of chivalry as based on masculine superiority: 'Who spares a woman's seeks not slumber's life' (III, 365).

The emptiness of this pretension to only 'open' honourable war is demonstrated by the fact that Seyd himself has spent the interval by considering which form of torture would give Conrad the most lingering death. Georg Lukács has commented that both Adam Ferguson and later Schiller pointed out the 'contrast between the splendidly naïve moral ingenuousness of the Greeks and the empty, exaggerated, and false conventions of bourgeois society in literary depictions of warfare'. He quotes Ferguson:

> The hero of Greek poetry proceeds on the maxims of animosity and hostile passion . . . The hero of modern romance professes a contempt for stratagem, as well as of danger, and unites in the same person characters and dispositions seemingly quite opposite: ferocity with gentleness, and the love of blood with sentiments of tenderness and pity.[17]

Byron is sufficiently aware of this discrepancy to point out the irony of such high-mindedness expressed by a helpless hero languishing in prison, awaiting the symbolic rape of a death by impalement. Yet he nevertheless shows his ambivalence towards the 'proverbial wiles, and ancient craft' of the Greeks (*The Giaour*, 157–60) by portraying the assassination of the sleeping Turk as a feminine act.

While Conrad prevaricates even about escape, worrying that the clanking of his chains will alert the guards, Gulnare determines to 'try the firmness of a female hand' (III, 380). He literally follows 'at her beck' down the winding dark passages, horrified to see by the spot of blood on her forehead, as she rejoins him, that she has not shown 'feminine' pity (III, 407), but has indeed killed her master.

> Again he looked, the wildness of her eye
> Starts from the day abrupt and fearfully.
> She stopped—threw back her dark far-floating hair,
> That nearly veiled her face and bosom fair:
>
> (III, 408–11)

The wildness of feminine passion, the floating hair, and the mark of Cain on a female brow all conjured up for the contemporary reader the image of Gulnare as a virago: symbol of the Terror. She would have brought to mind the feminist Théroigne de Méricourt, who had been cast 'in the eyes of her contemporaries, and of historians from Lamartine to Carlyle, as a symbol of the people's vengeance, a virago urging on the mob'. Théroigne became a mythologized figure: dressed in a blood-red riding habit, armed with sabre and pistols, she was accredited with leading the assault on the Bastille and the march of the women on Versailles.[18] The figure of Gulnare

[17] Georg Lukács, *Goethe and his Age*, trans. Robert Anchor (London, 1968), pp. 106–7.

[18] Linda Kelly, *Women of the French Revolution* (London, 1987), p. 11.

combined the virago with another threatening female image from the French Revolution: that of Charlotte Corday, the assassin of Marat.

Instead of depicting her in the traditional female role of obstacle to the hero's quest, like Dido or indeed Medora, Byron creates in Gulnare—as later in Kaled and Myrrha—a warrior maiden who not only accompanies the hero but proves herself indispensable to his mission. Southey's *Joan of Arc* was probably an influence. (One of her comrades in arms is named Conrade.) Brian Wilkie notes epic precedents for Southey's warrior-maiden: Camilla in the *Aeneid*, Clorinda in *Jerusalem Delivered*, Bradamant in *Orlando Furioso*, and Britomart in *The Faerie Queene*.[19] German drama, too, featured active female protagonists such as Goethe's Eugenie, Schiller's Johanna, and Kleist's Käthchen. While retaining the sensibility of earlier *Sturm und Drang* heroines, these active Amazonian heroines asserted themselves alongside men in the public arena, Johanna and Penthesilea actually becoming soldiers.[20]

The passive heroines discussed in Chapter 2 were dispossessed, mysterious, separate beings, their deaths inevitable in a world of power struggles between men. But then Byron transfers the bourgeois self-determination of his heroes to the active heroines, Gulnare, Kaled, and Myrrha. Gulnare becomes the leader of the Corsair's rescue, his equal and helpmeet. She has done the work of winning over Seyd's followers to revolt, and bribed the remainder to keep silent. She has a Greek ship waiting. She claps her hands, and her own band of vassals appear to remove Conrad's chains and to conduct him to a secret passage to the shore. As they sail away, she is his equivalent: a pirate chief, with her own ship and crew. Indeed the poet declares, had Conrad's own men known of her exploits, 'she were their queen' also (III, 510).

The spot of blood on her forehead now admits the Byronic heroine for the first time to the ranks of guilty mankind instead of idealized Other. Interestingly, this removes at a stroke her sexual attraction for the hero: 'That spot of blood, that light but guilty streak, | Had banished all the beauty from her cheek!' (III, 426–7).

[19] On the Dido and Aeneas theme in narrative poetry of the period see Wilkie, *Romantic Poets and Epic Tradition*, pp. 30–58.

[20] Julie D. Prandi, *Spirited Women Heroes: Major Female Characters in the Dramas of Goethe, Schiller and Kleist* (Berne, Frankfurt-on-Main, and New York, 1983), pp. 2–3.

When he compares her with the beau ideal of feminine fragility, Medora, he feels repugnance for Gulnare: 'He thought on her afar, his lonely bride: | He turned and saw—Gulnare the homicide!' (III, 462–3).

Conrad's comparison of Gulnare and Medora here, and the later death of Medora at the very moment he kisses Gulnare, shows how the autonomy of the female individualistic heroine conflicts with the traditional notion of 'femininity', formulated to serve the needs of fathers and husbands in a male-dominated society. Gulnare cannot be regarded as feminine whilst she holds an equal relationship with the hero. When she melts into tears, kneels at his feet, and begs forgiveness (III, 466–75), she shows acceptable humility. When they are met by Conrad's pirates, she excites their stares and curiosity, as a woman in a man's world. But instead of carrying on the role of initiator of the escape, she resigns leadership to Conrad, signalling this by resuming the conventional 'feminine' posture of silence and passivity: 'She drops her veil, and stands in silence by; | Her arms are meekly folded . . . ' (III, 517–18). Byron draws the reader's attention to the transformation. She 'now seemed changed and humble—faint and meek' (III, 531). Only when she demonstrates her subordinate role can Conrad accept her kiss in gratitude for his rescue.

The bold portrait of an active heroine had to be compromised at the end of the tale, if Conrad himself was not to be entirely eclipsed.[21] Contemporary critics expressed their relief at Gulnare's acceptance of a role of female passivity. The *Monthly Review* noted the lack of precedents in representing a female committing murder in poetry, and gratefully approved 'the return of that natural softness which must ever form a prevailing feature in the female character'.[22]

The alarming transformation of the heroine of sentiment into a blood-freezing homicide, an unnaturally passionate and active woman taking on a man's role, dramatized for Byron's readership their widespread fear of the subjective passions of rebellious subjects gaining the upper hand. Yet Gulnare's degradation as an oppressed subject had been sympathetically portrayed, and she is reassuringly shown after the murder as willing to accept the

[21] See Gloria T. Hull, 'The Byronic Heroine and Byron's *The Corsair*', *Ariel*, 9 (1978), 71–83 (81).

[22] Reiman, *Romantics Reviewed*, part B, iv. 1748.

authority of Conrad, her superior in rank, race, and sex. So although the ambivalence of the active heroine has been given its full weight, she is finally accepted as a worthy companion of the Byronic hero.

KALED

In *Lara*, the last of the series,[23] the idealization of femininity and Philhellenism are together abandoned. Now the hero and heroine lead a peasants' revolt against aristocratic rule in his own Western country. The heroine is correspondingly a warrior-maiden. But dangerous 'feminine' subjectivity in both Kaled and the serfs is seen to be controlled by the charismatic power of Lara's leadership by right of gender and rank.

The conventional romantic heroine, represented in the earlier tales as an unattainable beau ideal or muse figure has vanished entirely. Unlike all the other tales, there are no accounts of the quasi-spiritual nature of love in *Lara*. Kaled's devotion is of earthly dimensions. Kaled, like Gulnare, outlives her lover. She is not a ghostly chimera, or the object of Lara's quest, but his constant companion. This comradely relationship recalls the pre-sexual sibling relationship of Selim and Zuleika. But instead of an androgynous boy abjuring warfare we have the sexual role-reversal of a masculinized girl participating in the politics and battles of the public world.

As Gleckner has pointed out, Lara does not even know Kaled is a woman, otherwise there would be no reason for her disguise.[24] She has renounced her sex, class, family, and country for the sake of unrequited love (I, 524–5). It is now the disguised heroine who demonstrates the chivalrous self-sacrifice of courtly love and knightly service to her lover. The roles have been reversed. The strength and independence of female passion are no longer to be feared when put to the service of the 'feminine' virtue of selfless devotion. Kaled, like Gulnare, accepts the impossibility of a sexual relationship with her beloved. Her stoic containment of her passion

[23] Byron wrote of *The Giaour*, *The Bride*, *The Corsair*, and *Lara*: 'The last completes the series—and its very likeness renders it necessary to the others' (*L&J* iv. 165).

[24] Gleckner, *Byron and the Ruins of Paradise*, p. 163.

renders safe her unnatural 'masculine' independence and adoption of a masculine way of life. This was recognized by the *Eclectic Review*: 'The unfeminine and yet most womanly attachment of Kaled to her master—unfeminine only in its origin and in the degree of the passion—most womanly in its disinterestedness and secrecy and truth—is represented so as not to appear to offend against the dignity of her sex.'[25]

Kaled's disguise is not merely ornamental, like that of the irritating Edith in Scott's *The Lord of the Isles* (1814), whose frequent faintings and blushes signal her femininity. Kaled does not play, but really does enact a masculine role as friend and subordinate fellow-soldier to Lara. Byron does not allow the heroine equal pretensions to the gift of reason, as did Enlightenment thinkers and feminists like Mary Wollstonecraft. Neither did he link her right to independent conduct with her Christianity, as did many Evangelical woman writers of the period.[26] None of Byron's heroines puts religion before passion, and her capacity for feeling not thinking is her hallmark. But Kaled, like Gulnare, is now allowed a will to self-aggrandizement and individualism equal to the hero's. She changes her own destiny through her own actions. Her lack of a social and family background, her lack of a 'feminine' domestic role, absolves the poet from the convention of showing the detrimental effect of female passion on society.

Kaled is just as much a member of fallen humanity as her male partner. She is just as much a warrior, to be found in the thick of battle (II, 388–93). As in many recorded cases of eighteenth- and nineteenth-century female soldiers and sailors, her sex goes undetected until she needs medical attention. Her fierce individualism is equivalent to that of the typical Byronic hero: she denies Christian solace, by flinging back the crucifix proffered to the dying Lara (II, 476–89). There is every reason to believe that it was the devoted Kaled who carried out the murder of Ezzelin on behalf of Lara.[27]

The murder sets off the train of events which leads the pair to identify with the peasantry in rebellion and civil war, which in turn

[25] Reiman, *Romantics Reviewed*, part B, iii. 727.

[26] See e.g. the dramatization of a woman's right not to marry, but to form a female household devoted to Christian good living in Sarah Scott's *Millenium Hall* (1762). Novels like *Self Control* by Mary Brunton illustrated a woman's right to oppose her father, family, and friends in refusing to marry a known libertine: her independence is justified by her Christianity.

[27] See W. H. Marshall, *The Structure of Byron's Major Poems*, p. 52 ff.

condemns the hero to defeat by 'masculine' law, and the heroine to 'feminine' excessive subjectivity, resulting in madness. Their fate shows the inevitable doom of purely personal self-assertion, but it falls to Kaled alone to demonstrate at least the loyalty and self-sacrifice of a purely personal ideal of love.

Byron was probably not entirely disingenuous in being eager to have *Lara* published with Rogers's *Jacqueline*. Not only was he aware that the former was too inferior a production to stand alone, as he readily admitted, but he must also have realized that the heroines of the two poems would make a startling contrast. Jacqueline is an example of the sentimentalization of the domestic feminine ideal; Kaled demonstrates the new Byronic 'masculine' self-assertion of the passionate heroine.

Jacqueline initially runs away to marry her lover, but, unable to bear life without the blessing of her aristocratic widower father, returns to a scene of mutual forgiveness and reconciliation. The poem concludes with an encomium on the virtues of home and family. The *raison d'être* of the tale is the pathetic description of the grievous loss of Jacqueline felt by her venerable father, little brother, children of the village, recipients of her charitable work, and even family pets. The importance of woman's role as home-maker is extolled through grief for her absence, then joy at her return, and will be extended in her forthcoming marriage. The poem concludes with the image of autocracy, Louis XIV being introduced to induce the pity of the reader for the monarch in that he is denied the joys of hearth and home in spite of all his power. The middle-class readers—particularly women—are therefore indirectly asked to see home as an enclave of peace and freedom, preferable to the onerous and dirty business of politics and public life.

In Byron's tales, too, conjugal love has been idealized as a refuge from the public world in *The Bride* and *The Corsair*, though Byron implies that the exclusivity of the relationship may be antisocial rather than a means of socialization. Even so, the deaths of Zuleika and Medora serve only to obscure or smooth over the contradictions which begin to emerge in these tales. For the idealization of a monogamous love, consisting of a partnership between complementary but highly differentiated gendered roles, even if not a legal marriage, represents a constriction which coexists uneasily with the Byronic vision of masculinized individual freedom from social values. In *Lara* there is no conjugal relationship; the heroine has no separate social role; she participates in the perpetual masculine battle for power that constitutes Byron's view of history. The stereotype of femininity as passive beauty has been superseded by the stoic ideal of selfless unrequited love and service.

NEUHA

Byron's last romantic tale, *The Island* (1823), makes an intriguing contrast with the earlier series of Oriental tales. McGann has remarked of the latter: 'The . . . Oriental Tales are not merely a set of exotic adventure stories. They constitute a series of symbolic historical and political meditations on current European ideology and politics in the context of the relations between East and West after the break-up of the Roman Empire and the emergence of Islam.'[28]

The political background of the last tale, however, is the mutiny on the English ship, the *Bounty*, which took place on the significant date of 28 April 1789, a week before the meeting of the states-general which marked the beginning of the French Revolution. The nineteenth century was to mythologize the event in revolutionary terms, as the rightful deposition by the common seamen, under the leadership of the moody gentleman-officer, Fletcher Christian, of the tyrannical flogging captain, who was both the representative of the king and linked to the slave trade (his mission was to find cheap food for West Indian plantation owners)—a Byronic story if ever there was one. In fact, Jocelyn Dunphy comments on the discourse of liberal Romanticism utilized by the friends of Christian in their condemnation of Bligh, and quotes a poem by Isaac Wilkinson actually calling for Byron's sympathy and support for Christian's cause.[29]

But significantly, though Christian is characterized as a Byronic hero, he is only a minor character in *The Island*, and Byron chose to consult no accounts justifying the mutiny, only Bligh's own *Voyage*

[28] Jerome McGann, *The Beauty of Inflections: Literary Investigations in Historical Method and Theory* (Oxford, 1985), p. 262.

[29] Jocelyn Dunphy, 'Insurrection and Repression: Bligh's 1790 "Narrative of the Mutiny on board H.M. Ship Bounty"', in Francis Barker (ed.), *1789: Reading, Writing, Revolution* (Proceedings of the Essex Conference on the Sociology of Literature, July 1981 (University of Essex, 1982), pp. 281–301, (292)).

(1792), an expanded version of his *Narrative* (1790). In no way is Bligh characterized as a tyrant in the poem. That Byron made a deliberate choice not to do so is apparent from his letter to Leigh Hunt: '. . . I have two things to avoid—the first that of running foul of my own *Corsair* and style, so as to reproduce repetition and monotony—and the other not to run counter to the reigning stupidity altogether, otherwise they will say I am eulogizing *Mutiny*. This must produce tameness in some degree.'[30]

In fact, in *The Island*, as in the Oriental tales and in *Don Juan*, the politics of historical record are not foregrounded. McGann, in the comment above, concedes as much in his formulation 'symbolic . . . meditations'. It is sexual relationships which take centre stage. Critics have had a problem with what they deem to be Byron's trivial subject-matter, particularly those who wish to stress the historical context of the poetry. The crux of the matter is that the genre of the romance is still considered to be an inferior and effeminate one, as it was in Byron's day, and by the poet himself, who was always the first to disparage his own tales. Therefore critics prefer to elevate the subject-matter by treating it as allegory, rather than examining the ideological significance of Byron's treatment of romantic love itself. Daniel Watkins, for example, sees the Oriental tales as displaced explorations of the social and class structures of Regency England, though against the grain of problematic 'idealist and retrogressive tendencies in the Tales and in the later poetry'.[31] But this is to preference a traditional Marxist concern for the class struggle over the issue of gender, which is of paramount concern in this poetry.

Michèle Barrett has defined how the modern women's movement has established sexual politics as a significant area of struggle for Marxism:

> This achievement is predicated upon knowledge that sexual relationships are political because they are socially constructed and therefore could be different. A central element in this argument is recognition of the distinction between the physical characteristics of males and females and

[30] *L&J* x. 90.

[31] Daniel P. Watkins, *Social Relations in Byron's Eastern Tales* (London and Toronto, 1987), 138–9. Carl Woodring, however, comments that the tales—though subversive—are decontextualized, and therefore rendered politically harmless. See *Politics in English Romantic Poetry* (Harvard, 1970), p. 168.

the personality and behavioural characteristics deemed 'masculine' and 'feminine' in specific cultural and historical situations.[32]

Byron has in common with modern feminism (if nothing else), that for him, too, the personal *is* the political. Byron uses Bligh's account as the basis of *The Island* because the captain ascribes the cause of the revolt to the attractions of life with the women of Tahiti rather than oppression aboard ship. It was a vision of how sexual relationships could be different in a non-European cultural situation that inspired *The Island*, and constitutes the real revolutionary agenda of the poem. This was because, for Byron, sexual relationships are the basis of the workings of power in human society.

As P. D. Fleck comments: 'Neuha is herself the spirit or genius of the island.'[33] Byron uses a primitive society to emphasize the relativity of moral values, as had eighteenth-century writers like Diderot in *Supplément au Voyage de Bougainville*. He portrays Toobonai as a 'feminine' society which has not transcended its basis in the material, in comparison with the masculine, European, and hierarchical community aboard the *Bounty*.

The portrayal of a Tahitian heroine had been attempted before, by Mary Russell Mitford, in *Christina, the Maid of the South Seas* (1811). This poetic tale also took the mutiny as its starting-point, as well as featuring a wonderful cave. Christina is the daughter of Fletcher Christian and a native woman, thus exhibiting an ideal combination of British and Polynesian attributes. But Byron makes Neuha a true native. Bernard Smith has pointed out the salient fact that the letters of Jacques Arago, the artist of Freycinet's scientific expedition to the South Seas, were translated into English in the year that Byron wrote *The Island*, and he compares Arago's portrait of a Polynesian girl, *Reine des Carolines vue à Tinian*, with Byron's description of Neuha.[34]

Byron also used *An Account of the Natives of The Tonga Islands*, 'Compiled and Arranged from the Extensive Communications of Mr. William Mariner, by John Martin, M.D., 1817', from which he

[32] Michèle Barrett, *Women's Oppression Today: Problems in Marxist Feminist Analysis* (London, 1980), p. 43.

[33] P. D. Fleck, 'Romance in Byron's *The Island*', in J. D. Jump (ed.), *Byron: A Symposium* (London, 1975), pp. 163–83 (171).

[34] Bernard Smith, *European Vision and the South Pacific 1768–1850: A Study of the History of Art and Ideas* (Oxford, 1960), pp. 248–50. I have obtained my account of Mitford's *Christina, the Maid of the South Seas* from Smith.

obtained details of the scenery and folklore of the Friendly Islands.[35] The fictionalized romance of primitivism is placed between the factually-based account of the mutiny and the return of the English ship for the mutineers. Thus, as in *Beppo* and the Haidée episode of *Don Juan*, the heroine's love affair is framed by the expected return and reinstitution of male authority. As the patriarch Bligh is the exemplar of the 'manly courage' (I, 180), recorded by history, so woman is the true heroine of romance, whose laws are those of the sentiment disregarded by rational authority. The poem restores the woman's point of view, by incorporating the romance into the framework of Bligh's own account of events.

Byron based his poem loosely on the true account of a young midshipman, George Stewart, who stayed on Tahiti after the mutiny but was captured two years later by the *Pandora*. Stewart's Tahitian wife approached the ship in her canoe, and had to be removed by force and left on the beach. She died of grief and self-starvation two months later, leaving a baby girl.[36] However, it was Byron's decision to make his South Sea islander an active autonomous being rather than a passive victim that led him to change the story. So Neuha saves her mutineer lover from the retribution of English law by hiding him in a secret submarine cave. A man saves a woman this way in Mariner's *Account*, but Byron chooses to make his heroine the heroic rescuer. Zuleika, Haidée, Aholibamah, Anah, and now Neuha are all associated with caves. An enclosed space, secluded from the world, it represents womanhood—both her enforced confinement (compare the bowers of Zuleika and Medora) and her secret power. Neuha's blush is likened to a coral cave, in imagery reminiscent of the womb:

> The sun-born blood suffused her neck, and threw
> O'er her clear nut-brown skin a lucid hue,
> Like coral reddening through the darkened wave,
> Which draws the diver to the crimson cave. (II, 137–40)

In *The Island*, as in *Heaven and Earth*, woman is 'nature's goddess' (I, 211), a pagan deity, whose cave is a natural miracle. Her sudden disappearance from the sight of the pursuers is construed by the Englishmen's guilt-ridden Judaeo-Christian imagina-

[35] *CPW*, vii. 132.

[36] David Howarth, *Tahiti: A Paradise Lost* (London, 1983), p. 157.

tions as the supernatural punishment of hell (IV, 84–90). But Neuha's cave proves to be a holy sanctuary: 'a chapel of the seas', a cathedral 'upreared by Nature's architect' (IV, 145–60):

> And Neuha took her Torquil by the hand,
> And waved along the vault her kindled brand,
> And led him into each recess, and showed
> The secret places of their new abode. (IV, 161–4)

The cave is the symbol of 'feminine' sentiment: a refuge and source of power, hidden from the view of Northern rationalism.

The feelings and point of view of the female natives (and their offspring) are not taken into account in the English judgement of the events of the mutiny of the *Bounty*, concerned only with masculine discipline (I, 203; II, 270) and British patriotic duty (IV, 282). Yet Stanza xi of Canto II makes it clear that Neuha and Torquil are only a representative example of 'many a willing pair' of British men and native women on the island. Neuha sings the song of these women—Byron's translation of a Tonga folk-song. 'This ditty of Tradition's days' conveys 'a lingering fame' to the life of woman, yet a purely oral culture such as this 'leaves no record to the sceptic eye' (II, 79–102). The poet denigrates official records—'Hieroglyphics' and 'History's volumes'—compared to such poetry, 'the freshest bud of Feeling's soil'.

The 'infant world' (IV, 420) of Toobonai is portrayed as the realm of the female principle of materialism, fertility, and natural equality:

> The gushing fruits that Nature gave untilled;
> The wood without a path but where they willed;
> The field o'er which promiscuous plenty poured
> Her horn; the equal land without a lord. (I, 33–6)

As with Calypso's isle, an island of promiscuous plenty and its female inhabitants are a temptation to be resisted by masculine heroes like Bligh and Odysseus, whose duty to the military masculine ethos of epic transcends mere individual happiness. But in Byron's poem the mutineers, who are likened to 'wild beasts'—wolves, lions, deer, bears—when hunted down in retribution (III, 18; III, 60–70), are transformed (like the obverse of Circe's swine) from animals to men by life on Toobonai. The natural life

Tamed each rude wanderer to the sympathies
Of those who were more happy if less wise,
Did more than Europe's discipline had done,
And civilized civilization's son! (II, 268–71)

Torquil, who is described as a savage to Neuha's half-savage (II, 304–5), 'was tamed to that voluptuous state | At once Elysian and effeminate' by love for Neuha and abandons his martial ambitions. Love for Southern woman thus blunts the edge of Northern imperialism: 'Had Caesar known but Cleopatra's kiss, | Rome had been free, the world had not been his' (II, 318–19).

Though life on Toobonai is effeminate, compared to the 'discipline' of the men of the *Bounty*, it is not portrayed ironically like the drunken revelling of Haidée's rule in *Don Juan*. The island will only be corrupted from external influence—by the representatives of European civilization (I, 218–20). The primitive Southern island is presented as the mythical ideal society of sentimentalism, projected by eighteenth-century moral philosophers like Shaftesbury and David Hume, in which man is born with benevolent instincts, and is stimulated to do good—virtue being pleasurable to the individual because it gratifies his desire for approval. The pejorative association between the epicurean philosophy and degenerate luxury stressed in *Sardanapalus* is absent in *The Island*. Thus Neuha's selflessness is not portrayed as the abnegation of self expected by the contemporary ideology of femininity (as exemplified by Myrrha's suicide), but as a product of the pleasure principle itself:

Herself a billow in her energies,
To bear the bark of others' happiness,
Nor feel a sorrow till their joy grew less:
Her wild and warm yet faithful bosom knew
No joy like what it gave; (II, 142–6)

Sexual love is asserted to be productive of religious feeling (II, xvi). The life of a man devoted to woman is

Alike uplifted gloriously to God;
Or linked to all we know of Heaven below,
The other better self, whose joy or woe
Is more than ours; (II, 375–8)

Living close to nature teaches selflessness:

Who thinks of self when gazing on the sky?
And who, though gazing lower, ever thought,
In the young moments ere the heart is taught
Time's lesson, of man's baseness or his own?
All Nature is his realm, and Love his throne. (II, 393–7)

Byron also idealizes the island as a paradise of benevolent materialism by comparing this primitive society to that of the ancient Greeks (II, 217–19). Neuha's name, taken from that of a Tonga chieftain, is reminiscent of the Nereid to which she is compared (II, 231; III, 184; IV, 292), and her cave that of the Naiad (II, 155). She has a form 'like Aphrodite's in her shell' (II, 132), rising from the water. A native of the element (IV, 107), she is 'herself a billow in her energies' (II, 142–4).

This heroine is the central character of the poem, for the male hero, Torquil, is as much a cipher as Don Juan. Leslie Marchand comments that 'Byron has lavished more detail on the description of Neuha than on any of his fictional heroines, even Haidée.'[37] While Byron conforms to the stereotype of femininity by identifying woman with the realm of feeling, he abandons even further the portrayal of the heroine as a pathetic victim, whose weakness renders her tragic fate inevitable. This is evident, not just in the achievement of a 'happy ending', but in her characterization. Nothing could be further from the passivity of the first Byronic heroines than Neuha, who is described always in verbs of movement and activity, 'full of life' (II, 135), moving 'smoothly—bravely—brilliantly' (IV, 108) and with confidence, over and through the water. When the white man's ship arrives, she 'gazed and wondered', but fearlessly and curiously approaches in her canoe:

She, with her paddling oar and dancing prow,
Shot through the surf, like rein-deer through the snow,
Swift-gliding o'er the breaker's whitening edge,
Light as a Nereid in her ocean sledge . . .
(II, 228–31)

Like Haidée, Neuha is sexually precocious: 'In growth a woman, though in years a child' (II, 124). The Southern woman as 'Nature's Goddess' (I, 211) is the New World stretching its dusky hand to the

[37] Leslie A. Marchand, *Byron's Poetry: A Critical Introduction* (Boston, 1965), p. 73.

old (II, 239). Like Laura and Haidée she takes the sexual initiative. With no 'distracting world' or European society to regulate her conduct, she 'was all a wife' to Torquil, 'With faith and feelings naked as her form' (II, 340).

After the fight between the mutineers and the English sailors who have returned to exact retribution, it is Neuha who is 'the first' on the scene, 'springing on the strand' (III, 183). She could 'bear such sights' as Torquil's wound, and is practical enough to give escape greater priority (III, 191–4). She is the mutineers' only hope: '. . . All around them seemed arrayed | Against them, save the bride of Toobonai' (III, 217). Undaunted, she seizes the initiative, 'beckoned the natives round her', and places the mutineers in two canoes (III, 221–5). Like Gulnare, Neuha plans and executes escape from patriarchal vengeance, but without committing murder, and she takes command both of the Englishmen and her native crew. She chooses the black rock as rendezvous, and when the two canoes arrive there, 'by her command' the natives transfer to Christian's canoe, which takes a different course to divide or confuse the pursuers. She calmly and courteously overrides Christian's opposition to this plan (IV, 37–41). His fear for Torquil is mistakenly based on a supposition of her feminine weakness, for she is physically strong and perfectly capable of rowing to her destination:

> . . . her arm, though delicate, was free
> And firm as ever grappled with the sea,
> And yielded scarce to Torquil's manlier strength. (IV, 45–7)

When she arrived at the black rock, Neuha now 'uprose', pointed to the approaching English craft, and commanded Torquil to follow her (IV, 57–60) as she 'plunged into the deep' (IV, 105). A more 'expert' swimmer even than Torquil 'the nursling of the Northern seas', Neuha dived deep, her heels 'flashed like amphibious steel' (IV, 110), and she led the way to the secret cave. The conventional qualities of European femininity—modesty, chastity, submissiveness, silence—are all absent in Neuha. Though she is as devoted and protective of her lover as Kaled and Myrrha, she is the leader, not follower. Neither is she romantically contemplative or melancholy, but confident and joyous. Her first action on reaching the air of the cave is to laugh until the rock walls re-echo (IV, 116–19), and when he arrives, to clap her hands with joy at Torquil's surprise (IV, 128):

... she spread her little store with smiles,
The happiest daughter of the loving isles. (IV, 187–8)

As with Haidée, Neuha's love for the stranger is an inextricable blend of the sexual and the charitable. Having foreseen danger from the first sight of the English sail, she has spent the time Torquil has been fighting by stocking the cave with the necessities of life: a pine torch for light, a mat for rest, oil for the skin, water and fruits (IV, 137–88). At dawn the next morning she is first to swim to the surface to 'watch if aught approach'd the amphibious lair | Where lay her lover' (IV, 373–6) and ascertain that the English sail is departing. Again, her keen intelligence and practicality is shown by the detailing of how she had had the foresight and bravery to retrieve her abandoned drifting canoe the night before and secure it for their return to the island when the English had left (IV, 393–400). All Byron's energy of metre emphasizes the verbs of action in the final portrait of the active and resourceful heroine taking the initiative:

... All was Ocean, all was Joy!
Down plunged she through the cave to rouse her boy;
Told all she had seen, and all she hoped, and all
That happy love could augur or recall;
Sprung forth again, with Torquil following free
His bounding Nereid over the broad sea:
(IV, 387–92)

Only in the context of primitivism could Byron portray an active heroine unconstrained by the considerations of conventional femininity, who takes the sexual initiative, who does not know the meaning of modesty or Christian marriage, yet who is not portrayed, as convention dictated, coming to a tragic end. Neither the woman nor her society is portrayed as a tragic victim of oppression.

From the vantage point of *The Island*, we see that the presentation of the romance heroine has undergone considerable development. Originally a fragile slave murdered by an Oriental patriarch (Leila), she later loses her passivity to become the strong warrior/mistress (Gulnare, Kaled). Now Byron separates the heroine completely from a patriarchal society which condemns her sexuality. Though she is, from the European point of view, a fallen woman, Neuha is the first heroine whose independence and active sexuality are in no conflict with her own society. Just as it would be inappropriate to judge Neuha's love from the perspective of Northern Christian morality, so the heroism of Bligh is accepted as such in the context of his own European society. This is surely the reason why the poet did not consult any other versions of the mutiny, representing a viewpoint critical of Bligh. The 'masculine' and 'feminine' values of authority and sentiment are self-contained now and poles apart. The patriarchal Bligh and the autonomous heroine Neuha never meet, and are brought into conflict only obliquely, through the fate of Torquil. As in *Heaven and Earth*, written at the same period, the representatives of Christian law are all male; only the heroines can effect escape from both its ideology and its authority. In *The Island* two separate cultures of North and South are juxtaposed: the English ship represents the male hierarchical authority of God, King, and empire of a civilization based on the control of the libido of its subjects through Christian sexual morality; the island is democratic and sexually permissive.

In the Oriental tales, the ambivalent portrayal of Byron's heroines had encapsulated both the pathetic victimization and the feared subjectivity of those of inferior sex, rank, and race. By 1824 we see a divergence between a primitive woman, like Neuha, who is, in a state of nature, man's equal in every way, and the specifically 'feminine' moral role enjoined on Northern women of modern civilization, represented by the idealized portrait of the Englishwoman, Aurora Raby, in *Don Juan*. This Janus-faced relativism towards femininity is comparable to Byron's political dualism, in that he vested his zeal for ideal (republican) freedom in the national liberation of the Southern nations, Italy and Greece, but could not envisage the revolutionary breaking down of traditional class and patriarchal authority in England.[38]

[38] E. D. H. Johnson describes Byron as 'an eighteenth century Whig where England is concerned and a nineteenth century liberal on the continent'. See 'A Political Interpretation of Byron's *Marino Faliero*', *MLQ* 3 (1942), 417–25 (425).

4

'Quiet Cruising o'er the Ocean Woman': Byron's *Don Juan* and the Woman Question

> Should it be told to future ages, that the capricious dissolubility (if not the absolute nullity) of the nuptial tie and the annihilation of parental authority are among the blasphemies uttered by the moral instructors of these times . . . they would not ascribe the annihilation of thrones and altars to the arms of France, but to those principles which, by dissolving domestic confidence, and undermining private worth, paved the way for universal confusion.
>
> Jane West, *A Tale of the Times* (1799)

IN turning to *Don Juan*, one of the greatest long poems in English literature, we are also confronting a work of art consisting predominantly of a gallery of female portraits. This may seem self-evident, but in fact Byron is still habitually associated with the Byronic hero, in spite of the fact that none appears in his masterpiece. It has gone largely unrecognized that his subtle and complex representation of women in *Don Juan* is unrivalled in male-authored art of the period. Its concentration on different models of female social and sexual behaviour is comparable only with the novels of Jane Austen. This may seem a surprising observation, for Byron and Austen might be thought to have as little in common as possible for literary contemporaries who at one time shared a publisher. But this chapter will show that *Don Juan* and *Mansfield Park* emanated from a common climate of contemporary debate on the woman question.

It is well-known that Byron probably obtained the idea of writing a new version of the story of Don Juan from Coleridge's discussion of the character in Chapter 23 of *Biographia Literaria* (1817).[1] But

[1] S. T. Coleridge, *Collected Works*, ed. Walter Engell and W. Jackson Bate, 16 vols. (Princeton, 1983); *Biographia Literaria II*, vii. 208–33, esp. 214 and 229.

little attention has been paid to the context of sexual politics in which the comic epic came to be written. In his critique of Maturin's *Bertram*, Coleridge attacks as uncensorious its portrayal of adultery, commenting, 'The shocking spirit of Jacobinism seemed no longer confined to politics.' Coleridge compares Bertram to Don Juan, for as an adulterer he is no more than a libertine; and a libertine (as both free-thinker and subverter of sexual morality) represents a materialist philosophy and a denial of Christianity. The proper artistic function of such a character is didactic: a seventeenth-century morality play like Shadwell's *The Libertine* showed Don Juan rightly sent to hell. Furthermore, Coleridge states, if one wants a modern equivalent of hell-fire, for the retribution meted out to the materialism of the libertine doctrine, one need look no further than the Terror produced by revolutionary France, and he cites the careers of Carrier and Marat. Coleridge's linking of the subversion of sexual morality with Jacobinism gives us an important clue to the production of a text like Byron's *Don Juan* in the post-revolutionary climate.

Byron might have suspected that he himself was the indirect target of Coleridge's attack, since he had sponsored the play as head of the Drury Lane committee, which had subsequently rejected Coleridge's own play, *Zapolya*. Furthermore, the critique was written at the height of the separation scandal, when Byron himself was being castigated as a libertine, exploiter of both his wife and sister, and being accused by the Tory press of participating abroad in a 'league of incest' with Shelley and the two daughters of Godwin. His decision defiantly to take up Coleridge's hint of re-writing the Don Juan story in modern times may thus obviously be seen to have a quasi-autobiographical or mock-confessional purpose. This is familiar ground for Byron criticism.

But what I am concerned with here is the literary production of stereotypes of woman. The salient point is that Bertram is modelled on the Byronic outlaws of Byron's tales, and his love is reciprocated by the heroine. Moreover, as Kean grumbled, it is the adulterous Imogine who is the central character of *Bertram*; and Coleridge's critique—by attacking the male hero as a libertine—is designed to obscure the double standard behind the real issue: the effect of male-authored art on female morality. Byron himself was already being excoriated by the Tory reviewers as the corrupter of female morals in his poetry, and the epic poem which he now writes should be seen as his considered and devastating attack on—not women themselves—but the notion of reforming society through propagating an ideal of chaste femininity. This explains why Byron decides not to develop the Don as a Faustian anti-hero, as might have been expected, but makes him a passive cipher and focuses instead on a gallery of *female* characters, in a variety of nations.[2]

The 'sexual Jacobinism' or subversion of conventional sexual morality of the new poem would consist of a radical onslaught both on the sentimental hagiography of the family and on marriage as the basic unit of government under monarchy. As a Romantic individualist, Byron attacks the notion of the state as a collection of male-headed families. He responds with a psychological critique. The suppression and control of the female libido by men is not a good foundation for government, for the imbalance of power fuels male aggression and leads to female manipulativeness. The monarchical system of the *ancien régime* (now reinstituted) is therefore imperialist on the one hand, yet so lacking in true authority that women gain illicit influence.

The contemporary debate on the role of woman in society is therefore the context of Byron's decision to rewrite the Don Juan myth. Sexual politics are its subject-matter. That Byron has in his sights the Evangelical movement, now at its height, and the female writers of conduct books and novels propagating bourgeois domestic ideology is obvious enough. But this chapter will show that contemporary political theory specifically linked the need for subordination of woman in the family with historicizing the French Revolution, that Byron was aware of this, and that response to this formulation shaped his greatest work.

Byron said of his new poem: 'I *have* no plan—I *had* no plan—but I have or had materials.' McGann takes 'materials' to indicate the poet's personal sexual experience, and also, perhaps, his *Memoirs*, but it is unlikely that Byron would have used the latter, as he had made arrangements to have them published after his death.[3] I suggest that he was referring here to his library, which he had been forced to sell in 1816, including a large collection of histories and travel accounts, invaluable in constructing a detailed portrait of Europe on the eve of the French Revolution. Byron's declaration that he had no plan indicates the improvisatory process he adopted

[2] Peter Thorslev, *The Byronic Hero*, pp. 12–13, does not consider Don Juan a Byronic hero.

[3] Byron's comment is quoted by McGann, *CPW* v. 668.

in composing the individual episodes. But I believe that from the beginning he envisaged a specifically new version of the Don Juan myth as a sexual satire, and that the setting of the story at the time of the French Revolution shows his conscious decision to link sexual mores with strategies of government. The autobiographical impulse would be doubly transformed when fictionalized and inserted into this socio-political framework.

Amongst the various historical 'materials' in his library, relevant to the *ancien régime*, Byron had possessed two books on the woman question, neither published by Murray and so presumably deliberately purchased rather than merely acquired as gifts. These were *Women: Their Condition and Influence in Society*, by Joseph Alexandre Pierre Ségur, translated from the French and published by Longman in three volumes in 1803; and *History of the Female Sex* by Christoph Meiners, translated from the German, and published in London in four volumes in 1808.[4] (Significantly, Byron had referred to 'Meiners' four volumes upon womankind' in *The Waltz* (l. 75), an earlier but clumsy attempt at using sexual mores as the material for political satire.) These books applied Enlightenment relativist historicism to studying the status of woman in past eras and primitive countries, progressing through history to contemporary times. When we consider that Juan, on leaving his Spanish birthplace, travels first to a primitive Greek isle, then to despotic Turkey, followed by the 'enlightened despotism' of feudal Russia, and finally to the limited monarchy of England, we see that Byron follows a similar procedure. His poem is also structured to illustrate a secular and relativist view of sexual morality, in which the status of woman indicates the nature of a nation's government. Byron thus uses a doubled evolutionary model of sexuality to structure the poem. The story of Juan is a *Bildungsroman* which records the sexual history of a male individual from infancy to maturity, superimposed on a developmental view of sexual mores in society as a whole.

Meiners wrote his *History* over the revolutionary period, from 1788 to 1800; Ségur was writing *Women* from the heart of Republican France and mentions his own imprisonment during the Terror. Both acknowledge the influence of earlier writers on the subject: Ségur cites William Alexander's *The History Of Women*

[4] See W. H. Marshall, 'The Catalogues for Sale of Byron's Books', *Library Chronicle*, 34 (1968), 24–50.

From the Earliest Antiquity (1779); and both refer to A. L. Thomas's *An Account of the Character, Manners and Understanding of Women in Different Ages and Different Parts of the World* (1772). But unlike these eighteenth-century histories, or those by Boudier de Villemart or Pierre Joseph Caffiaux, these books of Ségur and Meiners are overshadowed by the spectre of the Terror, and it is in this context that they put forward an urgent call for a reformed role for women.

Don Juan is also set in the shadow of the Revolution. Byron told Murray that Juan would 'finish as Anacharsis Cloots in the French Revolution', and said to Medwin: 'He shall get into all sorts of scrapes, and at length end his career in France. Poor Juan shall be guillotined in the French Revolution!'[5] Though the details of Juan's career were not planned in advance, it is clear that from the outset Byron set the poem in the revolutionary period, for Julia refers to 'General Count O'Reilly, | Who took Algiers', as early as Canto I. Boyd dates the Julia episode in June 1789, and the English houseparty in Autumn 1791.[6] It seems certain that Juan was destined to travel to France during the Terror.

Needless to say, the French Revolution was a crisis for liberal ideology. The collapse into slaughter of the very society whose salons had stimulated Enlightenment questioning of the traditional basis of authority finally discredited belief in the simple progress of civilization through reason. The Revolution also made frighteningly clear the logical extension of liberalism in the direction of individualism and egalitarianism. Universal male suffrage would give over political power to the working class. But equal civil rights for women would challenge the whole economic basis of male primogeniture and property rights. To avoid such developments and to retrench their position now became the goal of most liberal thinkers of the period. Overridingly, to learn the lesson of France meant to recognize the need for reforming society to forestall revolution. The role of woman became central to this endeavour.

The France of the *ancien régime* had been a byword for the sexual promiscuity of its nobility and the prominence of women in its cultural and intellectual life. Their corrupting influence was therefore to be removed from the public arena. The question of

[5] *L&J* viii. 78; *Medwin*, p. 165.

[6] See Elizabeth Boyd, *Byron's* Don Juan: *A Critical Study* (New Brunswick, 1945; repr. New York, 1958), pp. 41–2.

political rights for women, raised in the ferment of revolutionary egalitarianism, would be countered by using sexual difference to propound an important new apolitical specifically female role of guardian of private morality. The reactionary nature of this new ideal was obscured by the fact that it conceded the argument for women's education, and even utilized the rhetoric of equality—equality in difference. Therefore the new role of woman, which comprised not only personal chastity, but also the reform of morals through private relationships in the family, became the precondition of the advancement of liberalism in the new century.

The detailed examination of Christoph Meiners and Joseph Alexandre Ségur which follows is intended not primarily to establish their role as sources or influences on the poem, but to demonstrate their importance in their own right as evidence that connections were overtly being made in Byron's time between the French Revolution and the role of woman in nineteenth-century society. It is not suggested that *Don Juan* merely reflects the views of these historians of women, but that his poem interrogates and engages with their thesis. These books, by the two most prominent contemporary male writers on women, are representative of the dominant sexual ideology of the post-revolutionary period—that of complementary gender roles. The connection between sexual mores and the French Revolution was also made by Jane West and Coleridge, as we have seen, and will later be shown to be an important factor in the development of the female-authored conduct novel. But Ségur and Meiners are worth considering in detail because their analysis openly situates the issue of female sexual morality in terms of a wider political debate.

Ségur and Meiners were synthesizers of Enlightenment thought for their middle-class readers, collecting together the scattered reflections of the *philosophes* on the role of women, but strenuously reinforcing existing arguments for their exclusion from public affairs by reference to the Revolution. Meiners was professor of philosophy at Göttingen, and a leader of Enlightenment thought in Germany. Ségur had been a frequenter of the Paris salons; Joseph Alexandre Pierre, Vicomte de Ségur was a member of a prominent aristocratic French family.[7] As one of the deputies of the nobility in

[7] On the Ségur family, see Harold Nicolson, *The Age of Reason (1700–1789)* (London, 1960), pp. 19–24. Interestingly, Philippe, Comte de Ségur, was appointed French Ambassador at the court of Catherine II of Russia. On the life of the Vicomte

the Estates General, he wrote some political pamphlets: *Réflections sur l'armée* (1789) and *Essai sur l'opinion* (1790). But he is better known as a libertine, a conversationalist, and a wit; for his editing of the scandalous memoirs of Besenval (1804–5); and for his lyric poetry, epistolary novels, and many dramatic pieces for the Comédie-Française and Opéra-Comique. His *Women: Their Condition and Influence in Society* was to achieve the status of a classic work on the subject, being reprinted in 1819, 1820, 1821, 1822, 1825, 1826, 1828 (twice), 1829, 1834 (twice), 1836, and 1852. After Ségur's death, Charles Nodier also wrote a sequel to it: *De l'influence des femmes sous l'Empire, et de notes historiques* (1820).

Ségur's discourse of Enlightenment scholarship is punctuated by occasional sugary effusions idealizing women, anecdotes, and even romantic tales. Like Byron's, his is the voice of the sophisticated liberal aristocrat, whose very libertinism gives him the authority to write on women. His stance is that of the chivalric defender of women's rights, for these 'divinities . . . are born to slavery or submission'. Women are compared to a colonized race: 'Their existence resembles that of a conquered people, who can only hope to ameliorate their situation by the address they can employ to please their masters, and to soften the injustice of their usurpation, and the severity of their caprices' (i. pp. xii-xiii). Compare Byron's odalisques of the Oriental tales, whose plight parallels that of the beautiful but oppressed land of Greece enslaved by her Turkish master. Ségur gives a moving account of the oppression of women in primitive societies. He cites polygamy, concubinage, the exchange of women as a commodity, tribal customs and taboos predicated on women's uncleanness, as evidence that it is only 'among barbarous countries (that) women are of no account; when the manners of men become more refined they are regarded as worthy of notice'.

Conjugal ties were the social basis of the first agricultural settlements (i. 65), and from then the melioration of the condition of women relates to the stages in the progress of civilization. The Middle Ages were the high point of European culture, when from the Northern Scandinavians and Celts came a 'masculine' military society which, when blended with the 'femininity' of Christianity, produced the ideal concept of courtly love which both elevated the

de Ségur, see Gabriel de Broglie, *Ségur sans cérémonie 1757–1805 ou la gaieté libertine* (Paris, 1977).

status of women and inspired the masculine code of chivalry. Ségur's emphasis on romantic love throughout *Women* is part of his quasi-Platonic theory of sexual complementarity, in which men and women are interdependent but different. The potentially egalitarian nature of Locke's emphasis on the contractual nature of marriage is thus sidestepped, replaced by a romanticization of medieval gender relationships as chivalry complemented by chastity. Women 'fixed themselves in the thoughts of their lovers and their husbands, between heaven, the throne and the altar'. Their chastity was ensured by the ideology of femininity: 'Our ancestors . . . left to their wives a liberty which was only restricted by the most salutary prejudice, and by a regard for their reputation; a restraint much stronger than all the subjection and all the chains' (i. 194).

The social status of woman is a reliable indication of the degree of governmental authority in a state: 'Their condition is a certain guide for the observations of a stranger who enters an unknown country' (i. 12). Compare Montesquieu's *Spirit of the Laws* (1748), Book VII, Chapter 9, 'The Condition of Women Under Diverse Governments', and Book XVI, Chapter 9, 'The Liaison Between Domestic and Political Government'. As in *The Persian Letters* (1721), Montesquieu related control of women to the strategies of political power. Scrutiny of the role of woman in various societies to evaluate the degree of liberty afforded by the government to the individual subject is also an important function of the Byronic heroine in *Don Juan*. Here the hero travels to various countries, encountering the daughters, wives, and queens of the *ancien régime*, and finding their condition symptomatic of the type of political authority wielded, whether patriarchal (Haidée), despotic (Dudu), feudal (Catherine is a mock queen of chivalry), or oligarchic (Adeline).

In his account of primitive societies Ségur had associated the increasing influence of women in society with the *progress* of civilization, but as the argument develops we find that this post-revolutionary treatise is just as concerned with the negative aspect of the argument. Too great an influence leads to degeneration and the collapse of authority. Though, like Byron in *Childe Harold*, Canto IV, Ségur praises the chastity and austerity of heroines of the Roman Republic (Veturia, Portia, Julia, Euphrasia), he castigates as 'unnatural' their 'masculinity', in that they 'acquired admiration by the elevation of the mind, rather than by the graces of the body, and by the solidity of their sentiments, rather than by the subtility of their wit'. He sees the correct balance between the sexes, like the maintenance of political stability in the state, as only achieved through ceaseless struggle between opposing forces. Stasis brings corruption. Therefore were obstacles to be removed from women's struggle for equality, they would degenerate morally. Ségur comments darkly: 'The time whereon the Roman matrons began to appear in public was a fatal moment' (i. 118). In Imperial Rome, when women achieved greater freedom and became active in the public sphere, they became promiscuous and even used birth control. As male authority waned, so came the degeneration of Roman civilization. The decline of the Greek and Roman civilizations is inevitably compared with the fate of France by both Ségur and Meiners.

Ségur's preoccupation with the organic evolution and dissolution of civilizations is shared by Byron. In *Sardanapalus*, too, the effeminization of the monarch and the undue influence of his mistress presages the end of an empire. When a female slave like Myrrha enters the masculine preserve of public affairs and even warfare she is portrayed with ambivalence as the embodiment of unnatural passion, like the 'Amazons' who led the mob in the early days of the French Revolution. When Gulnare in *The Corsair* wields the assassin's dagger she brings to mind Charlotte Corday. Lady Blessington commented: 'Byron has a false notion on the subject of women; he fancies they are all disposed to be tyrants, and the moment they know their power they abuse it'.[8]

In recounting the history of modern Europe, and France in particular, Ségur follows Montesquieu in identifying the prominence of women in fomenting intrigue and factionalism in troubled monarchies. The 'empire' of the women was the 'bon ton' of select society; they decided the direction of taste and fashion. When 'masculine' public affairs become subject to frivolous and arbitrary female influence this signals the corruption of the ruling class. In a passage comparable to the account of the 'gynocrasy' of the English cantos of *Don Juan* Ségur describes how, in the *ancien régime*, a young man, if he was to make his way in the world, must have his education superintended by his mother, so that he would have the

[8] *Blessington*, p. 123.

social graces to please the coteries of older women, who assisted such aspiring young men to obtain patronage and intrigued on their behalf (ii. 234–5). In their salons, society women formed 'alliances' with the pernicious philosophers who originated the principles that brought about the Revolution. 'In a certain degree the revolution was brought about by the influence of women' (iii. 11). In his account of the four main political factions Ségur maintains that the meddling of their respective female coteries was responsible for the failure to achieve a political resolution, and led to Revolution.

However, Ségur gives far more space to countless examples of female heroism in the Terror. Ségur's *Women*, together with Gabriel-Marie-Baptiste Legouvé's *Le Mérite des femmes: Poëme* (Paris, 1801), and their source, the Girondist Honoré Riouffée's *Mémoires d'un détenu pour servir de la tyrannie de Robespierre* (Paris, 1795), formed the basis of a mythological canon of revolutionary female bravery. Dorinda Outram comments that whereas males are credited with stoic heroic self-containment, women are credited with 'warm and generous outrage, and through maternal or married love or family affection of other kinds, perform acts of courage and sacrifice'.[9] Dangerous in the public sphere, women are capable of selfless heroism in a private capacity. (Compare the way the heroism of Byron's Gulnare, Kaled, Myrrha, and Marina is eventually cast into the reassuring 'feminine' mould of selfless service to their lovers.) Thus Charlotte Corday is an enigma to Ségur: a beautiful and apparently fragile young girl, who commits not a privately-motivated *crime passionel*, but a coolly premeditated political assassination. He quotes her own counsel who suggested in her defence that such 'unruffled serenity in a young woman of her age' in this context could hardly be 'natural', and put forward a plea of insanity (unsuccessfully) (iii. 52).

Finally, Ségur relates the role of woman to various forms of political government. Though female love of luxury, intrigue, and material advancement is least able to be indulged in small pastoral republics like Switzerland, he reserves his highest praise for the limited monarchy of England. The 'constraint' imposed on an upper-class Englishwoman (which he compares to that of Turkey) and her segregation from the centres of power (in that she lives on her country estate) effectively minimize her influence. Female

[9] Dorinda Outram, *The Body and the French Revolution: Sex, Class, and Political Culture* (New Haven, Conn., and London, 1989), pp. 84–5, 175.

chastity is rewarded by the high status of woman in England; but if 'she once falls, she renounces for ever that society in which she can no longer appear with respect'. (Compare *Don Juan*, XII, 77.) Ségur compares French equality between the sexes with this typical English marriage: 'There is established between his wife and himself a contract rather of power than of tenderness, of submission than of confidence, of concealed passion than of sympathy of sentiment and an unison of opinion' (iii. 175). Compare the Amundevilles' marriage in *Don Juan*: 'Their union was a model to behold, | Serene, and noble,—conjugal, but cold' (XIV, 86).

Because English women are segregated, and controlled by a rigorous expectation of chastity and decorum, their supposed influence towards individualistic and materialistic self-seeking is minimized. Men are consequently able to govern the country disinterestedly: 'In England, . . . the public spirit of the people never suffers the national interest to be eclipsed' (iii. 161).

Ségur does not cite scripture to endorse a hierarchical view of the creation. He categorically refutes the Judaic view of the intrinsic inferiority of women: the apportioning of the origin of evil to the female sex in the story of Eve; and the explanation in the Apocryphal Book of Enoch of the seduction of angels by earthly women, engendering a race of evil giants, as necessitating God's cleansing of the earth by the Flood (i. 296). (Compare Byron's sympathetic treatment of Anah and Aholibamah in *Heaven and Earth*.) Nevertheless, the usefulness of Christianity in maintaining female chastity and social stability is objectively evaluated. Women's 'natural sensibility'—so easily converted into dangerous passion—is transformed by religion into 'a mild and consolatory pity', and spends itself in good works (i. 136).

Ségur asserts that the fundamental characteristics of women are the same in all nationalities:

> Their virtues are the gifts of nature; while their defects are the result of a vicious education, or of particular laws and customs; and it is rather to men than to themselves, that their defects should be attributed, as men are the governors. (iii. 172)

Compare Byron's comment to Lady Blessington:

> I was, and am, penetrated with the conviction that women only know evil

from having experienced it through men; whereas men have no criterion to judge of purity or goodness but woman.[10]

Woman functions as an ideal only through negative qualities—her ignorance of the world and passive obedience—rather than through positive moral rigour. Ségur frankly acknowledges that women present a wonderful opportunity for social conditioning, as men 'compress or expand at their will the faculties of the women'. He compares them to marble 'which will receive whatever form or shape we (men) choose to give it' (iii. 173). Ségur adopts the Rousseauistic view that the function of women is to please and inspire men:

> To excite the object which they esteem to the love of glory; to sacrifice, likewise, their sentiments to his honour and his duty; to be our counsellors, our supporters, our consolations in sufferings, the source of our most perfect enjoyments: these are the ends for which they are placed with us on the earth. (i. 130)

Yet he asserts that he believes in the equality of the sexes: 'The design of my work is to demonstrate the equality of the two sexes, different as they may be; and to prove everything is compensated between them.' But he makes clear that his notion of sexual 'equality' is based on *complementary* roles strictly determined by biology:

> The hand which has regulated this vast universe, has assigned to each its part; each is born for a purpose which it ought to fulfil. If it deviates from that purpose, it infringes upon the general order; it is therefore punished because it acts counter to the eternal laws, from whence arose that consistency and harmony which nature never suffers to be violated with impunity. (ii. 26–7)

Feminine qualities are all related to the 'sacred destination' of motherhood. Because they live for their maternal and conjugal affection, women have greater compassion: 'They are made for love', but they are also immoderate and changeable in their emotions, characterized by their 'mobility'. Women should therefore be removed from the public sphere, but could be educated to perform the moral regeneration of society, as wives and mothers. Looking back at the two poles of first the lamentable oppression of woman by primitive societies, and then the peak of corrupting female influence in the *ancien régime* and the Revolution itself, he

[10] *Blessington*, p. 196.

suggests: 'After having fallen into two different species of excess, we have now nearly arrived at the true point and *the equality* of the two sexes will now perhaps be established' (iii. 346; Ségur's italics).

Comparing himself with earlier political writers on women's place in society (Plato, Sophocles, Condorcet, De Saint Lambert), Ségur calls upon the Napoleonic Code to stabilize society by rehabilitating women and enhancing the bourgeois hagiography of the family. In recognition of their important new status, he closes by proposing that the Napoleonic Civil Code allow women the disposal of their own property. Considering that, in fact, the Napoleonic Civil Code of 1804 actually rescinded the rights of woman gained in the Revolution, reinstituting unequal standards of divorce, and forbidding women to act as witnesses, to plead in court in their own name, or to own property in their own right, we may see Ségur as relatively enlightened.

We now turn to *History of the Female Sex* by Christoph Meiners. As professor of philosophy at Göttingen, Meiners together with Johann Feder published the anti-Kant *Philosophic Library* (1788–91). He believed philosophy should be based on psychology. One of the leaders of the Enlightenment in Germany, Meiners was a prodigous polymath, in the forefront of an attempt in Göttingen to apply historiography to a wide range of subjects. Coleridge's notebooks and letters of the 1790s provide evidence of the high regard in which he held Meiners's work, and in a letter to Sara written when he visited Göttingen in 1799 he included Meiners among the roll-call of distinguished professors.[11] This was at the very time Meiners was writing his study of women. Meiners began *History of the Female Sex* the year after the scientist Dorothea Schlözer became Germany's first woman Ph.D., hoping his book would help deliver Europe from the 'calamity of pedantic women'.[12]

[11] On the influence of Beddoes on Coleridge, and Beddoes's recommendation of Meiners as a leading thinker of the German Enlightenment, see E. S. Shaffer, '*Kubla Khan' and* The Fall of Jerusalem*: The Mythological School in Biblical Criticism and Secular Literature 1770–1880* (Cambridge, 1975), p. 29. For Coleridge's notes on Meiners's works, see *The Notebooks of Samuel Taylor Coleridge*, ed. Kathleen Coburn, 3 double vols. (London, 1957–73), i, 374–5 and nn. Coleridge was still ordering Meiners's works from a bookseller in 1819, and recommending them to a fellow-writer in 1826. See *Collected Letters of Samuel Taylor Coleridge*, ed. Earl Leslie Griggs, 6 vols. (Oxford, 1956–71), iv. 922–3; vi. 578–9. On Coleridge's visit to Göttingen and mention of Meiners, see Richard Holmes, *Coleridge: Early Visions* (London, 1989), p. 221.

[12] See Londa Schiebinger, *The Mind has No Sex?: Women in the Origins of Modern Science* (Cambridge, Mass., and London, 1989), p. 260.

Yet he begins in stirring style:

> The history of no people, of no other class of society, presents so revolting a spectacle that so powerfully excites the sentiments of horror and compassion, as the history of the condition of the female sex among most of the nations of the globe. The lot of slaves themselves was formerly enviable, when compared with that of women. (i. p. i)

But as we read on, we find that biological determinants of both race and sex account for this oppression and largely preclude change. Meiners's *History*, typical of synthesizing histories and theories of culture like De Staël's *De L'Allemagne* (1813) and Sismondi's *Histoires des Républiques Italienne du moyen âge* (1807–17), makes use of Montesquieu's theory of climate, in which the Southern nations are seen as inclined to lethargy and sensuality, and therefore tend to need despotic government. Meiners is particularly concerned with racial origin—he divides nations into 'Celtic' and the 'Oriental' types, to suggest a division by race of women into Northern chastity and Southern promiscuity. (His tendency towards racism is shown by his suggestion in *Moses und Christus* that physical dexterity, strength, wit, perspicacity, and judgement are characteristics essentially of the descendants of the Celts, to a far lesser extent of those of the Scythians and Slavs, and even less again of those of the 'Indostasians, to whom the Jews and Gypsies belong'.[13])

Meiners's account of the condition of women in the East, based mainly on Chardin and Rycaut, accords with Byron's own preoccupations in the Oriental tales and the Turkish cantos of *Don Juan*. He points out the paradox that the Mohammedan paradise consists in the embrace of houris, whilst earthly women are commonly deemed to have no souls (compare *The Giaour*, 480–9 and note[14]). He quotes an Eastern proverb that the only purpose of women is to provide enjoyment for men, and for the procreation of children (compare *The Corsair* III, 341–3). He provides much information of the extent of some harems into thousands; the degree of force and punishment used to control them; the 'horrible vices' (lesbianism) which result (compare *Don Juan*, V, 148–9; VI, 32–3, 39–40).

[13] Quoted by Henri Brunschwig, *Enlightenment and Romanticism in Eighteenth Century Prussia*, trans. Frank Jellinek (Chicago and London, 1974), p. 269.

[14] *CPW*, iii. 55, 419.

Meiners explains the lack of progress in the treatment of women in the Eastern nations as outwardly dictated by religious custom, but having two underlying causes, one biological and one political. Firstly, the early menarche of Eastern females makes them wives or concubines while still children, leading to the continued treatment and exploitation of them as such. For the same reason, and because of the climate which produces indolence, Meiners also attributes to them an insatiable lust, which leads to the necessity for oppressive control of their sexuality (i. 102). (Compare *Don Juan*, V, 157–8.) Despotism and concubinage/polygamy are also related, because having a harem precludes a ruler from forming 'a permanent connection in the realm, which might afford occasion for civil dissensions, jealousy and envy'. It can be seen that although Meiners's book begins with the same liberal rhetoric as Ségur's against the oppression of women by less advanced civilizations, in fact the status quo is simultaneously reinforced by the strong element of determinism which explains and rationalizes sexual and political tyranny as 'natural' in these nations through climate and biology.

When he has dealt extensively with the sexual customs of primitive tribal societies, the Southern and Eastern nations, he points out to his female German readers how fortunate is their condition by comparison. He attributes the comparative freedom of the women of the ancient German and Celtic nations to the fact that 'they might be abandoned without danger to their virgin modesty as the safest protection of their chastity' (i. 167). Again, this is biologically determined: a slower rate of puberty results in later marriages and consequently greater female independence, and the ensuing tendency for women to be treated as companions to their menfolk, demonstrated by Tacitus' accounts of women accompanying men to battle and even participating themselves. Meiners justifies the ancient Scandinavian custom of suicide of widows as the female equivalent of death in battle in a military society (compare Myrrha's suicide in *Sardanapalus*), and justifies the inability of females to inherit in Celtic society by the necessity to 'perpetuate noble families and to preserve their hereditary possessions entire' (i. 191). Only males capable of defending property could be deemed proprietors.

Underlying Meiners's thesis is the assumption that female sexuality is racially determined. When he considers the Muslim law governing polygamy which specifies that each wife is entitled to a certain number of conjugal embraces a month, he comments that this 'derives from notions which have never obtained in Northern Europe' (i. 110). Northern European women have no sexual desire, it is implied. The easier control over female sexuality in Northern Europe therefore facilitates the development of Western marriage, which is based not on physical restraint of women, but on cultural conditioning. Marriage is overtly linked by him to the hereditary dynastic transmission of property. In turn, the resulting creation of a class of wealthy landowners is an obstacle to a government by absolute despotism. The sexual mores of the female sex are thus perceived by Meiners as determinant of the economic and political nature of the whole society. Upon female chastity rests the whole edifice of middle-class property, liberty, and independence.

Meiners's accounts of the historical decline of great civilizations are similar to those of Ségur. His championship of female freedom evaporates when he comes to classical Rome and describes the evolution of female property rights: 'the most valuable prerogatives of the Roman citizens were annihilated' because the women and the slaves obtained 'one privilege after another' (i. 301). Meiners admits that he is contradicting the liberal premises with which he began his *History*, but explains the discrepancy by citing the self-evident need for male authority over female sexuality in the fact that these emancipated women took lovers just like men, and participated in political affairs. The 'liberties' or 'prerogatives' of the male citizens of a state are seen as preventative of monarchical despotism, on the one hand, yet are also perceived to be based on a hierarchical authority over both the lower classes and women.

In European history, too, women are related to the usurpation of male governmental authority. They are too prominent in the social life of the court; this in turn corrupts the capital, whose influence spreads via the other cities of the kingdom. Female sexual corruption flourished under the monarchical system of patronage, 'the eagerness after favour, places, and pensions . . . and the desire of making and advancing fortunes' (iii. 184). In a climate of sexual promiscuity, women obtain political influence for their favours, further weakening the rightful authority of ministers and counsellors. Purity of aristocratic blood was replaced by a purely mercenary bartering of women in the marriage market: 'The blood of the French nobility became depraved; the distinctions of rank were almost abolished, and wealth was the only standard by which the worth and consequence of persons and families was estimated' (iii. 186). We could compare *Don Juan*, XII, 3–16 where Byron desribes England as a society where cash rules love and all aspects of English society.

French dissolution is incessantly related by Meiners to lack of control of female sexuality and erosion of sexual difference: 'The men became effeminate, and the women masculine' (iii. 418). The climax of the book is his account of the Revolution itself, and his horror at the phenomenon of the 'amazon' or feminist Théroigne de Méricourt, who led the storming of the Tuileries, and the active participation of women in fighting and revolutionary politics: 'Who would imagine it possible, that the weaker sex, and the fairest part of that sex, could become the principal promoters and the principal victims of infuriate party rage?' (iv. 154).

Women in the Terror exemplify the extremes of passion: horrifying in their bloodthirsty call for revenge by the guillotine, or saintly in their faithfulness and self-sacrifice for their menfolk. Robespierre is scornfully likened to a priest with a coterie of female devotees (iv. 167). Meiners hopes that the 'masculinity' of Frenchwomen, their noted independence, loquacity, and even propensity for driving their own cabriolets, will disappear together with the fashion for the Revolutionary dress of trousers and caps of liberty, when the republic is more firmly established, to be replaced by a more modest demeanour, and eventually a retirement of women from public affairs altogether.

History Of the Female Sex concludes with a sustained attack on Wollstonecraft's *Vindication of the Rights of Woman* (1792), particularly her suggestion that the two sexes be educated together (iv. 270–348). Wollstonecraft's radicalism is castigated: she is 'a furious enemy of princes and nobles'. Her complaint of female servitude is entirely unfounded, also, since 'in no country do women possess more rational liberty . . . than in England'. England is 'a paradise for women', in comparison with other countries. Meiners notes that Wollstonecraft stops short of demanding full political and civil rights for women, for what to him are obvious reasons: '. . . either the men would be transformed into women, or . . . the women would be totally diverted from those objects for which nature designed them. . . . It is nature herself and not the cruelty of men that has denied them a participation in those rights, offices and pursuits from which they have been excluded in all ages among the nations of Europe' (iv. 328–9). He counsels his female readers to remain at home and to avoid such inflammatory doctrines. The high status of German women in society is based on their domestic role, and earned by the 'only indispensable female virtues—chastity and modesty'. Meiners consistently stresses the ideological importance of femininity. For the ideal of the supportive, obedient, chaste wife has been shown to be essential to the historical development of the independent propertied middle classes with their traditional liberties and privileges. The threats to female chastity from the desire to imitate aristocratic sophistication, on one side, and from the radical ideas of individualism, on the other, are countered both by Meiners's appeal to the 'natural' role of woman as biologically determined and his historical account of Western monogamous marriage based on romantic love as fundamental to the development of the modern state. He has shown female chastity in the bourgeois marriage to be essential to maintaining a middle class, which prevents the political extremes of both absolutism and egalitarian anarchy.

The importance of the debate on the woman question, and of Meiners and Ségur particularly, in framing a context in which to view Byron's 'sexual Jacobinism' is plain. In his comic epic, Byron employs the same procedure as these histories, of progressing from primitive to civilized countries; the same relativistic stance towards sexual morality; the same assumption of the influence of climate on Northern and Southern mores.[15] Most importantly, he too focuses on female morality as the perspective through which to test governmental authority over the individual subject. Ségur and Meiners portrayed the *ancien régime* as an effeminate civilization where the corruption of authority is measured by the ability of women to wield illicit power. This is the controlling perspective of the poem, too. For all the adult women of the poem are in positions of power or authority over Juan: his mother (Inez), elder (Julia), rescuer (Haidée), purchaser (Gulbeyaz), guide to harem life (Dudu), employer (Catherine), hostess (Adeline), and practical joker (Duchess). The poet begins by lamenting: 'I want a hero' (I, i). He portrays a Europe lacking in male public-spiritedness. England is a 'gynocrasy' (XII, 66; XVI, 52), whose aristocracy is maintained

[15] On Byron's imagery of climate, see Gerald Wood, 'The Metaphor of the Climates and *Don Juan*', *BJ* 6 (1978), 16–25.

by dynastic marriages arranged by female coteries (IV, 109; XIII, 82). Don Juan is thus a fitting modern 'hero', for he is shown to make his way in the world through the influence of women. All the male characters of the poem have lost the 'masculine' capacity to serve the state or to wield power disinterestedly, for universal justice. Lambro, the Greek poet, the Sultan, Johnson, Lord Henry —all have given way to dynastic or mercenary self-interest.

However, when we look more closely, there are some fundamental differences. The format of a progression from primitive Greek isle to Turkish despotism, to Catherine's attempt to graft enlightened monarchy on to Russian feudalism, and finally to British oligarchy, leads the reader to expect the same correlation between female chastity and the development of constitutional government as Meiners and Ségur had sought to establish. But the use of this framework as the background for repetitive stories of Don Juanism sets up a tension between the expectation of progress dictated by the format and the portrayal of actual human sexuality, unvarying, unchanged, and untamed, despite the differing mores. Byron undermines the concept of reforming society through endowing women with the role of guardian of morals by suggesting that the unalterable dynamics of human sexuality have appertained throughout time and place, and that woman is by nature as much a creature—or more—of sexual appetite as is man. Furthermore, as a republican, Byron castigates post-revolutionary European monarchy as just as effeminate as the *ancien régime*. He denigrates Britain's modern political and military leaders, Castlereagh and Wellington, the first as a moral eunuch, and both as self-seeking hirelings.

The poet's satiric strategy in *Don Juan* is that employed in *The Vision of Judgment*: he replicates the formula of an existing text in order to subvert it. Byron presents the same thesis as Ségur and Meiners that the development of a modern constitutional state necessitates ever-increasing control by women of their libido. However, with devastating comic irony he indicates in the English cantos the resulting choice between naïve idealism (Aurora), self-repression (Adeline), and outright hypocrisy (the Duchess) which represent three stages in an Englishwoman's life. The much-vaunted Northern ideal of female chastity is portrayed as merely an internalization of the traditional oppression of woman, which, however, is itself an inevitable feature of all organized societies. The poem offers no solutions to this impasse. Whilst Byron concurs with his historians in the diagnosis of *ancien régime* European monarchies as effeminate governments ruled by women, he also casts scorn on their notion of reforming society by apotheosizing woman as the angel of the house.

It could be said that his stance therefore makes Byron doubly anti-feminist—the more so when it is realized that women themselves were instrumental in forging the domestic ideology to which Ségur and Meiners subscribe. In their novels and their educational treatises, whether radical, liberal, or reactionary, writers like Catherine Macaulay, Maria Edgeworth, Anna Laetitia Barbauld, Mary Wollstonecraft, Mary Hays, Sarah Trimmer, Jane West, Mary Anne Radcliffe, and Hannah More all demanded that women put social and family duty above pleasure and, in return, call for a new public respect for motherhood as a specific vocation vital to the physical and spiritual well-being of the nation. More and Wollstonecraft—politically poles apart—concur in chastising aristocratic models of vanity, artifice, and irreligion, emphasizing instead women's moral and intellectual powers, and claiming the female sex to be less sexually passionate by nature than the male. Many women writers were influenced by the Evangelical movement, which reinforced middle-class ideology by channelling potentially revolutionary anti-aristocratic animus and reforming zeal away from politics and into the sphere of private morality. But, as Mitzi Myers asserts: 'Moral reform, radically or Evangelically permuted, offered such activist ideologues a body of legitimating imperatives and a vocabulary for venting female dissatisfaction and rendering telling critiques of a society governed by worldly libertine males, as well as for formulating counterpart models based on middle-class female values and priorities'.[16] Moreover, as Nancy Cott comments: 'By replacing sexual with moral motives and determinants, the ideology of passionlessness favored women's power and respect. It reversed the tradition of Christian mistrust based on woman's sexual treacherousness. It elevated women above the weakness of animal nature'.[17] The discourse of a specifically feminine moral role was empowering for women. The specifically male, aristocratic, libertine discourse of *Don Juan* is the

[16] Mitzi Myers, 'Reform or Ruin: "A Revolution in Female Manners" ', *Studies in the Eighteenth Century*, 11 (1982), 199–216 (204).

[17] Nancy F. Cott, 'Passionlessness: An Interpretation of Victorian Sexual Ideology 1790–1850', *Signs*, 2 (1978), 219–36 (228).

voice of opposition to this bourgeois, protestant ideology of femininity.

Byron's reactionary strategy is to replicate the flavour of the male-authored sexually explicit picaresque eighteenth-century comic novel,[18] but his concentration, not on the male protagonist, but on several contrasting female characters, shows that his real interest and target is what Ellen Moers has termed the 'heroinism' of feminocentric Regency female-authored novels, in which the new domestic ideology was represented and interrogated.[19] In a letter to Hobhouse Byron made explicit the way he saw his poem as part of a literary war of the sexes, undermining through comedy the novelistic cult of womanhood:

> Women all over the world always retain their freemasonry—and as that consists in the illusion of sentiment—which constitutes their sole empire—(all owing to Chivalry and the Goths—the Greeks knew better) all works which refer to the *comedy* of the passions—and laugh at sentimentalism—of course are proscribed by the whole *Sect*. I never knew a woman who did not admire Rousseau and hate *Gil Blas* and de Gramont and the like—for the same reason. And I have never met with a woman English or foreign who did not do as much by *Don Juan*.[20]

That Byron was an enthusiastic reader of what he disparaged as 'feminine trash' is apparent from the sale catalogues of his library.[21] These included De Staël's *Corinne* (1807); Fanny Burney's *Camilla* (1796); Mary Brunton's *Discipline* (1814); Edgeworth's *Harrington* and *Ormond* (1817), *Patronage* (1814), and *Tales of Fashionable Life* (1809); Amelia Opie's *Father and Daughter* (1801), *Simple Tales* (1806), and *Tales of Real Life*; Hannah More's *Coelebs in Search of a Wife* (1808); Mary Robinson's *Walsingham* (1805); several novels by Marie Cottin; and Lady Morgan's *Florence Macarthy* and her travel book *France* (1818). In *Childe Harold* (IV, 18) he praises the Gothic novels of Mrs Radcliffe, and comments in the notes to the second canto on Lady Morgan's *Ida of Athens* (1809), whose later book *The*

[18] András Horn, *Byron's 'Don Juan' and the Eighteenth Century Novel* (Winterthur, 1962, repr. 1969), p. 9.

[19] See Moers, *Literary Women*, pp. 125 ff.

[20] *L&J* viii. 148.

[21] See W. H. Marshall, 'The Catalogues for Sale of Byron's Books', *Library Chronicle*, 34 (1968), 24–50, and A. N. L. Munby (ed.), *Sale Catalogues of the Libraries of Eminent Persons*, vol. i (Poets and Men of Letters) (London, 1971).

Missionary (1811) he also read. In his journal he enthuses over Mrs Inchbald's *Nature and Art* (1796) and *A Simple Story* (1791).[22] He acknowledges in the preface that he based *Werner* on the story of 'Kruitzner, or the German's Tale' in Harriet and Sophia Lee's *Canterbury Tales* (1801). He was a friend of Mary Shelley and Madame De Staël, and knew Maria Edgeworth and Amelia Opie. He wrote to Murray, protesting at the *Quarterly*'s treatment of Lady Morgan; and praised her 'fearless and excellent' travel book *Italy*.[23]

Meiners and Ségur asserted that monogamous marriage is the basis of civilization itself. Women writers had made the heroine's preparation for marriage the subject-matter of the contemporary novel. *Don Juan* counters this by showing marriage (whether monogamous or polygamous) as destructive of the freedom of the individual for both sexes. All marriages depicted in the poem are unsatisfactory. Don José and Donna Inez are 'wishing each other, not divorced, but dead' (I, 26); the Fitz-Fulkes have 'that best of unions past all doubt, | Which never meets and therefore can't fall out' (XIV, 45). Marital unhappiness is also experienced by Julia and Alfonso, Gulbeyaz and the Sultan, Catherine and the Czar, Johnson in his second and third marriages, and the Amundevilles. In Canto III, 5–8, the poet overtly denies the bourgeois identification of romantic love with marriage:

> Marriage from love, like vinegar from wine—
> A sad, sour, sober beverage—by time
> Is sharpen'd from its high celestial flavour
> Down to a very homely household savour.

To Byron, the rhetoric of the social importance of domestic virtues actually masks the repression of the individual's sexual freedom. His original epigraph for the poem was 'Domestica facta . . . Horace'. Horace was referring to domestic governmental policy. Byron's pun not only hints at revelations about his own marriage, but also indicates that the personal is political. His satire of the new ideology of domesticity will link it with imperialist and reactionary governmental policy.

Ségur's hymning of complementary equality in difference between the roles of the sexes is also exposed as a sham, for even the highest

[22] *L&J* iii. 236.
[23] *L&J* viii. 186, 189.

social class cannot override the inferiority assigned a woman by gender, symbolized by the man-made shackle imposed on her:[24]

> The gilding wears so soon from off her fetter,
> That—but ask any woman if she'd choose
> (Take her at thirty, that is) to have been
> Female or male? a school-boy or a queen?
> (XIV, 25; Cf. II, 201)

The creation of a cult of feminine morality combined with a simultaneous relegation of women to the tasks enjoined by the material aspects of existence is a waste: 'Their love, their virtue, beauty, education, | But form good housekeepers, to breed a nation' (XIV, 24).

Although Byron, like Ségur and Meiners, took a critical view of the effeminization of public life, he was nevertheless not prepared to endow the domestic sphere with a neo-spiritual sanctity in his poetry, like Coleridge and Wordsworth, or make the nuclear family the central plank of his liberalism. The poem begins in Canto I, with a savage denunciation of the bourgeois hagiography of the family, which for Ségur and Meiners was the basis of political stability, and for women the foundation of their new importance. Byron attacks it for personal, literary, and political reasons: his anger at his own failed marriage; contempt for the bourgeois protestant ethos which characterized contemporary English poetry; his perception that the new emphasis on sexual morality signalled the extension of the concerns of power into all aspects of life. The poem's stylistic features—irony, cosmopolitanism, and refusal of closure—are all designed to expose the small-mindedness and insularity of the cant of personal morality, by reference to a cosmopolitan, aristocratic perspective.

INEZ

Thus the portrait of Donna Inez, the moralizing mother, is not just a personal attack on Annabella and Mrs Byron, but has a wider satiric purpose. The poet parodies contemporary effusions on the ideal mother. Inez is 'perfect past all parallel' (I, 17); 'a prodigy' (I, 12), 'with virtues equall'd by her wit alone' (I, 10); she made 'the good with inward envy groan', and 'her noblest virtue was her

[24] I am indebted to Susan Wolfson for this point.

magnanimity' (I, 12). As well as demonstrating the insipidity of the ideal (I, 18), the poet shows Inez to have internalized the feminine ideal of morality and obedience to such an extent that, whereas primitive women had to be physically oppressed to ensure their chastity, the modern woman is 'an all-in-all-sufficient self-director' (I, 15). The moralizing mother then becomes the tool of institutional authority in policing others. She is compared to Romilly 'the Law's expounder and the State's corrector', and is shown to be in league with the legal and medical professions and the Church to conquer and bring about the death of Don José (I, 34). The new domestic ideal is portrayed as not 'natural' to woman as Meiners and Ségur assert, but a deliberately cultivated, artificial aura of perfection (I, 18), an ideology of femininity propounded by texts and manuals:

> In short, she was a walking calculation,
> Miss Edgeworth's novels stepping from their covers,
> Or Mrs. Trimmer's books on education,
> Or 'Coeleb's Wife' set out in search of lovers,
> Morality's prim personification. (I, 16)

Maria Edgeworth, Sarah Trimmer, and Hannah More are cited here as writers on woman's role and education, who have themselves internalized male expectations of female propriety and transformed their own subservience into a source of pride, a viewpoint to which the modern critic Lynne Agress also subscribes.[25] In Edgeworth's *Belinda* (1801), for example, the dutiful heroine is extolled in comparison with the worldly Lady Delacour, the 'amazon' Harriet Freke, and the child of nature brought up in seclusion, Virginia. The aristocracy, feminism (of Wollstonecraft), and primitivism (of Bernadin de Saint-Pierre) are all rejected as sources of models for female behaviour, in favour of bourgeois decorum. Maria Edgeworth, like the other women writers cited by Byron, was also an educationalist, and published, with her father, *The Parent's Assistant: or, Stories for Children* (1796), a book of moralistic children's stories.

Sarah Trimmer (1741–1810) wrote numerous religious textbooks for children, and a treatise on the formation and management of

[25] Lynne Agress, *The Feminine Irony* (Rutherford, NJ, and London, 1981). For the relationship between the Evangelical movement and the origins of feminism, see Jane Rendall, *The Origin of Modern Feminism: Women in Britain, France, and the United States 1780–1860* (London, 1985), pp. 73–107; and Myers and Cott cited above.

Sunday schools. Alison Adburgham gives an account of her inauguration of the *Family Magazine* in 1788, designed for 'cottagers and servants'.[26] The supposed author is the charity-dispensing wife of the squire of a country village, a Mrs Andrews. (Pamela's social elevation from the servant-class through her virtue makes her an ideal role model.) Apart from sermons and improving tales, each number also contained a pejorative account of a foreign country—often France—written from a jingoistic viewpoint.

Hannah More, the redoubtable tract-writer of the Evangelical Clapham sect, was also a pioneer of the Sunday School movement.[27] The anti-Jacobin nature of the Evangelical moral revival may be seen from More's strenuous attempts, by way of tracts and conduct books alike, to stem subversion both from the lower orders and from women. She wrote *Coelebs* (1808) specifically to refute de Staël's *Corinne* (1807), in which the idealized Italian heroine is financially and socially independent: an artist, not a wife and mother. More takes de Staël's Lucile, the repressed victim of English mores, and turns her into Lucilla Stanley: the self-effacing Christian wife as heroine. Both *Coelebs* and *Corinne* were best-sellers. They represent the dialectic of sense and sensibility in women's writing of the period. Byron's Canto I takes on both Christian and sentimental heroines in its satiric portraits of Inez and Julia.

Inez's function in life is to devote herself to the personal superintendence of her child's education, the role outlined by Rousseau, and elaborated by female educationalists like Trimmer, Edgeworth, and More. Like Émile, Juan is supervised for all his waking hours (I, 49), but his curriculum is circumscribed by the new wave of puritanism deriving from the Evangelical movement, resulting in the philistinism of Inez ensuring that his studies do not include natural history (I, 39), a large part of the classics (I, 40–5), or even the Confessions of Saint Augustine (I, 47–8). The whole Rousseauistic theory of the importance of woman's nurturing and educational role in the upbringing of children is ridiculed in the fact that—despite this rigorous regime—the boy in question grows up

[26] See Adburgham, *Women in Print*, p. 187; see also Agress, *Feminine Irony*, pp. 88–9.

[27] On Hannah More see Katharine Rogers, *Feminism in Eighteenth Century England* (Brighton, 1982), ch. 7; Moers, *Literary Women*, pp. 125 ff.; and Agress, *Feminine Irony*, pp. 61 ff.

to become Don Juan. The force of Nature is comically too strong for Nurture to overcome.

When he leaves Spain, Inez, like Trimmer and More, applies her educational philosophy to the children of the poor:

> In the mean time, to pass her hours away,
> Brave Inez set up a Sunday school
> For naughty children, who would rather play
> (Like truant rogues) the devil, or the fool;
> Infants of three years old were taught that day,
> Dunces were whipt, or set upon a stool:
> Their manners mending, and their morals curing,
> She taught them to suppress their vice and urine.
> (II, 10; the final couplet was censored in the proofs.)[28]

Byron plainly portrays the appeal of the role of moralizing mother to women as a sublimated power strategy. The poet's technique of accretion enables him subsequently to reveal Inez to have been a hypocrite: though she acted the part of the wronged wife with Don José, she herself has had an affair with Alfonso (I, 146), and schemes to break up his marriage in order to marry him herself (I, 101). Her adherence to the state religion is also linked with material ambition. In her letter to Juan commending Catherine's 'maternal' friendship for her son, Inez advises him to conceal his Catholicism and presumably to adopt the religious orthodoxy of his new country, so as not to impair his advancement (X, 31–4).

JULIA

In rejected stanzas to Canto II Byron refers to 'Rousseau's Julietta' in connection with Donna Julia. The very use of the name would

[28] Byron may well have had in mind Hannah More's story 'The Sunday School', which appeared in *Stories for the Middle Ranks of Society and Tales for the Common People*, 2 vols. (London, 1818). We may compare Byron's stanza with her remarks: 'It is something gained to rescue children from idling away their Sabbath in the fields or the streets. . . . It is no small thing to keep them from those tricks to which a day of leisure tempts the idle and the ignorant.' (p. 361.) The anti-Jacobin motive of her didactic fictions (one of which attempts to counter the influence of Thomas Paine) is made clear in the Advertisement: 'As an appetite for reading had from various causes been increasing among the inferior ranks, it was judged expedient at this critical period to supply such wholesome aliment as might give a

instantly indicate to contemporaries a long line of novelistic heroines deriving from Rousseau's novel of sentiment. The contrast between Inez and Julia is the familiar device of conduct novelists, like Edgeworth and Austen, whose Carolines and Eleanors adopted a rational, prudent approach to marriage, instead of the unstable sensibility of a Marianne or Julia. Byron satirizes both types of heroine in Canto I, but Inez's unpunished hypocrisy is finally the more repellent. He therefore reverses the usual value judgement in order to reintroduce the claims of sentiment. The comedy at the expense of Julia is thus double-edged and defensive, for it prepares the way for his own ideal romantic heroine in Canto II. Haidée will not discourse on the passions, like the Julias of eighteenth-century epistolary novels, but will act upon them directly and spontaneously. Sentiment will be newly interpreted as the spontaneous response to nature and biology.

Byron's essentialism is apparent in the way that Julia's heredity identifies her with paganism and Southern passion. She has an 'Oriental eye' deriving from her 'heathenish' Moorish blood (I, 56), which has ruined the purity of her family's noble ancestry, but much improved its physical stock (I, 57). At twenty-three she is the victim of an arranged marriage to a man of fifty, but with the help of Christianity she struggles to 'chasten down' her biologically determined feminine subjectivity to passion, heightened both by her oriental blood and the external influence of the sun:

> 'Tis a sad thing, I cannot choose but say,
> And all the fault of that indecent sun,
> Who cannot leave alone our helpless clay,
> But will keep baking, broiling, burning on,
> That howsoever people fast and pray,
> The flesh is frail, and so the soul undone:
> What men call gallantry, and gods adultery,
> Is much more common where the climate's sultry. (I, 63)

Julia first tries to put into practice the decision of Rousseau's Julie to remain faithful to her elderly husband, and yet to retain a purely Platonic love for St Preux (I, 77–83; I, 111; I, 116). But her attempt to live the literary ideal is doomed to failure. The poet represents the resulting love affair as the comical triumph of

new direction to the public taste, and abate the relish for those corrupt and impious publications which the consequences of the French Revolution have been fatally pouring in upon us.'

biology—Julia's libido (I, 60) and Juan's puberty (I, 93)—over ideology. When Alfonso, supported by all the husbands of the city, storms into her bedroom, to make Julia an example to all the other women (I, 138), she improvises a dramatic scene, playing the part of the wronged wife so effectively that she believes and even weeps at her own self-martyrdom (I, 145–58). But after the lovers have been disgraced and parted, it is in her letter to Juan that she most clearly shows her affinity with the epistolatory sentimental heroines, particularly Corinne, who died of a broken heart when her lover left her.

The letter voices woman's protest that it is always she who is punished for both transgressors, by society's sexual double standard. The anguish of the cry is fully acknowledged—yet it is simultaneously undercut by ironic stress on the carefulness of its textualization:

> The note was written upon gilt-edged paper
> With a neat little crow-quill, slight and new;
> Her small white hand could scarcely reach the taper,
> It trembled as magnetic needles do,
> And yet she did not let one tear escape her;
> The seal a sun-flower; '*Elle vous suit partout*,'
> The motto, cut upon a white cornelian;
> The wax was superfine, its hue vermilion. (I, 198)

The tearing-up of Julia's letter by the survivors of the shipwreck in Canto II, to draw lots to decide who is to be eaten, is a macabre symbol of the primacy of appetite over both the textual art of civilization (and specifically women's writing?) and over the protest the letter contained. In the contemporary literary controversy on the role of woman conducted by female novelists the female sexual appetite was ignored and deemed not to exist, even though the difficulty of guaranteeing the legitimacy of male heirs was the unacknowledged *raison d'être* of the debate itself. Women in *Don Juan*, however, are consistently presented as creatures of appetite and will, from the time that Julia seduces the sixteen-year-old son of her friend.

Women novelists themselves had not challenged the strictures of conventional sexual morality since the revolutionary decade of the 1790s.[29] Radical novelists, like Wollstonecraft in *Wrongs of*

[29] See Rogers, *Feminism in Eighteenth Century England*, pp. 195 ff.; Jane Spencer, *The Rise of the Woman Novelist* (Oxford, 1986), p. 137.

Woman (1798), and Inchbald in *Nature and Art*, had graphically portrayed the double sexual standard: both depicted a fallen woman condemned by a male judge. Wollstonecraft's Maria attempts to justify the adultery with which she is accused, after having met her lover in the madhouse in which her husband has had her locked up while he enjoys her fortune. Wollstonecraft has the judge answer that 'we did not want French principles in public or private life—and, if women were allowed to plead their feelings, as an excuse or palliation of infidelity, it was opening a flood-gate for immorality'.[30] Wollstonecraft thus acknowledges that the establishment habitually identified female sexual subversion with Jacobinism.

By 1819 the notion of female passionlessness had achieved such a consensus that it was rare for any female-authored novel to feature a sexually passionate woman, unless as an aberrant minor character always punished with death. In *Don Juan*, Canto I, Byron has comically exposed as cant both the didactic novel's morally idealized heroine of unstained virtue, and the sentimentalist's pathetic fallen woman as victim in order to explode entirely the notion (so irresistible to women) of the superior refinement and moral purity of 'femininity'.

Don Juan has so far been shown as a poem endorsing contemporary political critiques which related the rule of women with the degeneration of the *ancien régime* that led to the French Revolution, and also satirizing the idealization by women writers and ideologues of a new bourgeois feminine role that would ensure the stability of the property-owning class and reform the nation's morals. In the next chapter I shall examine the positive, rather than merely negative, contribution Byron makes to the debate.

[30] Mary Wollstonecraft, *Mary* and *The Wrongs of Woman*, ed. Gary Kelly (Oxford, 1980), p. 199.

5

'Each Was Radiant in Her Proper Sphere': Byron's Theory of Repression from Greece to the 'Gynocrasy'

> Women are now respected and excluded; under the old regime they were despised and powerful.
>
> Olympe de Gouges, *Les Droits de la Femme* (1791)

THOSE of the generation that had experienced the French Revolution, like Coleridge, Ségur, and Meiners, were seeking to re-establish the authority of male over female, and imbue woman's familial role with moral sanctity, as a bulwark against rampant individualism, a protest against aristocratic promiscuity, and an affirmation of the importance of the hereditary transmission of property. Because he was of the second generation of liberals, an emigré, an aristocrat and libertine himself, and above all an individualist, Byron was in a unique position to challenge the new puritanism.

Evolutionist accounts of woman's social position were used by male writers like Meiners or Thomas Gisborne (in *An Enquiry into the Duties of the Female Sex* (1813)) in anti-feminist discourse. Feminists (such as Lady Morgan in *Woman and Her Master* (1844)) and socialists later in the century would begin to write counter-arguments using the same cross-cultural approach. Byron's poem (typically) takes a paradoxical point of view: the text both defensively proclaims its anti-feminist stance and yet also anticipates to some extent the way early socialists would adopt a historical approach to the developing role of women, in arguing against the institution of marriage. The Owenites of the 1830s were influenced by the French socialist, Charles Fourier, who argued: 'Social progress and changes of period are brought about by virtue of the progress of women towards liberty, and social retrogression occurs as a result of a diminution of the liberty of women.'[1] Although

[1] See Barbara Taylor, *Eve and the New Jerusalem: Socialism and Feminism in the Nineteenth Century* (London, 1983), pp. 28–9.

Fourier's elaborate cosmology was little known in Britain or America in 1819–24, I shall be arguing in this chapter that, like Fourier, Byron sees sexual passion as the driving force of power politics—as the psychology of history itself. Byron's sexual satire is Romantic in its stress on the indivisibility of the individual, biologistic in insisting on the common physicality of all humanity as expressed in the libido. But at the same time essentialism with regard to gender is also interrogated in that the characteristics traditionally associated with sexual difference—masculinity and femininity—are often seen in the poem as secondary, being socially and culturally determined.

In nineteenth-century feminist discourse there was an unresolved tension between the desire to minimize sexual difference, preferencing humanist universalism, and the need to assert a difference in women's favour, thus adapting the notion of woman's unique moral mission to a call for civil equality. But there was also, in this period, a fracture between male and female radical writers with regard to the question of sexual passion. Godwin, Shelley, Owen, and Byron adopt a necessitarian or functionalist view of sexuality, the last three celebrating the liberated libido, whereas feminists like Mary Wollstonecraft, and later Anna Wheeler, advocate reason over passion.[2] If we compare *Don Juan* with Wollstonecraft's *A Vindication*, we find that Wollstonecraft attempts to minimize sexual difference by attacking femininity only, whereas Byron's critique of a culturally determined sexual role applies to both sexes alike.

Both Byron and Wollstonecraft seek to challenge Rousseau's insistence in *Émile* on the necessity of dividing the public life of the citizen from the private life of the family through sharply differentiated sexual roles (which is the basis of Meiners's and Ségur's thesis, but applying the lessons of the Revolution). Wollstonecraft rejects Rousseau's identification of the feminine with irrational sentiment, and wants both the 'masculine' public and the 'feminine' private spheres to be judged by the universal standard of Enlightenment rationalism. This leads her to denigrate sexual passion even within marriage: '. . . a master and mistress of a family ought not to continue to love each other with passion. I mean to say that they ought not to indulge those emotions which

[2] Ibid. 30–47.

disturb the order of society.'[3] Wollstonecraft still sees motherhood as a woman's primary vocation, but her own ideal is that of the strong, independent Republican matron. In rejecting Rousseau's insistence that a woman should always be using feminine wiles to attract and keep a husband, Wollstonecraft repudiates the whole idea of female sexual passion as necessarily degrading to woman. The tendency in radical twentieth-century feminism to privilege sexuality itself as the central fact of women's oppression, and to problematize female subjectivity as regressive, may be traced back to Wollstonecraft. Cora Kaplan comments:

> Wollstonecraft saw sentiment and the sensual as reinforcing an already dominant, approved and enslaving sexual norm, which led women to choose a subordinate social and subjective place in culture . . . In *A Vindication* women's subjection is repeatedly compared to all illegitimate hierarchies of power, but especially to aristocratic hegemony. At every possible point in her text, Wollstonecraft links the liberation of women from the sensual into the rational literally and symbolically to the egalitarian transformation of the whole society . . . [4]

But because the basis of her argument rests on an acceptance of the dichotomy between nature and culture Wollstonecraft's attempt to envisage a sexually neutral society and a universal morality, as Moira Gatens comments, 'involves a collapsing of sexual difference into what has, historically, been associated with masculinity'.[5]

However, Byron's Romantic sexual satire gives preference to individualism over social duty, and therefore challenges the very basis of the reason/sentiment, culture/nature dichotomy itself. Ursula Vogel has contrasted rationalism and Romanticism as two divergent strategies for women's liberation in this period. She comments on the Romantic position:

> Not 'rational fellowship' among citizens, but romantic love freed from the confines of conventional sexual roles points towards the utopia of a regenerated world. . . . While the rationalist associates the oppression of women, and the defects of present society in general with the all-pervasive effects of social and political inequality, the romantic critic focuses on the

[3] Wollstonecraft, *Vindication*, p. 114.

[4] Kaplan, 'Pandora's Box: Subjectivity, Class and Sexuality in Socialist Feminist Criticism', p. 160.

[5] Moira Gatens, 'Rousseau and Wollstonecraft: Nature vs. Reason', *Australian Journal of Philosophy*, supplement to vol. 64 (1986), 1–15 (14).

hypocrisy and pettiness of bourgeois philistine morality in which he sees the most telling signs of the profound corruption of modern culture.[6]

Romantic thinkers repudiated the constraint on individuality of character imposed by sexual stereotyping. Both Meiners and Ségur had deplored the sexual equality of the ancient Spartan republic, as destructive of femininity. But Friedrich Schlegel, in *Theorie der Weiblichkeit*, admired both the strength and independence of Spartan women and the gentleness of the men, compared to the exaggerated sexual differences of modern times: 'Both the impatient will to dominate in man and the self-denying submissiveness in woman are exaggerated and ugly. Only self-reliant womanhood and gentle manhood deserve to be called good and beautiful.'[7] In 'Über die weiblichen Charaktere in den griechischen Dichtern' and 'Über die Diotima', published in the 1790s, he articulated his thesis that the measure of a just society was the freedom it granted to both males and females to overcome the behavioural extremes culturally associated with gender. Sara Friedrichsmeyer points out that early German Romantic poets hailed the love of man and woman as an indivisible combination of the sensual and the spiritual, and their union as a concrete means of synthesizing opposing qualities within individuals.[8] In his novel *Lucinde* (1799) Schlegel illustrates this conception of love: Julius and Lucinde are erotically portrayed experimenting with role-reversal in their love-making, delighting both in their sexual difference and their ability to transcend that difference. Like Byron, Schlegel claimed that the sensual passion of Southern women was more natural than the 'northern frostiness' held up as a feminine norm in Europe.

This notion of romantic love is often automatically perceived by contemporary Marxist and feminist critics (heirs of Wollstonecraft) as irrational, regressive, and hostile to feminism. It is interesting that Kaplan's discussion of this question, cited above, takes off

[6] Ursula Vogel, 'Rationalism and Romanticism: Two Strategies for Women's Liberation', in Judith Evans *et al.* (eds.), *Feminism and Political Theory* (London, 1986), pp. 17–46. On the comparison between the attitudes of the Rationalists and the Romantics to sexual difference and to romantic love, see also H .G. Schenk, *The Mind of the European Romantics* (London, 1966; repr. Oxford, 1979), pp. 151–8.

[7] Quoted by Vogel, 'Rationalism and Romanticism', p. 37.

[8] Sara Friedrichsmeyer, 'Romanticism and the Dream of Androgynous Perfection', in Theodore G. Gish and Sandra G. Frieden (eds.), *English and German Romanticism: Cross-currents and Controversy*, *Houston German Studies*, 5 (1984), 67–75 (70–1).

from Mary Jacobus's and Judith Lowder Newton's opposite points of view towards the contradictions between feminism and the evocation of female desire in Charlotte Brontë's *Villette*. Representations of woman's sexual and romantic longings may be seen, from a psychoanalytic point of view, as potentially radical in a Victorian context, yet can also be interpreted, by modern Marxists, as self-indulgent subjectivity in conflict with a rational appraisal of sexual and social oppression. If we compare Brontë with Austen, it is apparent that whereas Austen is writing from the heart of the female-authored counter-revolutionary debate on the role of woman, discussed in the last chapter, Brontë's work of a generation later has assimilated and adapted Romanticism—specifically Byronism, in fact—to the rational, Christian feminism of her female forebears. For in the early nineteenth century, with the possible exception of the sentimental novelist Germaine de Staël, it was male Romantic writers who included the liberation of woman's sexuality in their idea of female independence. They saw romantic love as a means of personal liberation. Vogel comments: 'In early Romantic theory it is credited with a power that encourages the discovery of the self. To love is to inspire another person's development, each releases in the other energies that will bring them closer to what they might achieve as human beings.'[9]

Byron sees liberation in terms of personal relationships which will challenge the individual to extend the boundaries of self. Therefore, rather than positing reform on the basis of the separation of public and private, by the reinstituting of sexual difference, Byron's poem diagnoses the lack of true male heroism as actually the *result* of such reductive dualism—based as it is on a false dichotomy between nature and culture. The lack of true male public-spiritness is not attributed to the female attempt to wield 'petticoat influence' (as in Meiners and Ségur), but to the splitting-off of public from private spheres and the consequent overvaluing of policy over sentiment.

Julia's letter, on the other hand, voices the plight of woman, whose whole life is now conceived entirely in sexual terms:

> 'Man's love is of his life a thing apart,
> 'Tis a woman's whole existence; man may range

[9] Vogel, 'Rationalism and Romanticism', p. 41.

The court, camp, church, the vessel, and the mart,
Sword, fame, ambition to fill up his heart,
And few there are whom these can not estrange;
Man has all these resources, we but one,
To love again, and be again undone.' (I, 194)

The development of the poem casts an ironic light on Julia's envy of the masculine prerogative to separate love from life and to derive satisfaction from both the private and public spheres. An anti-epic, it calls into question the masculine ethos of love as 'a thing apart' and in inevitable conflict with duty. The masculine honour of the court, camp, church, vessel, and mart will each be shown in the poem to have degenerated into pragmatism and selfish materialism, as a result of relegating subjectivity to the feminine (and therefore inferior) sphere of the private life. Military glory, fame, and ambition are contemptuously portrayed by Byron as motivating the men of an age of bronze, instead of true patriotism and love of liberty. A further irony is that Juan does not fill up his heart with public affairs like most men, anyway, but by appropriating the feminine role of a life devoted only to love manages to retain his innocence and natural goodness. The expression of the sentiments through even promiscuous sexuality is thus shown to be less morally harmful to the individual than the separation of his private from his public life to facilitate the concerns of policy. Both the Romantic idealization of illicit love in the Haidée episode and the corrosive satire of imperialist warfare in the Siege of Ismail thus emanate from the heart of the poem's interrogation of the notion of gender as complementary. Venus' 'feminine' domain of love is associated with the psychology of the defeated in Haidée's Greece, while Mars' 'masculine' code of military glory has degenerated into the rationalization of militarist aggrandizement by Eastern and Western great powers.

Byron's critique of complementarity and its concomitant ideo logy of female passionlessness was viewed in the last chapter in largely negative terms as the basis of anti-feminist satire. But in the Haidée story we have an outright celebration of female sexuality, the like of which cannot be found in women's writing of the period. We have to look to the feminist Cythna, in Shelley's *The Revolt of Islam* (1817), for another heroine presented as sexually autonomous. The comparison with Shelley is significant. At the centre of

Byron's Romantic irony are what Bakhtin terms 'dialogics', or the competing discourses of libertinism and libertarianism. For the poem emanates not only from the poet's attack on the women who humiliated him in the separation scandal, but also from his association in Italy with the Shelley/Godwin/Wollstonecraft circle, its free-thinking and its feminism.

HAIDÉE

The Romantic primitivism of the Greek island episode is presented with deep ambivalence. It thus forms the centre of a web of Byronic irony, which makes these cantos the site of Byron's most profound investigation of the relationship between woman's autonomy and sexual freedom for the individual, but also of the link between effeminacy and degeneracy in a defeated society. Ségur and Meiners had identified barbaric Southern and Eastern societies with patriarchal physical oppression and enslavement of women. By contrast, their evolutionary accounts of the history of Europe demonstrated that Christian marriage was woman's salvation. Northern chivalric protection of woman signalled the superior civilization of Christendom compared to that of Islam; Western female chastity and submissiveness demonstrated the possibility of authority based on conditioning rather than coercion. Romantic literary medievalism centred on this ideology, as we saw in Chapter 1, with all its concomitant implications for sexual politics, missionary activity, and imperialism. But Byron takes a different Romantic view of the North/South or West/East divide. In *Cain*, *Heaven and Earth*, *The Island*, and in the Greek cantos of *Don Juan*, he portrays primitive societies' freedom from the Christian heritage of sexual guilt as more natural, particularly to the young: a Golden Age of spontaneity. Though Byron is careful to stress the relativity of sexual mores in *The Island* and *Don Juan* the comparison he makes between Haidée and Aurora problematizes the mutual incompatibility (for him) of two models of female autonomy: the Southern, based on lack of sexual inhibition; and the Northern, with its feminist stress on moral and intellectual equality.

What happens in the Haidée episode is that we are first presented with Byron's outright celebration of the liberated female libido. If a woman's sexual freedom is the measure of the freedom of an individual in her society, then the story of Haidée posits a pagan libertarian paradise—a dream linked, for the poet, with the romance of Philhellenism. But of course it is a dream. As the romance deconstructs into tragedy, we become aware that the illusory nature of the paradise was always apparent, in that it was artificially created by the absence of the patriarch, Lambro, and the half-Moorish Haidée's forgetting of her Christian upbringing (II, 193). Significantly, the father's impending return frames the complex irony of the interpolation of 'The Isles of Greece', in which the concepts of 'masculinity' and 'femininity' are questioned in relation to nationhood, politics, and poetry, as well as sexuality. For the tragedy both of love and Philhellenism is that female equality and free sexuality are associated by the poet only with effeminate societies: in the context of contemporary Western imperialism these are either vulnerable to colonialization, like Tahiti, or already conquered, like Greece. The masculine authority necessary to achieve national self-determination always entails the dynastic control of female fertility as central to its socio-political organization, and thus curtails the sexual autonomy of the individual.

So though it first appears that Juan has been washed up on a desert island ('The shore looked wild without a trace of man' (II, 104)), and then that the inhabitants are commanding and autonomous women, in fact Byron quickly contextualizes Haidée —'I'll tell you who they were, this female pair . . . ' (II, 124). Haidée's kinship relations are simplified into the usual configuration of father/ruler and only daughter/heir, so that youthful female sexuality is presented in stark confrontation with patriarchal dynastic considerations. We are briefly forewarned of the possibility of conflict. Haidée has already independently 'rejected several suitors' (II, 128), and rescues Juan only by concealing him from her slaver father (II, 130). It is only by subsequently allowing the particularized social, familial, and historical context of this heroine to fade away with the disappearance of Lambro that Byron is able to present a temporary vision of free love and the equality of the sexes, before bringing in Nemesis in the mock-heroic return of the patriarch—a modern and fallen Odysseus.

Much of the irony of these cantos rests upon the unspoken dichotomy between the ancient Greeks and the contemporary Christian population of this part of the Ottoman empire, unaware of its classical history. Haidée's story is firmly situated in 1790, during the Russo-Turkish War of 1787–91. It is therefore not based on the literary classics, but taken from the realm of folk-tale. The specific prototype was a Romaic transcription of an oral Cretan romance. *The Voskopoula*, or Shepherdess, published in Venice in 1627.[10] Marchand has commented that Byron selected the Romaic names of Haidée and Zoë for his female characters, as those most common in contemporary Romaic ballads.[11]

The ambivalence of contemporary Europeans towards the Greeks was demonstrated by their careful use of the separate words 'Hellenic' and 'Romaic' to distinguish between the revered classical and the supposedly degenerate contemporary civilizations.[12] Of the notable Philhellenes of the period, neither Shelley nor Goethe nor Winckelmann visited modern Greece. Only Byron had the courage to face the discrepancy between the ideal Hellas of myth and the real country with its contemporary poverty and degradation.[13]

This discrepancy had been portrayed indirectly in the Oriental tales by means of the ambivalence with which the heroine's sexuality was viewed. Her beauty, associated with that of her land, had been idealized, whilst simultaneously her sexual degradation at the hands of her Turkish master was graphically presented. But in Haidée's story both the island and the heroine have acquired an artificial aura of self-determination, so the emphasis changes from sensationalizing Turkish masculine oppression to interrogating effeminate Greece's capacity for independence. The character of Haidée therefore epitomizes the poet's ambivalence about feminine autonomy—as it concerns both the individual woman and her conquered oriental country.

Haidée at first seems an active heroine rather than a passive victim. She is very tall, she is no slave, and has a commanding presence:

> . . . in her air
> There was a something which bespoke command,
> As one who was a lady in the land. (II, 116)

[10] See Panos Morphopoulos, 'Byron's Translation and Use of Modern Greek Writings', *MLN* 54 (1939), 317–26 (324); Kiriakoula Solomou, 'The Influence of Greek Poetry on Byron', *BJ* 10 (1982), 4–19. [11] Marchand, *Byron's Poetry*, p. 73.

[12] See John Buxton, 'Greece in the Imagery of Byron and Shelley', *BJ* 4 (1976), 76–89 (80).

[13] Gilbert Highet, *The Classical Tradition: Greek and Roman Influences On Western Literature* (Oxford, 1949), 360–9.

Rather than fruitlessly waiting, like Leila, for rescue by her foreign lover, it is Haidée who saves his life. Rather than her seduction demonstrating the weakness of feminine innocence, the sexual attraction of the pair is mutual (II, 185–6). Her courage in adversity is shown to be equal to a man's, when she confronts her angry father:

> ... 'twas strange
> How like they look'd! the expression was the same;
> Serenely savage ...
> For she too was as one who could avenge,
> If cause should be—a lioness, though tame:
> Her father's blood before her father's face
> Boil'd up, and proved her truly of his race. (IV, 44)

Though Haidée's collapse into madness and death is comparable to the fate of the most passive and fragile heroines of the early tales, only 16 stanzas out of the 288 are devoted to her demise. The emphasis of the episode as a whole is on her vitality: 'Round her she made an atmosphere of life' (III, 74).

Associated from her first appearance as rescuer of the half-drowned boy, with the life-giving gifts of the material world, warmth, shelter, food and drink, she represents Epicurean rather than Stoic values—a turning away from masculine military and governmental achievements in favour of individual fulfilment (II, 205–7). Ceres and Bacchus are cited as assisting Venus, when breakfast is served in Haidée's cave (II, 169–70). We remember Nausicaa's rescue of the shipwrecked Odysseus in Book VI of the *Odyssey*. But to underline the poet's affirmation that the modern Greeks have an equal capacity for noble deeds, Byron lays stress on Haidée's *Romaic* speech in the very stanzas describing her spontaneous good-heartedness:

> ... she told him, in good modern Greek,
> With an Ionian accent, low and sweet,
> That he was faint, and must not talk, but eat. (II, 150)

He goes on to devote another stanza to the beautiful music of Haidée's Romaic language to the foreign ear (151); a further stanza to her volubility in Romaic (161); and yet five more to Juan's delight in learning the language from her (163–7).

The island love idyll endorses natural equality between the sexes, as in the Rousseau-inspired tale of *Paul et Virginie.* But Byron identifies sexual freedom (not chastity) with innocence. (Saint-Pierre's Virginie is so naturally modest that she chooses to drown during a shipwreck, rather than either take off her clothes to swim, or be saved by a naked sailor.) As in Longus' *Daphnis and Chloe*, Haidée's naturalness is represented as the frank expression of her sexuality and the absence of prudery. Like Nausicaa she rescues a shipwrecked hero and admires his naked body. Though nominally a Christian (II, 193), Haidée easily forgets the threat of eternal punishment, and never thinks of extorting vows and promises in return for her favours (II, 190). Byron follows Montesquieu in ascribing sexual precocity to the Southern nations, for the lovers are 'children' (IV, 15); they were 'all summer' in years (IV, 9). Byron's essentialism can be seen to take the form of racial rather than gender stereotyping by identifying both Julia's (I, 56) and Haidée's capacity for passion with their Moorish blood: 'Afric is all the sun's, and as her earth | Her human clay is kindled' (IV, 56). Marilyn Butler sees *Don Juan* as part of a Romantic cult of the South, in which the glorification of sexual love in a liberal, extrovert mode, in a Mediterranean setting, challenges Judaic-Christian moral orthodoxy.[14]

In the positive portrayal of the love affair, the victory of Hellenic sexual freedom over Romaic Christian sinfulness is celebrated, as Haidée's pagan Southern blood influences her to re-enact the eroticism of classical amatory art:

> She sits upon his knee and drinks his sighs,
> He hers, until they end in broken gasps;
> And thus they form a group that's quite antique,
> Half-naked, loving, natural, and Greek. (II, 194)

Haidée evokes, albeit temporarily, a lost Golden Age of erotic libertarianism. The fertilizing power of the sun drenches the poetry. Byron hails the pagan sun-god Apollo as his muse (IV, 7). Juan and Haidée fall in love in summer, and the word 'sun' is used sixteen times in Canto II. Haidée is sister to the dawn (II, 142); her breath like the South wind over a bed of roses (II, 168); her cheek like a

[14] Marilyn Butler, *Romantics, Rebels, and Reactionaries* (Oxford, 1981), p. 137.

sunset (II, 115). The lovers' feelings are as 'universal as the sun' (II, 167); their love is consummated at sunset, when it seemed 'as if the whole earth it bounded, | Circling all nature' (II, 183). Their kiss focuses all the sun's rays, their blood is lava and pulse a blaze (II, 186).

> Haidée was Passion's child, born where the sun
> Showers triple light, and scorches even the kiss
> Of his gazelle-eyed daughters; (II, 202)

When she becomes queen of the island, on the supposed death of her father, the now-pregnant Haidée recreates a society devoted to the female principle of love and fertility. True to her life-affirming role in the rescue of Juan, she establishes an atmosphere of love, festivity, peace, drinking, and feasting in her court. The rule of Venus has replaced that of Mars—symbolized by the children's wreathing with flowers the horns of an old ram, 'the patriarch of the flock' (III, 32). Traditional art flourishes in the new leisure in the form of music, story-telling, and poetry. The happy pair are surrounded by the merry-making of the whole community. The values of pagan materialism so joyfully, if briefly, portrayed here are in stark contrast to the use of Christianity as an endorsement for the brutality of the Siege of Ismail, later in the poem.

But even while Haidée's life-giving feminine values are celebrated as an expression of her individual autonomy, they begin to take on a more sinister light when she usurps masculine rule. A latter-day priestess of Aphrodite, Haidée turns Lambro's austere warriors' hall into a shrine for the senses, surrounding herself with beautiful furniture, food, hangings, carpets, clothes, jewellery, and exotic servants (III, 61–78). Though as a woman she is close to nature, she is also prone to luxury. Her materialism smacks of decadence already, as the economic basis of her magnificent court is the ill-gotten gains of piracy and slave-trading.

Haidée is the most idealized heroine in *Don Juan*, the incarnation of female passion. In this primitivist romance, Byron celebrates the female libido as natural, and associates free sexuality with individual freedom. It is this enclave of personal freedom, which Haidée has created, which re-awakens the almost-forgotten desire for political liberty of her Philhellenist poet. Yet, ironically, the decadence and effeminacy of her court is also seen by him as inimical to its achievement, and thus her rule is subjected to a masculine critique within the poem, in the lyric 'The Isles of Greece'. A different view of Hellenic sexuality now counterpoints the Romantic primitivism of the episode. The strict division of sexual role and subjugation of women in the Greek *polis* is the unspoken but implied factor in this comparison of then and now.

Haidée's feminine rule of love is not attacked from the point of view of orthodox Christian morality, but because it needs to be matched by a complementary true masculine heroism if it is not to degenerate into mere epicurean luxury. In the lyric, the history of Greece is construed as the ceaseless striving of the male and female principles: between war and peace (l. 691), between heroic and amatory art (l. 695), between tyranny and slavery (st. 12). The modern poet singing to Haidée, the female ruler of a pleasure-loving throng, reproaches his own people as effeminate degenerate slaves of the Turks and calls in vain for the return of the masculine heroism of the classical Greek republics.

The poem, a pastiche of modern Greek patriotic songs such as Rigas's 'Greek Marseillaise' which Byron had himself translated years earlier, is often abstracted from its context as an anthology piece, but is actually made to allude directly to Haidée's court as detailed in Canto III. Its ironic refrain 'Fill high the cup with Samian wine' simultaneously reproaches both the islanders' hedonistic festivity and their political apathy, for Samos was the adopted home of Anacreon, whose poetry celebrated pleasure and ridiculed heroic and military values.[15] Furthermore, the decisive battle of the Persian Wars was lost by the treachery of Samos, a wine-producing area. The Greek poet's challenges, questions, and responses to his audience (see sts. 7–9) indicate the supposedly extempore nature of his exhortation. When he calls for assent to his proposal for 'a new Thermopylae' he is greeted by silence, but his ironic injunction to 'shed the blood of Scio's vine' is willingly obeyed by each 'bold bacchanal' of the company. The poet's scathing reference to the Pyrrhic dance which has outlived the 'nobler and the manlier' tradition of the Pyrrhic phalanx (st. 10) and to the dancing virgins (st. 115) alludes to the courtyard scene we have just witnessed through Lambro's eyes (III, 29–30). Moreover the 'glowing maid'

[15] *CPW* v. 701. On the trimmer poet see Jerome McGann, *The Beauty of Inflections: Literary Investigations in Historical Method and Theory* (Oxford, 1988), pp. 271–86.

whose 'breasts must suckle slaves' recalls Haidée herself, who we will shortly find out is already pregnant.

The possibility of the degeneration of the rule of Venus into hedonism and luxury had certainly been implied in the narrative account of the sumptuous extravagance of Haidée's jewelled clothes and banquet of 'about a hundred dishes' (III, 62). Yet the court poet's contempt for the modern Greeks as degenerate and effeminate is also held at an ironic distance by the device of qualifying the criticism by characterizing the bard himself as a 'sad trimmer' (III, 78–86), who is only emboldened to speak his mind by the certainty that in present company there was no 'danger of a riot' (III, 83).

While he eulogizes Greece as a natural paradise in the figure of his heroine Haidée, the poet also calls in 'The Isles of Greece' for a complementary masculine heroism to be worthy of her. However, the lyric is framed by complex irony, for its bard is impugned at length (III, 78–86) as a Southeyan hack, who has abandoned the republicanism of his 'hot youth'; significantly, his career reflects Byron's own earlier role as salon Philhellenist (III, 83–4). Interestingly, Byron told Medwin that the lyric was originally written in 1811, at the same period as *Childe Harold* I and II.[16] In other words, Byron now qualifies his own earlier contempt for the contemporary Greeks as an effeminate conquered people by placing the lyric in quotation marks.

The effect of this is that, while the masculine critique still stands, its (and by implication Byron's) own heroic credibility is undermined. Philhellenism (an imported Western notion) is shown to be based on a history and literature of which the contemporary Greeks are unaware (st. 2); it is espoused by a renegade who is willing to play lip-service to every other European tyranny, only because he knows Greek freedom to be a hopeless Utopian ideal unlikely to be implemented. Moreover, this poet who bases his own martial masculine ethos on the values of ancient epic to denounce the effeminacy of the Romaic people actually uses the medium of a romantic lyric, beginning with a tribute to the eulogist of the feminine principle and priestess of Aphrodite, 'burning Sappho', and concluding on a defeatist note of swanlike martyrdom

[16] *Medwin*, pp. 231–3. Lovell notes that of the six unrevised stanzas of Canto III, four appear in this lyric (stanzas 7, 10, 11, 16), and speculates that at least part of it may well have been written much earlier than 1819.

reminiscent of de Staël's *Delphine* (st. 16). Behind the rhetoric of the lyric, we thus glimpse Byron's ironic perception of himself uneasily uniting the role of feminized Romantic poet and liberal scourge of an effeminate society. So, even while 'The Isles of Greece' suggests that the feminine natural paradise of Haidée's isle could be criticized negatively for lack of sufficient male heroism to enforce political authority, that view itself is open to question. Is Philhellenism merely the displacement on to a primitive land of the liberal ideals frustrated by the perpetuation, in Northern Europe, of its own *ancien régime*?

Lambro returns as if in response to the poet's call, to restore masculine discipline, in the manner of Odysseus returning to Ithaca. Patriarchal leadership is certainly not idealized here. Even the most heroic modern patriot (Lambro was based on Lambros Katsanes[17]) turns out to be an individualistic opportunist, interested only in enough independence from the Turks to establish (absolute) rule over his household and retainers and to make money by whatever unscrupulous means. Lambro even provides slaves for the Turkish overlords of his country in return for personal wealth and the rule of his own small island (III, 53). Nevertheless, the patriarch must inevitably return because (as 'The Isles of Greece' showed) political authority is definitively masculine. Indeed, this is the lesson of the poem as a whole. (Catherine II, another female usurper of male rule, succeeds only because she herself adopts a masculine, militaristic ethos.) Haidée's 'rule' merely marked the absence of rule. And because government is patriarchal and dynastic in all countries represented in the poem, female sexuality, synonymous as it is with the freedom of the individual, is inevitably repressed.

The ironic impugning of the court poet; the failure of the song to arouse its audience; the reimposition of patriarchal rule; the death of Haidée and her unborn child, followed by the disintegration of the whole community: these are the hammer blows of Byron's pessimism with regard to the Utopian dreams of Philhellenism, or of reinstituting the Golden Age of sexual libertarianism.

It could be said that Byron gives Haidée the death conventionally reserved for fallen women, despite all the endorsement of her

[17] On Byron, contemporary Greece, and Philhellenism, see William St. Clair, *That Greece Might Still Be Free* (Oxford, 1972). See also E. T. Helmick, 'Hellenism in Byron and Keats', *K-SMB* 22 (1971), 18–27.

natural passion. 'If she loved rashly, her life paid for wrong' (IV, 73). But the narrator gives an alternative explanation. Were their story to continue, they would inevitably lose their love (IV, 12), which would be even more tragic:

> . . . they could not be
> Meant to grow old, but die in happy spring,
> Before one charm or hope had taken wing. (IV, 8)

In an earlier digression, the narrator also admits that the free expression of her sexuality he has extolled in Haidée makes woman vulnerable to the sexual double standard of society:

> Alas, the love of women! It is known
> To be a lovely and a dangerous thing,
> For all of theirs upon that die is thrown,
> And if 'tis lost, life hath no more to bring
> To them but mockeries of the past alone . . . (II, 199)

Even while the intensity of Haidée's love is portrayed as she watches over her sleeping lover, the poet points out the capacity for female passion to transform into 'the tiger's spring' of deadly revenge when such a woman is deceived or abandoned. This is not cast in essentialist terms, but contextualized in terms of sexual politics. The 'unnatural situation' of woman, 'from the dull palace to the dirty hovel', is to be content with a role in society based entirely on her sexuality, yet simultaneously to be constrained to act only the part of modesty, passive obedience, and passionlessness. If she is not to lose 'the advantages of a virtuous station', she must live a life of repression:

> . . . for man, to man so oft unjust,
> Is always so to women. One sole bond
> Awaits them, treachery is all their trust.
> Taught to conceal, their bursting hearts despond
> Over their idol, till some wealthier lust
> Buys them in marriage—and what rests beyond?
> A thankless husband, next a faithless lover,
> Then dressing, nursing, praying, and all's over. (II, 200)

The epigrammatic intensity of 'dressing, nursing, praying' as the sum of woman's conventional role has a vigour comparable to that of Wollstonecraft herself.

So it is made clear that Haidée can act as 'Nature's bride' and 'passion's child' only because of her remoteness from European civilization and her youthful disregard for the future:

> . . . What was said or done
> Elsewhere was nothing. She had nought to fear,
> Hope, care, nor love beyond; her heart beat here. (II, 202)

The comparison between Haidée and the English Aurora Raby demonstrates how inapplicable would be the ideal of woman's free sexuality in the context of an advanced society:

> Yet each was radiant in her proper sphere.
> The island girl, bred up by the lone sea,
> More warm, as lovely, and not less sincere,
> Was Nature's all. Aurora could not be
> Nor would be thus. The difference in them
> Was such as lies between a flower and gem. (XV, 58)

We see a relativistic, if not Janus-faced, attitude towards women of East and West here. It corresponds to the dialogics or competing discourses which operate throughout the poem via the narrator, either to enter sympathetically into the experience of the heroines and their sentimental young lover or to maintain an ironic distance by employing the cynical persona of middle-aged libertine narrator. The underlying suggestion is, of course, that hero and narrator are age-related aspects of the same man (the poet), but this does not necessarily imply a hierarchy of view.

The libertine pose, particularly evident in Canto I, is the source of anti-feminist satire of the new importance of woman as guardian of society's morals. The narrator's tactic is to reassert the traditional, but now-discredited, view of woman as dangerously close to nature, a creature of insatiable appetite, an ensnarer of men. There are routine jokes about the bluestockings, and he disinters stereotypical characterizations of women as loquacious (VI, 57); capable of extreme rage (XII, 50); revengeful (I, 124); and obtaining sway by the use of tears (V, 118), lies (XI, 36), and through matchmaking (XV, 31). The tone is patronizingly teasing, but it rarely shows the outright contempt of Pope's anti-feminist satire, or the repulsion towards women we find in Swift, although the notion of the sexuality of older women is assumed to be automatically humorous (see the treatment of Catherine II, and the stanzas joking about geriatric rape, VIII, 130–2).

The aristocratic, masculine, and colloquial language of the worldly narrator signals the poet's preference for the notoriously immoral Whig aristocratic ruling class of the past, over the present Tory administration which was influenced by the Evangelical mercantile classes. In fact, he identifies himself with the very salon society that Meiners and Ségur had accused of paving the way to Revolution through their free-thinking and sexual laxity. In this respect, as Paulson comments, Byron's sexual comedy looks back to the libertarian ethos of Sheridan and Rowlandson, that of the Foxite Whigs of the 1790s.[18] In France too, sexual licence had characterized the first phase of the Revolution—the period in which the poem is set. The Liberty tree and Phrygian cap derived from Roman fertility rites before becoming the emblems of Liberty, and were often portrayed as phallic symbols in cartoons of the period. Hostile English reviewers of *Don Juan* linked the poem's free sexuality with those early days of revolutionary fervour in France, by comparing Byron to Louvet and Laclos, who were both revolutionaries and authors of sexually-explicit novels.[19]

Of course, when Robespierre came to power, erotic libertarianism went out of favour, and the Jacobins reverted to defining the state as a collection of male-headed families. The second phase of the revolution was sectarian and homophile in character, and saw the guillotining of the female revolutionaries and feminists. As the victim of the re-emergence of puritanical moral law in the purges of the Terror, the Don would thus become a comic martyr for sexual liberty, if his career was cut short on the block. The poet would thus neatly combine his hero's aristocracy with his potential for a subversion of society too radical even for the Revolution.

The aristocratic and masculinist discourse of *Don Juan* is chiefly a controlling principle in the poem, satirically deflating or contextualizing the competing voice which hymns romantic love in lyrical description, and empathizes with the subjectivity of the

[18] Paulson, *Representations of Revolution*, p. 279. On *Don Juan* and libertinism, see also Leonard W. Deen, 'Liberty and Licence in Byron's *Don Juan*', *TSLL* 8 (1968), 345–57; and Sheila J. McDonald, 'The Impact of Libertinism on Byron's *Don Juan*', *Bulletin of Research in the Humanities*, 86:3 (1983–5), 291–317.

[19] Reiman, *Romantics Reviewed*, part B, i. 307, 207.

lovers in their dreams, interior monologues, and indirect reported speech (for example I, 75–96; IV, 9–35). This second discourse of romantic antinomianism, which dominates the Haidée episode, attacks as unnatural the institution of marriage itself, in passages like the reverential description of Juan and Haidée's natural 'marriage' on the beach (II, 204), itself quickly followed by a digression accepting the mutability of human desire.

> The heart is like the sky, a part of heaven,
> And changes night and day too, like the sky. (II, 214)

The libido is linked to appetite:

> . . . some good lessons
> Are learned from Ceres and from Bacchus,
> Without whom Venus will not long attack us.
>
> (II, 169; cf. XVI, 86)

The inflation—deflation pattern of each *ottava rima* stanza, like the shape of each amatory episode, follows the cyclical rhythm of bodily appetites—the waxing and waning of desire—in opposition to fixed moral absolutes.

The poem's emphasis on the physicality of the individual is egalitarian in its implications. Instead of the traditional notion of a libertine as sexual/class predator, Byron's Don is an ordinary man released from the confines of social mores, who acts in accord with his emotions. The spontaneity of the fictional hero's love affairs (and by implication the poet's) makes the moral rigour of the men and women of the 'literary lower empire' (XI, 62) appear unnatural by comparison. Far from enabling the latter to act disinterestedly for the public good (as had been claimed by Ségur and Meiners), the repression of their natural sexuality is portrayed by Byron as causing the corresponding swelling of their diseased imaginations with delusions of grandeur. Thus Worsdworth is compared to Joanna Southcott, a mystic who thought her dropsy meant she had been impregnated by God, and to other messianic fanatics—Swedenborg, Brothers, Tozer, di Cagliostro, and the Baroness de Krüdener (Prose preface, ll. 24 ff.). Sexual impotence is linked with linguistic incoherence in the comparison of Southey's empty bombast with sexual intercourse without emission (Dedication, 3), and in the comparison of Wordsworth's introspection and Coleridge's metaphysics with the confused yearnings of Juan's puberty

(I, 90–3). Castlereagh, too, is simultaneously mocked for his inarticulacy and for his homosexuality, he is an 'it', a time-serving eunuch, 'emasculated to the marrow' (Preface to Cantos VI–VIII), taking a perverted sadistic pleasure in subjugating Ireland (Dedication, 12).[20]

This notion of repressed or perverted sexual energy causing physical symptoms of disease, mental disturbances, and aggression is not merely a device for satirizing individuals, but a fundamental principle of the poem. Byron analyses the cause of imperial aggrandizement—represented by the Siege of Ismail—in psychological terms. The monarchs of Turkey and Russia are described as having perverted their sexuality into an unnatural exercise of power over others, expressed in their amassing of both harems and armies. The energy created by this distortion of the libido can only find its outlet through genocide. The only alternative would be a therapeutic imperial copulation:

> There was a way to end their strife . . .
> She to dismiss her guards and he his harem,
> And for other matters, meet and share 'em. (VI, 95)

Compare Swift's 'A Digression concerning Madness', in *A Tale of a Tub*. Both Byron and Swift use a materialist perspective derived from Lucretius' *On the Nature of the Universe* to explain the sexual basis of their satire of imperial warfare. Swift attributes the military aggrandizement of Henry IV of France to unfulfilled lust for the Princesse de Condé:

> . . . the collected part of the Semen, raised and enflamed, became adust, converted to Choler, turned head upon the spinal Duct, and ascended to the Brain. The very same Principle that influences a *Bully* to break the Windows of a Whore, who has jilted him, naturally stirs up a Great Prince to raise mighty armies, and dream of nothing but Sieges, Battles, and Victories.
> . . . *Teterrima belli causa* . . .[21]

[20] Frederick Garber has noted that this crude abuse of Castlereagh and others, for their impotence or chastity, can be compared to the origin of satire, as described by Robert C. Elliot's *The Power of Satire*, in fertility festivals. See his 'Self and the Language of Satire in *Don Juan*', *Thalia: Studies in Literary Humor* (University of Ottawa), 5 (1982), 35–44, p. 40.

[21] Jonathan Swift, *A Tale of a Tub*, ed. Kathleen Williams (London, 1975), pp. 103–4.

Byron quotes the same Horace tag (*Sat.*, I. iii. 107), and emphasizes that he takes the unspoken word 'cunnus' as the cause of war, rather than—by synecdoche—woman: 'Oh thou *teterrima causa* of all *belli*— | Thou gate of life and death' (IX, 55). The vagina is metonymic of the libido itself, which is hailed as the driving force of both love and war:

> From thee we come, to thee we go, and why
> To get thee not batter down a wall
> Or waste a world, since no one can deny
> Thou dost replenish worlds both great and small? (IX, 56)

The libido functions beneficially in furthering procreation under Venus, yet is converted into the death-dealing aggression of Mars if thwarted or perverted, engendering hysteria on a world scale. Sexual stereotyping is overturned by having Catherine make the martial decision to take the city at any cost, and likening Juan in his military uniform to Cupid, the god of love. This emphasizes that the libido works both positively and negatively in both sexes alike. In fact the selection of the Siege of Ismail as an image of carnage, in which the warring nations are headed by a male and a female monarch, illustrates that the dynamics of sexuality and power operate in exactly the same way in men and women. This pan-sexual diagnosis of both personal and political aggression is biological in emphasis. It therefore undermines the relativist, cross-cultural format of the poem that Byron has appropriated from his histories of women. Byron's viewpoint is fundamentally psychological and essentialist. His identification of sexual perversion and/or repression with political authoritarianism anticipates the ideas of Freud and Wilhelm Reich. The notion of repression—a significant strand of modern Marxist and feminist thought—arose specifically to challenge the basis of the nineteenth-century sexual double standard and assertion of woman's passionlessness in bourgeois progressivist accounts of European civilization.

On the other hand, 'feminine' and 'masculine' roles are shown not to be predetermined by biological gender, but social constructs, moulding the essential sexual self according to the balance of power. The poem specifically attacks both the notion of woman's role as reformer of the nation's morals, and the masculine military ethos lauded by traditional epic. Central to this endeavour is Byron's use of the comedy of sexual role reversal. His version of the

Don Juan story is innovative in that his Juan is a passive cipher; the women seduce him. This satirizes the notion of female desire as either non-existent or purely maternal. Frederick Beaty has suggested that Byron was probably inspired by the pantomime tradition, and may have read Hazlitt's review in *The Examiner* for 25 May 1817 of a new after-piece, based on *The Libertine*, in which Don Juan was for the first time portrayed as the victim of female circumstance 'forced into acts of villany against his will'.[22] However, Byron's use of sexual role reversal differs from this pantomime as from *Joseph Andrews*, in that he makes Juan not a chaste and reluctant victim, but vulnerable to seduction through his capacity for emotion. The purpose of the sexual role reversal is thus extended: showing men as equally capable of 'feminine' sentiment, as well as women not above indulging in 'masculine' appetite.

GULBEYAZ AND CATHERINE

In the Turkish episode Byron explores from the inside (in two senses) the oppression of women and the repression of female sexuality at its most extreme—in the Sultan's harem. Drawing on the transvestite tradition of pantomime, carnival, and masquerade, Byron has Juan not only entering the all-female community of the seraglio, but also taking on female identity, when he experiences the double powerlessness of a woman slave. The surprising ease with which cosmetics, clothing, and a modest demeanour transform Juan into a simulacrum of femininity, convincing enough to deceive both the Sultan and the other odalisques, unsettles any simplistic essentialist notions regarding 'masculinity' and 'femininity'. Juan goes on voluntarily to act the part of male courtesan in the court of Catherine II. The reversal of roles, in both the Turkish and the Russian episodes, works to attack the double standard of sexual morality. Juan is dressed and/or treated as a concubine, and evaluated by his owner/employer in purely physiological terms. In Russia he is medically examined, and has his sexual prowess tested by Catherine's lady-in-waiting, 'l'Éprouveuse', before his services are engaged (IX, 84–5). The unusual view of a man used in this way

[22] Frederick L. Beaty, 'Harlequin Don Juan', *JEGP* 67 (1968), 395–405.

brings home to the reader the humiliating sexual exploitation of women accepted as normal in many societies. The satire simultaneously shows women in authority, like Catherine and Gulbeyaz, to be as capable as men of using sexuality in the context of a power relationship. Juan initially reacts to Turkish threats of force with tears and protests (V, 118); but sacrifices his honour in Russia through vanity (IX, 68) and for material gain (IX, 79), as women conventionally do. The Russian courtiers behave in response to the role-reversal: the women enviously 'cast some leers' at Juan, while jealous 'tears of rivalship rose in each clouded eye' of the men (IX, 78). Clearly, the poem demonstrates 'feminine' and 'masculine' behaviour as culturally rather than biologically determined.

However, the exploration of sexual politics in these cantos is not straightforwardly feminist. For the device of inverting the scenario of the Turkish tales by casting Juan as victim and woman as tyrant also allows the poet to portray the sexual urge of the experienced woman as overpowering in the imperious poignard-wearing Gulbeyaz, and plainly disgusting in the menopausal Catherine. Juan is threatened with castration (V, 75) and death (VI, 113) in Turkey, and in Russia suffers life-threatening debility from servicing the empress (X, 39, 43). Susan Wolfson cites Byron's wavering between defensiveness and feminist analysis, expressed in his letters describing his own role of *cavalier servente* to Teresa Guiccioli, to show his ambivalence at experiencing 'polygamy' with the roles reversed. This was obviously one of the inspirations of this part of the poem, written in despite of Teresa's prohibition. Wolfson uses 'the myth of a male-authored and male-centred psychoanalytic tradition' to suggest that Juan's transvestism in the harem creates the fantasy of a 'phallic woman' to assert the male hero's superiority in the presence of strong women.[23]

The Turkish and Russian cantos juxtapose the extreme of woman's 'passive obedience' (VII, 67) in the Eastern harem with the ultimate example of her usurpation of masculine authority in a Western monarchy—Catherine's disposal of her husband to rule in his place. There is none of the pathos or indignation of the Oriental tales in the treatment of the subjugation of women in the seraglio

[23] See Susan J. Wolfson, '"Their She Condition": Cross-Dressing and the Politics of Gender in *Don Juan*', *ELH* 54 (1987), 585–617 (604, 607). See also Katherine Kernberger, 'Power and Sex: The Implications of Role Reversal in Catherine's Russia', *BJ* 10 (1982), 42–9.

episode of *Don Juan*. The emphasis falls instead on examining woman's defiance of this, in Gulbeyaz's attempt to copy masculine sexual behaviour by buying her own male concubine. Her arranged marriage to the fifty-nine-year-old sultan, whose sexual favours she shares with three other wives and fifteen hundred concubines, is briefly mentioned in extenuation: 'The fair Sultana erred from inanition' (VI, 9); and the harem is also described as a hothouse of sexual repression: 'A thousand bosoms there | Beating for love as the caged birds for air' (VI, 26). Her bravery is acknowledged, for 'she also risked her life to get him [Juan]' (V, 122). But the portrait of the imperious Gulbeyaz is essentially the Rousseauistic image of the female aristocrat as a symbol of unnatural power. This theme continues in the Russian cantos, with the chilling picture of Catherine as sexually empowered woman going on to select her favourites from the most 'gigantic gentlemen' (IX, 54), and to appropriate the masculine 'pastime' of warfare and power politics—equalling the sultan in her ruthless enjoyment of slaughter (IX, 59–60).

The Turkish cantos problematize feminism from a masculine viewpoint, by counterpointing the blunt defiance any self-respecting man (Juan) would express if treated as a female concubine with the repulsion he feels for a woman who rejects 'feminine' subservience altogether in making a sexual advance on her own account. Instead of hinting while simulating reluctance like Julia (I, 117), Gulbeyaz 'rather ordered than was granting' (V, 109), demanding 'Christian, canst thou love?' (V, 116), and throwing herself upon him (V, 125). Juan replies Byronically:

> In this vile garb, the distaff, web, and woof
> Were fitter for me. Love is for the free! (V, 127)

In the feminine 'vile garb' which denotes inferiority, freedom to love is not possible.

As in Wollstonecraft's *Vindication*, the image of a woman who has attained reflected power through sexual relationships with male aristocrats is castigated. The purple-robed Gulbeyaz requires her slave to kiss her foot (V, 102). She is compared with powerful women of the court culture of the past—Mary, Queen of Scots, and Ninon de l'Enclos (V, 98). From a Republican point of view, Gulbeyaz's power—'royal rights o'er men'—is doubly illegitimate, being derived from blood and beauty (V, 112). From a masculine point of view, the combination of despotism with the outward signs of femininity is a contradiction in terms:

> Her very *smile* was haughty, though *so sweet*;
> Her very *nod* was not an inclination.
> There was a self-will even in her *small feet*,
> As though they were quite conscious of her station;
> They trod upon necks. And to complete
> Her state (it is the custom of her nation),
> A poniard decked her *girdle*, as the sign
> She was a sultan's *bride* (thank heaven, not mine). (V, 111)

(Italics and underlining mine, to denote respectively 'feminine' words and phrases and those appertaining to despotism.)

Only when the fearsome Gulbeyaz, on being rejected, 'felt humbled', experienced 'her sex's shame', and was reduced to womanly tears did Juan's principled stand even begin to dissolve (V, 137, 141). Gulbeyaz is the only woman he refuses in the poem. So unsettling is the configuration of emasculated man confronted by empowered repressed woman that Juan's potency and woman's femininity must be restated—in his tricking and deflowering of the seventeen-year-old virgin, Dudu. Another large Oriental woman, Dudu is, however, reassuringly the epitome of passivity: 'languishing and lazy' (VI, 41),'sleepy' (VI, 42), 'not violently lively' (VI, 43), 'quiet, inoffensive, silent, shy' (VI, 49), 'a soft landscape of mild earth | Where all was harmony and calm and quiet' (VI, 53). Not only this, but while the narrator declares 'I love the sex', he means by this he envies a tyrant's ability to demonstrate his power in the sheer number of women he keeps for his sexual pleasure at one time (VI, 27–8). The Sultan's ability to keep the odalisques cool, controlled, and disciplined is admired: 'The Turks do well to shut, at least sometimes, | Their women up . . . ' (V, 157), especially when we are reminded of the extent of their repression by their reversion to wildness when freed from their guards (VI, 32–4). It is, significantly, when they are again still and silent (in sleep), that the beauty of the women of the harem is described—their half-naked bodies made over to the narrator's male gaze (VI, 64–9).

The contradictions and ambiguities of the treatment of Gulbeyaz and Catherine are apparent in passages where the narrator reverts to exclamations on the mysterious and unfathomable nature of female psychology.

Men with their heads reflect on this or that,
But women with their hearts or heaven knows what! (VI, 2)

What a strange thing is man, and what a stranger
Is woman! What a whirlwind is her head,
And what a whirlpool full of depth and danger
Is all the rest about her! (IX, 64)

The pun on 'stranger' stresses sexual difference, as does the suggestion that female biology substitutes for thought. This is so even for English bluestockings:

What after all can signify the site
Of ladies' lucubrations? So they lead
In safety to the place for which you start;
What matters if the road be head or heart? (XI, 34)

Elemental imagery characterizes woman: she changes her mind like the wind (IX, 64); fire flashes from the sultana's eyes (V, 134); her rage makes her 'a beautiful embodied storm' (V, 135); wordless woman is 'silent thunder' (VI, 57). Yet, in a stanza indirectly referring to Gulbeyaz, this apparently inexplicable feminine capacity for extremes of passion is actually contextualized as the result of powerlessness:

And yet a headlong, headstrong, downright she,
Young, beautiful, and daring, who would risk
A throne, the world, the universe to be
Beloved in her own way, and rather whisk
The stars from out the sky than not be free
As are the billows when the breeze is brisk—
Though such a she's a devil (if that there be one),
Yet she would make full many a Manichean. (VI, 3)

But even here, admiration for female rebellion is conditional on the woman being young, beautiful, and in search of love.

Catherine II, being old, fat, and powerful, cannot be Byronically idealized, and her prodigious sexual appetite provides scope for a good deal of innuendo and obscene word-play. However, surprisingly, the humour is at least as much at the expense of the ambition (and exhaustion) of the hero as of the Empress herself. Both Gulbeyaz's and Juan's faking of enthusiasm for making love to their elderly monarchs are satirized (VI, 13–20; IX, 68–72; X, 22–

4). The feminist Mary Hays featured a long section on Catherine II in her *Memoirs of Queens, Illustrious and Celebrated* (1821), whose purpose, stated in the preface, was to demonstrate 'one moral standard of excellence for mankind, whether male or female'. With regard to Catherine's 'ambition and avarice' Hays comments: 'Catherine went on adding kingdom to kingdom, state to state, by force, by negotiation, or by intrigue'. On her sexuality: 'She changed lovers with as little scruple, or even affectation of concealment, as a despot or a sultan changes his mistresses.'[24] In *Don Juan*, also, the 'masculine' behaviour of Catherine demonstrates the irrelevance of biological gender to the characteristic deployment of power on the battlefield and in the boudoir. This is counter-pointed by Juan's 'feminine' capacity for tears at the memory of Haidée (V, 117–18), and for 'maternal' feelings in his rescue and care for the orphan Leila.

The sexual politics of each country visited by the androgynous Juan reflect the degree of governmental control exercised over the libido/autonomy of the individual subject. In Greece Juan finds an island paradise of free love and material pleasure. In the despotism of Turkey he is enslaved like the women; in the absolute monarchy of Russia he prostitutes himself for gain and status. It is apposite, then, that in the constitutional state of Britain Juan contemplates making a marriage contract.

When he arrives in England, Juan voices the approval reserved for the 'island of the free' (X, 64) by progressive histories like that of Meiners:

> 'And here,' he cried, 'is Freedom's chosen station;
> Here peals the people's voice, nor can entomb it
> Racks, prisons, inquisitions; resurrection
> Awaits it, each new meeting or election.' (XI, 9)

The constitutional government is paralleled by high moral standards, for 'Here are chaste wives, pure lives . . . ' (XI, 10). Juan's illusions are somewhat deflated when he discovers that political rights for the gentry leave unchanged the economics of the class system. The common people have turned to sharp practice (X, 70), robbery (XI, 11), and prostitution (XI, 30). Moreover, England, which to Meiners was 'a paradise for women', where they enjoyed 'rational

[24] Mary Hays, *Memoirs of Queens, Illustrious and Celebrated* (London, 1821), pp. 241–2, 230.

liberty', is shown at length in Cantos XI–XII to possess the most highly-organized system of bartering women for money: the aristocratic marriage market (XI, 48–9; XII, 13–16, 58–61), which forms an ironic point of comparison with the Turkish slave market of Canto V (7, 10, 26–30). Marriage is here a matter of lawsuits not passion (XII, 68), and money above all (XII, 32–8). In fact England is sardonically revealed to be an aristocratic oligarchy in the process of transforming from a basis in land to one in capital. The English ideology of strict female propriety facilitates this transition, for wealth is acquired by the noble 'twice two thousand' (XI, 45) via intermarriage with the merchant classes, whilst political power is retained by a dynastic system of political patronage. Though women are a commodity, a unit of exchange between male property-holders, this dynastic furtherance of power operates with the connivance of the women themselves, the 'gynocrasy', who obtain a modicum of political influence through their participation (XV, 33–4).

Joan B. Landes comments that in the *ancien régime*, upper-class women did indeed have greater status under monarchy than they would under a future nation-state, being essential to the generational reproduction of class power. Through their sexual relationships with ministers and courtiers, they could also act as power-brokers.[25] To a certain extent all subjects shared a subordinate posture beneath a king, but as parliamentary privilege became increasingly accepted as the basis of British government, from the late seventeenth to the nineteenth century, the citizenry were stratified according to gender and class. After the dissemination in the French Revolution of theories of natural rights and even universal suffrage, such categories of difference had to be re-affirmed. Hence the development of theories of complementary gender roles, which would preclude women from civil rights.

Don Juan is therefore very much the product of its time—reacting to the transformation of the absolutist public sphere into the bourgeois state with its gendered citizenship. The structure of the poem, which it shares with the histories of women in Byron's library, hinges on the contrast between the despotic treatment of women in the East and their social dominance in Western monarchical society: the subtext is Rousseau's depiction of

[25] Joan B. Landes, *Women and the Public Sphere in the Age of the French Revolution* (Ithaca, NY, and London, 1988), pp. 20–1.

republicanism as fostering a truly heroic masculinity, nostalgically viewed in a past classical golden age or eulogized in a Utopian future. *Don Juan* thus combines an anti-feminist critique of the undue influence of society women in the effeminate *ancien régime* with an equally anti-feminist repudiation of the new bourgeois ideal of the moralizing mother. So what is the ideal role of women in modern society? What happens to the poem's radical and emancipatory celebration of female sexuality in the Greek cantos, by the time Juan has travelled from the primitive simplicity of civilization's childhood and eventually comes of age in England? We find an impasse has been reached, and Byron falls back on the uneasy relativism of the comparison between Haidée and Aurora, that 'each was radiant in her proper sphere'. Aurora is close to being a feminist heroine, in her independent outlook. But she is also insistently characterized as virginal. Compare Pierre-Antoine Choderlos de Laclos in his unpublished *Des Femmes et de leur éducation* (1783), who argued that because, in the present state of society, women are slaves, they would become unhappy or positively dangerous if they received a full liberal education instead of mere conditioning. No true educational improvement can be effected unless a social revolution simultaneously gives them the same freedom to make moral choices as men, rather than merely conforming in fear of a social stigma enforced by the double standard. Reaching an impasse, Laclos turns to discuss 'natural' women, in primitive lands, since his argument hinges on the fundamental opposition between nature and society.[26]

AURORA

Bernard Beatty has rightly pointed out that critics have tended to ignore Aurora Raby, or to concur in Adeline's judgement of her as 'prim' (XV, 55).[27] However, as Beatty demonstrates, Aurora represents a genuine ideal of womanhood in the poem, and one which is linked with her Northern Christianity. Nevertheless, it is unnecessary, on the basis of this, to postulate an elaborate

[26] Jean H. Bloch, 'Women and the Reform of the Nation', in Eva Jacobs *et al.* (eds.), *Woman and Society in Eighteenth Century France: Essays in Honour of John Stephenson Spink* (London, 1979) pp. 3–18 (13).

[27] Bernard Beatty, *Byron's* Don Juan (London, 1985), ch. 4.

argument demonstrating the teleological development of the importance of religion in the poem, as Beatty does. Aurora's significance is social, not existential. She represents Byron's attempt to create a heroine comparable to Haidée in idealization, yet appropriate to an advanced European civilization.

For, by juxtaposing Aurora with the lustful duchess, Byron indicates that the ideals of pagan free sexuality would be inapplicable in a highly-structured and corrupt modern civilization. So Aurora is a heroine neither passionate like Haidée nor repressed like Adeline. Her description emphasizes mind, not body. The sixteen-year-old 'little Aurora' (XV, 55) has none of the threatening sexuality of the mature woman. Like the little Nell and little Dorrit of future Dickens novels, she is 'infantine in figure' (XV, 45), 'scarcely formed or moulded' (XV, 43). Though so young, she is 'grave' and 'mournful' (XV, 45): 'she had so much, or little of the child' (XV, 55). A 'sincere' and even 'austere' Christian (XV, 46), she is contemptuous of pleasure-seeking high society (XV, 47). An orphan, scorned by the fine lady of the house, the bookish Aurora is a Cinderella figure, whose loneliness and rejection, despite her self-evident worth, constitute a reproach to the landed gentry for their worldly and materialist outlook. Austen's Fanny Price performs a similar function in *Mansfield Park*.

Formerly, the product of the pens of Maria Edgeworth, Hannah More, and Sarah Trimmer had merely been satirized in the portrayal of Inez as a manipulative hypocrite. But in the creation of Aurora the poet pays tribute to this novelistic heroine as the true feminine antithesis of his own idealization of male individual aggrandizement in the Byronic heroes. He makes clear that Aurora is not superior to Haidée: 'Each was radiant in her proper sphere' (XV, 58). But though Aurora's gemlike moral strength is less joyous, it demonstrates an equivalent ability of woman to exercise individual autonomy—not sexually, but through rational control of her subjectivity. Whereas Haidée is Juan's counterpart, Aurora is his complement. As Beatty has pointed out, the unlikely association of Southern sensual Don Juan with the Christian English virgin is an inversion of Goethe's pairing of the Northern introspective Faust with the pagan Southern Helen (to produce the Byronic Euphorion) in Part 2 of *Faust*.

Where Byron parts company with most of his contemporary female novelists, however, is that, rather than developing her moral sense the better to fulfil her pre-ordained familial role, his heroine stands proudly aside from society: 'She gazed upon a world she scarcely knew | As seeking not to know it' (XV, 47). Byron thus makes Aurora's chastity a matter of individual choice and independence rather than obedience and propriety. As an unmarried orphan (XV, 44) Aurora is not subject to male control. As an heiress she is financially independent. As a bluestocking she is Juan's intellectual equal, if not superior (see XV, 85; XI, 51). She is strong-minded (XV, 47) and serious, despising frivolity (XV, 53). She has the Northern woman's 'natural' control of her own sexuality. As a Christian she is confident of the equality of her soul with that of man. All these elements combine to give her a sense of self-worth based not on a man's romantic love for her, but on her intrinsic value as an individual: 'Such was her coldness or her self-possession' (XV, 57). Aurora is Byron's portrait of the modern woman: newly confident of her moral value to society, she refuses to be continually judged through the medium of her sexuality.

Although she has noticed his beauty (XV, 85–6), Aurora judges the Don only by his moral worth, and finds him superficial (XV, 83). She is indifferent to Juan's charm, hardly bothering to reply to his 'gay nothings' (XV, 78). Refusing to indulge in superficial banter, she makes an abrupt transition from ignoring his flirtatious gambits to initiating a conversation on her own terms—asking him direct questions. Ironically, a serious conversation between a man and a woman is construed as boldness bordering on impropriety by Adeline, the pillar of society (XV, 81). On another occasion, he is discomposed to catch her amused smile at his clumsiness in serving fish at the dinner-table. This rare smile has no coquetry (XVI, 92); and she returns his look with serenity. Unlike the passive and docile romantic heroines of the Oriental tales, Aurora does not blush or cast down her eyes submissively (XVI, 94). Indeed, it is Juan who 'grew carnation with vexation' (XVI, 93). Instead of responding to him sexually, she only shows her approval of him morally, when she mistakenly believes his abstention from the 'skirmish of wits' at the expense of the departed guests is an act of charity (XVI, 106).

What gives the portrayal of Aurora its distinctively Byronic twist, however, is her Catholicism. I am not convinced by Beatty's view that Byron was expressing Burkean nostalgia for the mediaeval, combined with neo-Catholicism, in linking Aurora with the Virgin Mary who presides over the Abbey. His purpose was much simpler.

Aurora is in many respects, as we have seen, the type of heroine approved by the didactic or moralistic female-authored novel. But these writers were inspired by the Evangelical movement, which was low-church and politically conservative. Catholicism was anathema to them. Byron's strategy is to present them with an impeccable heroine—both chaste and religious—yet one who exposes the prejudices of both her fictional English society and the contemporary reader. Neither was able to identify with a Papist.

As C. J. Clancy suggests: 'Aurora is a rebel whose religious practice has a political dimension.'[28] The advancement of Catholics to civil rights was a Whig policy, with particular significance for the question of Ireland. Byron draws our attention to the secular motives for Aurora's loyalty to Catholicism: 'perhaps because 'twas fallen', and because her family: 'had never bent or bow'd | To novel power'. (Compare the Muslim orphan Leila's refusal to be converted to Christianity (X, 55).) Aurora's minority religion gives her an individualism which she proudly refuses to relinquish for mere social conformity (XV, 46). In fact the Protestant authors, Germaine de Staël and Sydney Owenson Morgan, had also made their sentimental heroines Corinne and Glorvina Catholics, specifically to refute Protestant moral rigour and to raise the issue of religious toleration. Aurora's Catholicism is not indicative of the nostalgic escape to the Gothic past which would characterize the Oxford movement, but shows Byron slyly subverting, even while paying sincere tribute to, the idealized heroine of the female-authored novel.

As with Edgeworth's Belinda and Burney's Evelina, Aurora's honesty shows up the superficiality of her fashionable aristocratic milieu. But whereas Richardsonian novels like Mary Brunton's *Self Control* relate the adventures of a Christian heroine pursued by an unscrupulous libertine, it was rare after Fielding's satirizing of Richardson's *Pamela*, to find authors attempting the dangerous ground of portraying a love match between the moral heroine and the (repentant) rake. Byron's unfinished story of 'little Aurora' may have fed back into the history of the female-authored novel, by influencing Charlotte Brontë to take on the challenge of a love story between the lonely orphan Jane Eyre, a rational, Christian, and independent heroine, and the Byronic gentleman who also has

[28] C. J. Clancy, 'Aurora Raby in *Don Juan*: a Byronic Heroine', *K-SJ* 28 (1979), 28–34.

returned from his travels with a female 'ward' and whose name is synonymous with libertinism.

Aurora's intellectual equality and Haidée's free sexuality are contrasting or complementary versions of female autonomy: the products of the most and least civilized societies of the poem, they are implied to be mutually exclusive. As a fierce individualist, Aurora is also an atypical English heroine. It is the conformist Adeline who is most representative of the fate of British women, and whose portrait is most fully drawn. The character of Lady Adeline is a complex analysis of the artificiality of western femininity: both a masculinist satire of a salon *précieuse* and political hostess and yet, most importantly, a sympathetic rendering of the self-repression of the female libido demanded by English society.

ADELINE

Compare Adeline with Hannah More's Lucilla Stanley or, for that matter, Rousseau's Julie. Byron's sardonic portrait of Adeline's *ennui* punctures these inflated novelistic claims for the vitally important role played by the chaste and obedient lady of the manor, in creating familial harmony and bonds of reciprocal duty between the classes, to pre-empt civil dissent. After two years of apparent power during courtship, when 'a hecatomb of suitors' panted at her feet (XIV, 55), Adeline marries, bears an heir, but then finds her lifetime role of political and social hostess 'a dreary void' (XIV, 79), stretching ahead of her. Adeline, as circumspect mistress of her country house and hostess to the local gentry, is not shown fulfilling a redemptive moral role in provincial society, but coldly performing an artificial and uncongenial exercise in political management and public relations.

Norman Abbey is an emblem of Northern marriage. The juxtaposition of its ruined church and opulent mansion indicates that the decline of the Church's influence in the state has contributed to the power of the landowning dynasties. Its carved religious symbols are gone: only the female icon of virgin mother and child is left to preside over an empty arch (XIII, 61–4), just as the only vestige of Christianity in public life is the vapid sentimentalization of domesticity. The ghost of the black Friar haunts the Amundevilles' marriage-bed (XVI, 340–1). Adeline's role as wife and mother is thus symbolically constrained by the life-denying morality of a largely defunct religion. She could cast it off by night, as the Duchess casts off her cowl, to play the game of adultery, but only at the risk of her social position. The ghost's first, and apparently genuine, appearance to Juan (on which the opportunist Duchess capitalizes) suggests imminent bad fortune in the Amundeville family, possibly through a lapse of Adeline's chastity. Unlike Laura in *Beppo*, Adeline would be entirely ruined by one such error, owing to the stricter sexual mores in England (XII, 78). This is a measure of how little the English social system allows for natural impulse in women.

The 'splendid mansion' of Adeline's heart is vacant (XIV, 85), which, it is hinted, could undermine the whole matrimonial edifice upon which English society is built. The pre-election dinner for the local gentry over which she presides is a mockery of genuine reciprocal social bonds. The spontaneous mutability of the feelings, natural on the Greek island (II, 208–16), becomes in Adeline a civilized 'vivacious versatility' (XVI, 97) and 'mobility' of temperament which oil the social wheels so smoothly that Juan 'began to feel | Some doubt how much of Adeline was *real*' (XVI, 96).

The cost of keeping up the façade is Northern self-repression. To love Lord Henry, who treats her 'like an aged sister' (XIV, 69), takes a great effort (XIV, 88). Adeline, like England, has had the briefest of summers ('The London winter's ended in July' (XIII, 43)), and as its 'gloomy clouds'. . . 'put the sun out like a taper' (X, 83), so Adeline's effervescence is 'frozen into a very vinous ice' (XIII, 37). While her husband is motivated by the iceberg of self-love (XIV, 102), Adeline is frozen champagne, the North-West Passage which may lead a Don Juan to 'glowing India' or just the North Pole (XIII, 37–9).

When the poet travels with Juan to England, the pace of the poem slows, and its sexual satire modulates into novelistic complexity. While the comedy continues in the mock-Gothic ghost story and Juan's midnight encounter with the lusty and cowled Duchess, the putative marriage of the hero to Aurora and fall of Adeline, which constitute the real interest of the English cantos, are merely narrative possibilities frozen into lack of closure by Byron's death. What we are left with, in the comparison between Aurora and

Adeline, is the unresolved tension between modern woman's assertion of moral and intellectual equality, and the repression of her sexuality which this nineteenth-century feminism entails. This, indeed, was where the poem began, in the comparison between Inez and Julia. But Aurora and Adeline are far more sympathetically drawn, subtle characters, related specifically to their social milieu.

What we may be sure of, in the way the poem may have continued, is that marriage would not have constituted a happy ending. Byron only considered it as an alternative to Juan's decapitation in the French Revolution, as another way of representing the Hell of the original myth![29] The poem as a whole strenuously opposes the cult of domesticity and the moral mother, an ideology which would go from strength to strength in the Victorian age. To the voice of cynical detractor of female virtue was added that of the Romantic individualist, who hymns self-fulfilment for both sexes and denies that romantic love has anything to do with the institution of marriage.

The poem's attack on Northern sexual repression is subversive, not only of orthodox Christian morality, but of one of the fundamental tenets of liberal ideology: the notion of the state as a collection of male-headed families whose ability to transmit hereditary property rests on the ideology of female submission and chastity. Just as the revolutionary concept of universal suffrage threatened the political authority of these property-owners, so sexual individualism would undermine male primogeniture and dissipate their economic power. Byron took from Coleridge the idea of a new treatment of Don Juan, ending his days in the Terror, in order to vent his scorn, not just on the Tories, but at the bourgeois and reactionary turn liberalism had taken after the French Revolution.

Had he completed the poem, Juan's death on the guillotine would have explicitly underlined the relationship of the political and sexual, which has been virtually ignored by the modern reader. As the subverter of dynastic marriages all over Europe, the aristocratic Don Juan is a sexual Jacobin, and one who continued to pose a threat to the contemporary re-establishment of the *ancien régime*, since all known social and governmental systems have been shown in the poem to be based on control of female sexuality to

[29] *L&J* viii. 78.

further dynastic alliances. Sexual libertarianism, such as the Don's, was an aspect of the Natural Law which, it had been thought in the earliest days of the Revolution, would replace the authority of Church and King. But the guillotining of Juan by the Jacobins themselves, in the purges of 1793, would also show how incompatible are true individualism and political government of any colour.

The political danger of sexual libertarianism was clear at the time. The Poet Laureate thundered: 'This evil is political as well as moral, for indeed moral evils are inseparably connected . . . there is no means whereby that corruption can be so surely and rapidly diffused as by poisoning the waters of literature.'[30] Southey was particularly worried that Byron's attack on the Evangelical emphasis on sexual morality would influence two sections of the poem's readership: women and the working class. The poem was being brought out in numerous pirated editions by Radical publishers like Benbow, Onwhyn, and Sherwin in half-a-crown duodecimo volumes, which would enable the poorer classes to buy it.[31] Women formed a large part of Byron's readership. Women and the working class were both characterized as so susceptible to subjectivity and irrationality that they would be more easily corrupted by the dangerous individualism of the poem into subversive lawlessness. It is a historical irony that it was a libertine who was in a position to challenge the consensus on the necessity for female chastity, and an aristocrat who could discern the bourgeois nature of contemporary liberal thought.

Southey need not have worried. Byron's attack on the hagiography of the family in *Don Juan* was almost as much a voice in the wilderness as that of Wollstonecraftian feminism, a generation earlier. Wollstonecraft's rejection of conventional 'femininity' and Byron's celebration of the female libido were both anathema to the majority of women, who found that stressing their feminine sentiment and saintliness was more effective in gaining concessions from the male hegemony than attacking the ideology of sexual difference itself. The notion of woman's role as biologically and culturally determined to be

[30] Robert Southey, Preface to *A Vision of Judgement*, *The Poetical Works of Robert Southey* (London, 1837–8), x. 206.

[31] See Hugh J. Luke Jr., 'The Publishing of Byron's *Don Juan*', *PMLA* 80 (1965), 199–209. See also N. Stephen Bauer, 'Romantic Poets and Radical Journalists', *NM* 79 (1978), 266–75; and William St. Clair, 'The Impact of Byron's Writings: An Evaluative Approach', in Andrew Rutherford (ed.), *Byron: Augustan and Romantic* (Basingstoke, 1990), pp. 1–25.

guardian of morals in the family was used as an argument to press for reforms in female education, and later even to demand the vote.

In the post-war reconstruction of society after the anarchy of the Revolution, the personal had become the political. Writers like Meiners, Ségur, and Coleridge, and the Evangelical women novelists, saw female chastity as the measure of effective political authority. Byron's poem accepts the premise. He merely restates it in terms of individual freedom. Freedom over his/her sexuality is the measure of the individual's degree of autonomy.

6

'Why, What Is Virtue If It Needs a Victim?': Heroic Heroines in Regency Drama

BYRON'S experimentation with genre in both *Don Juan* and the dramas he wrote from 1820 to 1825 was motivated largely by his determination to eschew sentimentalism. The whole enterprise of qualifying Romantic subjectivity through satire, or dramatic objectivity, was coloured by Byron's perception of Romanticism as effeminate and his desire to masculinize his art. The authorial voice, source of the subjective in the lyrics, *Childe Harold*, and even *Don Juan* would be eliminated by the adoption of the dramatic mode. The plays were to be austerely neo-classical; romantic love would form no part of the subject-matter. However, as with *Don Juan*, elements of romance re-emerged in the later plays, and of course all the protagonists do voice Byronic sentiment.

The literary production of Byron's plays will now be considered in their historical context. Byron wrote eight plays altogether—more than any other Romantic poet. All were tragedies—in defiance of the popular taste of the theatre-goers of the time for melodrama and domestic comedies. Only one was staged in the poet's lifetime; they were therefore published as closet drama. In the preface to *Marino Faliero* Byron repudiates the theatrical audience.[1] This was becoming increasingly dominated by the lower classes, and a fracture had developed between popular theatre and drama as literature, to be enjoyed by the individual reader in the study.[2] As chief member of the Drury Lane committee in 1815, he

[1] *CPW* iv. 302.

[2] The development of 'closet drama' is discussed by Joseph Donohue, *Theatre in the Age of Kean* (Oxford, 1975), pp. 161–75. For the 19th-cent. theatre and its audience, see Michael R. Booth, *et al.* (eds.), *The Revels History of Drama in English*, vi. 1750–1880, (London, 1975), pp. 3–57. On Gothic drama, see Bertrand Evans, *Gothic Drama from Walpole to Shelley* (London, 1947).

had sifted through the stock of '400 fallow dramas' as well as considering unsolicited manuscripts like Maturin's *Bertram*, and suggesting dramatic projects to established writers like Scott, Moore, and Coleridge.[3] In considering what Alastair Fowler terms 'the generic horizon'[4] of his closet drama, therefore, we need to bear in mind Byron's extensive experience and knowledge of the contemporary theatre he was reacting against.

In a survey of English nineteenth-century drama, James Ellis has observed:

> The most pervasive feature of nineteenth-century English drama, that which stamps tragedy, melodrama, comedy, farce, pantomime, and extravaganza alike as of that time, is domesticity. Hearth and home, the closeness of parents and children (especially fathers and daughters), the purity and devotion of women, the protectiveness and duty of men, form the warp and woof of virtually every play.[5]

The heroines of this popular stage drama were feminine stereotypes similar to those of the Regency verse-tales. Predominant was the damsel in distress. She might be the daughter of a 'bankrupt broken-hearted' Bohemian father and pursued by a robber-miller, as in Isaac Pocock's immensely popular melodrama *The Miller and his Men* (Covent Garden, 1813); or chaste daughter of a venerable Roman and threatened with rape by a tyrant, as in James Sheridan Knowles's verse tragedy *Virginius* (C.G., 1820); or feature in any number of exotic or homely settings. Such a heroine was sometimes portrayed as intelligent and articulate, as was the resourceful Florence in John Tobin's Gothic drama *The Curfew* (Drury Lane, 1807). But the audience was simultaneously reassured of her 'femininity' in a play of this genre, by her demonstrable vulnerability to physical danger and sexual attack, and the eventual necessity for male protection. As with the verse-tales, her relationship with her father is at the emotional heart of many plays. Virginia responds, on being falsely informed that she is an adopted slave: 'I could not live, an he were not | My father' (I, 119). As with the Regency verse romances considered in Chapter 1, such concentration on filial love

[3] *L&J* v. 319.

[4] Alastair Fowler, *Kinds of Literature: An Introduction to the Theory of Genres and Modes* (Oxford, 1982), p. 262.

[5] See James Ellis, 'A Great Reckoning in a Little Room: English Plays of the Nineteenth Century', *Nineteenth Century Theatre Research*, 5 (1977), 27–42.

stresses the patriarchal identity of the father and bolsters the necessity of patrilineal control over female generativity.

If the heroine is seduced, it is still her estrangement from and eventual reconciliation with her father which forms the focal point of the drama. Even in a popular comedy like Colman's *John Bull; or, An Englishman's Fire-side* (C.G., 1803) the reconciliation of father and erring daughter is the emotional climax of the play. Here the ethos of John Bull is identified with the inviolable right of a middle-class father to stand up to his social superiors in defence of his daughter's rights; her seduction is representative of any threat (from above) to his control and superintendence of his family and property: 'No one deserves forgiveness who refuses to make amends when he has disturbed the happiness of an Englishman's fireside!' (III, 142).

When George III died on 27 April 1820 and the theatres were no longer prohibited from playing *King Lear* (the spectacle of a mad king had been considered in bad taste!), the theme received a fresh impetus, in the reunion of Lear with Cordelia. This was, of course, the text revised by Nahum Tate with its happy ending, in which the gods do indeed love old men, both Lear and Gloucester surviving. The theme is filial piety rewarded, as the aged fathers smile upon the union of Edgar and Cordelia:

> But Edgar, I defer thy joys too long.
> Thou served'st distressed Cordelia; take her crowned,
> Th'Imperial grace fresh blooming on her brow.
> Nay Gloster, thou hast here a father's right,
> Thy helping hand t'heap blessings on their heads.
>
> (V, vi, 135–9)

As well as revivals of Shakespeare's play, theatre-goers were treated to a melodrama created by its translation to the realms of domesticity: Moncrieff's *The Lear of Private Life!, or Father and Daughter* (Coburg, 1820). (This was an adaptation of Amelia Opie's novel *The Father and Daughter*.) The seduced and abandoned heroine returns home with her baby, and in a raging snowstorm encounters her father who, having been driven mad by her loss, has temporarily escaped from a lunatic asylum. Unlike Shakespeare's Lear, this father is portrayed as without fault. The heroine is made to condemn her own wickedness which has made him insane with grief:

This is the recompense bestowed on him by the daughter he loved and trusted for years of unparalleled fondness and indulgence! Horrible! Horrible! (III, iii)

In preference to popular theatre such as this Byron commended, in the preface to *Marino Faliero*, the genre of historical/biblical blank-verse tragedies, instancing Joanna Baillie's (*Ethwald* and *De Montfort*); the Revd H. H. Milman's (*Fall of Jerusalem*); and John Wilson's (*City of the Plague*). Before he left England Byron had been instrumental in instigating a temporary revival of blank-verse tragedy in the theatre, in having Maturin's *Bertram* produced at Drury Lane in 1816. Richard Lalor Sheil's *Evadne* (C.G., 1819) and Milman's *Fazio* (C.G., 1818) followed, as well as Knowles's *Virginius*, and later Byron's own *Marino Faliero*, of course. But these tragedies had only a limited success, being predominantly closet drama. Most were set in mediaeval or Renaissance times, reflecting nineteenth-century nostalgia for a mythical past when politics could be portrayed in an aristocratic ambience in terms of chivalric concern for individual honour. The father/daughter configuration is still a common feature, but, as in Byron's *The Two Foscari* and Shelley's *The Cenci*, many of these dramas present a heroine who is stronger than or even critical of the patriarch, rather than a pathetic victim; and the context is one of political or religious struggle in the public arena, rather than domestic life.

Joanna Baillie published eighteen verse tragedies and numerous comedies and musical works, as well as verse, and was hailed as the Shakespeare of her time. The theatre of the 1780s and 1790s had been dominated by women playwrights such as Frances Brooke, Hannah Parkhurst Cowley, Elizabeth Inchbald, and Hannah More.[6] Baillie, a close friend of Scott and friend of Annabella and her family, was particularly highly regarded by Byron, who tried to have *De Montfort* revived whilst at Drury Lane. His letters provide abundant evidence of his admiration of her tragedies.[7] In her three series of *Plays on the Passions* (Vol. I, 1798; Vol. II, 1802; Vol. III, 1812), Baillie often contrasts the fatal passion of the (almost always) male protagonist with the stoic, nurturing endurance of the heroine. *Marino Faliero*, *Sardanapalus*, and *Cain* reflect exactly this configuration.

[6] Stuart Curran, 'The I Altered', in *Romanticism and Feminism*, ed. Mellor, pp. 185–207.

[7] *L&J* iv. 336. On Byron's admiration of Baillie as a tragedian, see *L&J* iii. 109, 180; iv. 290, 336. Concerning his request for her works from Murray, along with those of his most respected contemporaries, in contrast with the 'trash' he no longer wishes to receive, see v. 207.

In Baillie's early play *Basil*, the Countess of Albini is given privileged discourse in her assertion that a woman should be valued for fulfilment of 'an useful state' rather than sexual beauty. She echoes the sentiments of Wollstonecraft arguing against Rousseau's endorsement of feminine wiles:

> For she who only finds her self-esteem
> In others' admiration, begs an alms;
> Depends on others for her daily food,
> And is the very servant of her slaves;
> Though oftentimes, in a fanastic hour,
> O'er men she may a childish pow'r exert,
> Which not ennobles, but degrades her state. (II, iv)[8]

Jane, in *De Montfort*, is likewise a heroine whose virtues are illustrated by a familial but not sexual role. Like Charlotte in Goethe's *Werther*, she is fulfilling a useful station in life as a mother-substitute to her siblings, and is made to gain in dignity from her obliviousness to romantic love:

> The virgin mother of an orphan race
> Her dying parents left, this noble woman
> Did, like a Roman matron, proudly sit
> Despising all the blandishments of love;
> While many a youth his helpless love conceal'd,
> Or, humbly distant, woo'd her like a queen. (II, ii)

Jane is specifically compared to other (superficial) women: her dress is simpler because her mind is on more important matters; they become petty through sexual jealousy, whilst she earns men's respect through her efforts on behalf of her brother.

Whilst her brother is obsessed with hatred for and plotting secret vengeance on his enemy, she endeavours to bring about a reconciliation. At first this appears to have succeeded, but even when De Montfort has brutally murdered the innocent man Jane refuses to desert her brother. She helps him regain his nobility by ensuring that he prays for forgiveness and thus attains a tranquil death. A further scene follows, (significantly) cut in Kemble's stage adaptation, in which the heroine is apotheosized—surrounded and praised by all her brother's servants and friends. In this final tableau Jane stands in dignity, with these men in postures of

[8] *The Dramatic and Poetical Works of Joanna Baillie* (London, 1851), p. 27. All quotations from Baillie are taken from this edition.

subservience: one is embracing her knees and another reverently touching her robe. Monks and nuns are grouped around also, to endorse her Christian ethics. The whole purpose of the play has been to demonstrate the heroine's saintliness. The ideology of the play identifies woman's familial role with an important civilizing influence on the primitive passions of the man of action.

Baillie's heroines were undoubtedly an influence on Byron's, as contemporary reviewers noticed. His Zuleika had previously been compared to Bertha in *Ethwald*, and later the *Examiner* praised the character of Angiolina in *Marino Faliero* as '. . . an exquisite conception of female dignity and loveliness, in the spirit of Jane de Montfort of Miss Bailey (*sic*) . . . Looking down upon the miserable scurrility which has so enraged her husband, with the calm content of conscious virtue and unruffled intellect, she is skillfully made to lay open the peculiarity of his temperament . . . Every scene in which she appears is excellent . . . '[9]

Adah, in *Cain*, is even closer to Baillie's Jane. Here the heroine is shown fulfilling her domestic duties and actively putting the ethics of love and forgiveness into practice. She also attempts a reconciliation between her brother and his adversary; she too forgives her brother and supports him after he has murdered Abel. Like Baillie, Byron emphasizes the equality of the sibling relationship, the naturalness of friendship arising from a common childhood. In the case of Cain and Adah, marriage and parenthood are added to this; the effect is to characterize love between the hero and heroine as a rational, equal relationship, not an artificial social arrangement or a destructive passion.

In *Constantine Paleologus: The Last of the Caesars* (*Miscellaneous Plays*, 1804), Joanna Baillie had taken as subject Gibbon's account of the siege of Constantinople by the Turks in the fifteenth century. In the introduction, she describes the emperor as '. . . nursed in a luxurious court in habits of indulgence and indolence; without ambition, even without hope, rousing himself up on the approach of unavoidable ruin, . . . deserted by his own worthless and enervated subjects, supported alone by a generous band, chiefly of strangers, devoting themselves to him from generous attachment . . .'.[10] The resemblance of the theme to that adopted by Byron in *Sardanapalus* (1821) is sufficiently obvious. But compare the

[9] Reiman, *Romantics Reviewed*, part B, iii. 101.

[10] Baillie, *Works*, p. 390.

heroines of these plays. The similarities and the differences are illuminating. Baillie's Valeria is the emperor's wife, not concubine. This marriage is close, monogamous, and based on mutual respect. Mahomet, on the other hand, disciplines both his harem and his soldiers by means of the bowstring, even on an unsubstantiated suspicion. The real climax of the play occurs, as in *De Montfort*, after the defeat and death of the male protagonist, when the victorious Turk enters the city to claim Valeria for his harem. Her proud repudiation of him puzzles the Turks:

> It does indeed a wondrous mixture seem
> Of woman's loveliness with manly state;
> And, yet, methinks, I feel as though it were
> Strange, and perplexing, and unsuitable.
> 'Tis not in nature. (V, iii)

Baillie portrays concepts of 'femininity' as culturally produced. The Turks regard self-assertion as 'masculine'; they find Valeria's assumption of dignity unnatural in a woman. When Valeria further demonstrates her Romaic heroism by putting herself beyond his power by stabbing herself in the breast, Mahomet is converted to wonder and admiration: 'O live, thou wondrous creature, and be aught | Thy soul desires to be!' (V, iii). Valeria explains her action; that she wishes to share her husband's eternal rest 'without reproach'. Mahomet is amazed at this concept of monogamous marriage for life: 'Prophet of God, be there such ties as these!' As in *De Montfort*, the play closes with a tableau centred around the heroine, who sits dying whilst four male Greek nobles kneel in reverence to her. When she dies Mahomet makes obeisance to her body, as he exclaims incredulously: 'Great God of heav'n! was this a woman's spirit | That took its flight?' Byron's Myrrha also heroically commits suicide rather than outlive her lover. But his Greek heroine educates the Eastern potentate about woman's capacity for heroism, altruism, and monogamous mutuality, through her unwilling love, not repudiation of him. Compare a comic verion of the theme—Bickerstaffe's *The Sultan* (D.L., 1775). Here, Roxalana, an Englishwoman captured for the sultan's seraglio, astonishes and finally moves him to love and respect by her self-assertion. She lectures him on women's rights, and finally secures the freedom of all his wives.

Constantine and *Sardanapalus* both show liberal-minded monarchs presiding over empires stagnating into extinction through aristocratic luxury and lack of political purpose. Autocracy stands waiting in the wings, ready to take over. The heroine plays a double role. As a potential victim of rape, she focuses the horror of a return to despotism; yet her heroism is a patriotic symbol of the resistance of even the weakest section of society—its women. Her defiance is not threatening, because it is framed as a personal commitment of love to the deposed ruler, not participation in politics; and her suicide emphasizes her dependence on him to give her life meaning.

Perhaps the most extraordinary example of a verse tragedy which linked female heroism and patriotism was Arthur Murphy's *The Grecian Daughter* (D.L., 1772), which was regularly performed for fifty years, and the story of which Byron extols in *Childe Harold* IV (148–51). It is perhaps the ultimate expression of the father and daughter theme so prevalent in all genres of the period. Euphrasia is both daughter of the imperilled patriarch, as well as wife and mother of the male heirs to power. When the tyrant captures her venerable father Evander, and is in the process of starving him to death, she manages to keep him alive by breast-feeding him in his cell. When Dionysius discovers the reason for Evander's surprising survival and is about to cut him down, she saves her father again by stabbing the tyrant:

> A daughter's arm, fell monster, strikes the blow.
> ... Ye slaves, look there;
> Kneel to your rightful king: the blow for freedom
> Gives you the rights of men! (V, iii)[11]

The woman herself holds no immanent power, yet endows soldiers with 'the rights of men'. The heroine's role in relation to the male members of her family is representative of the citizen's in the state, without autonomy yet a crucial support. The play shows that in this crisis only she can sustain (literally) the patriarch of imperilled liberal tradition. Though she herself will not rule, she gives life and nourishment to future heirs. This image of female heroism contrives to use the emotive role of motherhood to endorse patriarchal rule, but to remove from it any connotations of female sexuality, which might present a potential threat to social order. The importance of

[11] Quotations are from Arthur Murphy, *The Grecian Daughter: A Tragedy in Five Acts*, ed. Mrs Inchbald (London, 1816).

motherhood is conceded: dynastic rule depends on it. But when female nurture is devoted asexually to the father the daughter's generativity is seen to be controlled by patriarchy, and, in the case of Euphrasia put to the service of the state. So heroic is Euphrasia, that Evander makes her temporary ruler of Sicily until Timoleon returns, 'a parent to her people'.

Menenius Agrippa's fable of the belly, found in Plutarch and used in *Coriolanus*, was commonly quoted in political argument of the day (by Scott, for example) to illustrate the function of the lower classes to provide food for the body politic (the nobility) and so enable the head (monarch) to make executive decisions. In this play, the heroine's breast-feeding of her father is a variation of this metaphorical role of the disenfranchised subjects, and a macabre attempt to glorify it. The political relationship between ruler and ruled is translated into the terms of reciprocal love and nurture. 'Feminine' values are therefore appropriated to endorse patriarchal rule. In *The Grecian Daughter* a specifically female stoic heroism is thus patriotically made to endorse a Whiggish ideology of aristocratic republicanism.

The Revd H. H. Milman's apocalyptic play *The Fall of Jerusalem* (1820) also features a strong and nurturing daughter. Miriam is a secret Christian in a Judaic Jerusalem besieged by the Romans. Torn between love for a Christian, who wants to help her escape, and duty to her father, she chooses the latter, though he is shown to be a tyrannical murderer, and even at the cost of concealing her Christianity. The correctness of her choice is underlined by her citing of Judaic law on filial duty. The imagery of the heroine feeding her father is again utilized in this play, as Miriam only meets Javan in order to procure food for her starving father. Byron admired Milman as a dramatist,[12] but uses a similarly apocalyptic setting in *Heaven and Earth* to refute entirely Milman's eulogy on filial loyalty in an atmosphere redolent with the fear of divine wrath. Anah and Aholibamah repudiate Judaic patriarchalism, and human love is preferenced to obedience to moral laws in Byron's play.

This brief sketch of the contemporary context of Byron's plays is sufficient to show that, like other writers of closet drama, he rejected both bourgeois naturalism and popular sensationalism, in favour of a

[12] On Byron's opinion of Milman, and his comments on Heber's comparison of them as dramatists, see *Medwin*, pp. 122–4.

drama of ideas: 'I want to make a *regular* English drama—no matter whether for the Stage or not—which is not my object—but a *mental* theatre.'[13] Religion and politics were to be the subject-matter. Compare Shelley in *A Defence of Poetry*: 'The connection of poetry and social good is more observable in the drama than in whatever other form: and it is indisputable that the highest perfection of human society has ever corresponded with the highest dramatic excellence.'[14]

The ideal was Greek drama. The development of literary theory at this period was inextricably linked to the idealization of antiquity. A. W. Schlegel had asserted the connection between the Athenian socio-political system and its drama in *Lectures on Dramatic Literature*, translated into English in 1815. For Byron, as for other Liberal writers, the possibility of re-creating the democratic Greek *polis* functions as an unattainable Utopian political ideal (*Marino Faliero*, III, 168–75). Classical antiquity was also perceived as an era of ideal humanism before the integrity of mankind had been separated into body and soul by Judaeo-Christian moral consciousness, and this is the subtext of the Biblical dramas *Cain* and *Heaven and Earth*. While popular modern drama was entirely given over to the realm of the private and the subjective, it seemed therefore both an aesthetic and a political imperative for a serious dramatist to look to classical art as a model when attempting to reassert public themes in drama. In his political Venetian plays, therefore, Byron followed the neo-classical tradition of Addison's *Cato* and the republican tragedies of Alfieri, with their meticulous observation of the unities.

Both by championing the neo-classical tradition, and because he sees the dramatist as fulfilling a public role as critic of his society, Byron defines tragedy as a specifically masculine genre: 'Women—saving Joanna Baillie—cannot write tragedy; they have not seen enough nor felt enough of life for it.'[15] Byron regularly associated the possession of literary genius with male sexual potency. He sardonically quotes Voltaire on women's inability to write tragedy: '"Ah (said the Patriarch) the composition of a tragedy requires *testicles*." If this be true Lord knows what Joanna Baillie does . . . '.

[13] *L&J*, viii. 187.

[14] *Shelley's Poetry and Prose*, ed. Donald H. Reiman and Sharon B. Powers (New York, 1977), pp. 491–2.

[15] *L&J* v. 203.

The letter in which these sentiments occur, written to Murray on 2 April 1817, is worth examining more closely for the light it sheds on Byron's desire to masculinize drama. He had just finished *Manfred* and sent it for publication, accompanied by a plethora of self-deprecatory references to its Gothic elements (considered 'feminine'). His thoughts are already turning to a new project: to rework the themes of Otway's *Venice Preserv'd* in a play on the revolt of Marino Faliero. Byron declares his respect for the seventeenth-century dramatist, except for his heroine: ' . . . that maudlin bitch of chaste lewdness and blubbering curiosity . . . whom I utterly despise, abhor and detest . . . '.

The violence of the language shows that the role of the heroine was of central concern. Byron's project was to turn back the clock to the period before the 'masculine' genre of tragedy first became corrupted by its concentration upon the sentimental heroine, in the 'she-tragedies' of Banks, Rowe, Southerne, and Otway. The features of these plays which gave rise to the later development of full-blown sentimentalism in drama are defined by Arthur Sherbo as the prominence of the heroines, the prolonged treatment of their pathetic situations, the absence of conflict, and the acquiescent submission and acceptance of death and defeat by the protagonists.[16] (These features of sentimentalism are, of course, exhibited in varying degrees in Byron's own early tales.) Central to Byron's dramatic project, therefore, is his determination to avoid the sentimental portrayal of victimized heroines, and to concentrate instead on the masculine subject of a political/religious dilemma in a historical/biblical setting.

The following chapters will show that in *Marino Faliero*, *The Two Foscari*, *Sardanapalus*, and *Cain*, while the dramatic heroines are of secondary importance to the male hero, they are never victims, but heroic, strong characters, like those of Baillie. Their stoicism and nurturing support of their men, in the political plays, reflects a republican writer's adaptation of the role of women in classical times to the nineteenth-century idealization of the wife and mother. Indeed, in *Marino Faliero* his effort to avoid emotionalism is such that Byron makes the marriage and, by extension, the whole dilemma of the Doge a mere formality. As a result, the play is lifeless and stilted. Rather than dramatizing sexual jealousy as the

[16] Arthur Sherbo, *English Sentimental Drama* (East Lansing, Mich., 1957), p. 139.

spur to a strange and problematic alliance between the duke and plebeians, Byron makes the political question an abstract debating problem: the hero must choose between chivalric loyalty towards his friends and his obligations to his friend's daughter.

The play illustrates perfectly the extent of that split which developed in the nineteenth century between popular theatre eulogizing the private life, and a stylized closet drama of ideas. Georg Lukács attributes this fracture to the cleavage of modern man into private individual and citizen, so that in political drama which 'resolutely rejected the expression of the particular and private as Alfieri did . . . large-scale but lifeless and abstract outlines of potential tragedies were created'. Lukács quotes Schiller on the difficulty of the modern dramatist's attempt to synthesize the public and private in drama:

> The palaces of kings are closed now. The tribunals have withdrawn from the gates of the cities to the interior of the houses; writing has supplanted the living word; the people itself, the palpable living mass, when it does not operate as a brute force, has become the state, and thereby an abstract idea; the gods have returned within the bosom of man. The poet must reopen the palaces, bring the tribunals out into the open air, resurrect the gods; he must restore everything immediate which the artificial frame of real life has abolished . . . [17]

Lukács comments that in his dramas Schiller attempted '. . . to create by artistic means an artificial milieu in which the purely private realm is inflated idealistically into the public realm. Into this artificial milieu of an artifically stylized public realm, he had to insert dramatic figures whose private relationships are equally submitted to a subjectivist exaggeration of this sort.'

Schiller's 'republican tragedy' *Fiesco*, which Byron preferred even to *The Robbers*, is a case in point. The three stereotypical female characters operate entirely as political symbols. Bertha, the virgin only daughter of the venerable republican patriarch Verrina, is raped, like Genoa, by the tyrant. In a bizarre ritual curse her father vows that until he obtains revenge on the tyrant he will himself torture his daughter (allegorically indicating the civil war, which now ensues). Bertha accompanies her lover, Bourg, into battle dressed as a page, and the latter slays the tyrant: 'Violator of the

[17] Lukács, *Goethe and His Age*, pp. 109–12.

republic and of my bride! | . . . Freedom to Genoa and my Bertha!' (V, iii).[18] The couple are ritually married and the curse revoked, amidst scenes of slaughter and republican victory.

In contrast, Julia, the tyrant's sister, embodies aristocratic corruption: her sexual attraction has distracted the liberal noble Fiesco both from his wife Leonora and from his republican ideals. Fiesco's return to civic and sexual virtue is depicted symbolically when, in a ritualistic unmasking scene, with Leonora watching behind a screen, he lets Julia express the extent of her passion for him, then ceremoniously humiliates her, culminating in her prostrating herself before him only to be contemptuously spurned. Julia's 'feminine wiles' symbolize the romantic notions used by the aristocracy to disguise personal ambition; female sexuality itself is for Schiller, as for Rousseau, an image of unnatural hunger for power.

Leonora, Fiesco's faithful wife, suffers silently Fiesco's open infidelities, for he does not consider confiding in her that his libertinism is a pose to cover his political activity. Leonora, like Bertha, fights in the republican cause, but she is accidentally killed by her own husband. The portrayal of Leonora shows the ideal virtues of an obedient and chaste wife to be congruent with those of the well-governed kingdom. Fiesco's personal ambition is dangerous to the republican ideal; by implication it is compared with destroying one's wife through one's own libertinism.

As in *Fiesco*, so in *Don Carlos* the chastity of a loyal wife is the apex of Schiller's hierarchy of values. In the latter play Philip explicitly compares his treatment of his wife (he puts guards on her bedroom door) with his rule of Flanders, and complains that female ability to contaminate the heredity of the male dynastic line is the only weak link in the chain of his absolute rule. Elizabeth's romantic love for her stepson parallels her political sympathy with Flanders, but her chastity is the *sine qua non* of the play. It represents the guarantee of the hereditary transference of property and power; the rule of law; respect for authority, and for the institution of marriage and monarchy, even if the man himself is a tyrant. The audience is permitted to sympathize with the critique of absolutism in the play because the ideal of female obedience is vaunted as the highest moral value dramatized and this guarantees

[18] *The Works of Frederick Schiller: Early Dramas and Romances* (London, 1849).

that the necessity is recognized for society to remain stable, civilized, and under the command of its rightful rulers (like a virtuous wife).

Byron's republican tragedies, like *Fiesco* and *Don Carlos*, feature stoical republican matrons as feminine ideals. But the following chapters will show that Byron's heroines are much more self-assertive, challenging the male representatives of secular authority through personal commitment to their husbands. Furthermore, in *Cain* and *Heaven and Earth*, where the poet attacks the Judaeo-Christian notion of original sin, the heroines preference loyalty in love to obedience to both secular and spiritual patriarchal authority. In the verse tragedies of Byron's contemporaries there are also some heroines who are sympathetically depicted despite committing faults, sins, even crimes because of complex circumstances. A notorious example was Imogine in Maturin's *Bertram*. The plot is similar to that of Hannah More's *Percy* (1778), where a young woman renounces her intended husband for another for the sake of her father. But in the later play this plot is used to mitigate the heroine's adultery with her former lover (compare adaptations of Kotzebue, like Benjamin Thompson's *The Stranger* (D.L., 1798)). This was a controversial undertaking, for adulteresses were by literary convention always strictly condemned. With the advent of the Evangelical movement, even a playwright like Hannah More began to think play-going wrong, and the popularity in the 1790s of the permissive Kotzebue was now turning to censure, as illustrated by the *Lovers' Vows* episode in Austen's *Mansfield Park*. *Bertram* thus provoked Coleridge's famous attack in *Biographia Literaria*.

An avowed feminist, Shelley went even further in *The Cenci* (1819). Influenced by Bianca in Milman's *Fazio* (C.G., 1818), he portrays his heroine initially as enmeshed in a situation over which she has no control, but then transforms a merely pitiable victim into a formidable and ambivalent avenger of tyranny. Beatrice is driven to murder her father, who has has raped her. Cenci represents the corrupt male secular and spiritual leaders of Rome, preying on those in their power. Shelley has entirely reversed the use of the father and daughter theme so prevalent in the literature of the period, to explain in psycho-sexual terms (though, as he states in the preface, not to condone) a revolutionary retaliation against patriarchal oppression.

Shelley in *The Cenci* and Byron in *Heaven and Earth* were innovative and shocking in using heroic heroines not as loyal supporters of a male ruler, but specifically to illustrate the patriarchal nature of political tyranny and the religious ideology underpinning it. As Richard Cave comments, Beatrice discovers 'that beyond the battle with Cenci lies a greater battle with a paternalistic Deity, that tyranny is the true nature of a principle in the universe to which till now she has given unquestioning assent.'[19]

Though Byron affirmed the 'piety' of his Biblical plays with all the solemnity with which Hannah More had written of her *Sacred Dramas* (1782), the backcloth of divine tyranny undermines and mitigates our condemnation of his defiant protagonists. Ranged against Anah and Aholibamah and their sinful act (which is more innovative and shocking than Beatrice's because expressive of female sexuality, not in defence of virginity) are the combined forces of patriarchal authority of both Earth and Heaven. What Shelley attempted to represent symbolically, Byron presented literally, and thus far more effectively. Byron avoids the awkwardness of Beatrice's assertion of her innocence in spite of her technical criminal guilt, by simply refusing either to put his heroines on trial at all or to show the deaths to which sinful women in literature were always condemned.

All the dramatic heroines of Byron's plays considered here exemplify a specifically feminine version of stoic heroism. The republican ideology of the loyal wives of the Venetian tragedies will be considered first, then, in Chapter 8, those heroines whose bravery is linked with defiance of moral orthodoxy.

[19] Richard Cave, 'Romantic Drama in Performance', in Richard Cave (ed.), *The Romantic Theatre: An International Symposium* (Gerrards Cross, 1986), pp. 79–104 (90). In the same volume, see Stuart Curran, 'Shelleyan Drama', pp. 61–78, and Giorgio Melchiori, 'The Dramas of Byron', pp. 47–60.

7

'My Hope Was to Bring Forth Heroes': The Fostering of Masculine *Virtù* by the Stoical Heroines of the Political Plays

> Thought of the state of women under the ancient Greeks—convenient enough. Present state a remnant of the barbarism of the chivalry [chivalric?] and feudal ages—artificial and unnatural. They ought to mind home and be well fed and clothed—but not mixed in society. Well educated too, in religion, but to read neither poetry or politics—nothing but books of piety and cookery. Music—drawing—dancing—also a little gardening and ploughing now and then. I have seen them mending the roads in Epirus with good success. Why not, as well as haymaking and milking?
>
> (Byron's Journal of 6 January 1821)

WHILE the burlesque world of *Don Juan* is one of monarchical tyranny and female domination, that of the political plays set in Venice is its obverse: an androcentric republic. In both the mock epic and the political plays the poet's concern is with the question of re-establishing republican masculinity. According to Enlightenment political thinkers such as Montesquieu and Rousseau, the classical republics had been successful in ensuring the disinterested patriotic service of the (male) citizen, because private interests were rigorously separated from the public arena. This had been achieved by rigid sexual role differentiation, and the low status of women, as Byron sardonically observed in his journal. Writing from the perspective of the failure of the French Revolution, but in the years which saw revolutionary conspiracies in both England and Italy, he now questioned the neo-classical ideology of a gendered nation-state which underpinned his own republicanism.

Marino Faliero and *The Two Foscari* were amongst a group of political plays which appeared at this period, set in classical or mediaeval Italy.[1] We could compare the American playwright John Payne's *Brutus; or The Fall of Tarquin* (D.L., 1818), and a later play in the idiom, Mary Russell Mitford's *Rienzi* (D.L., 1828). Like James Sheridan Knowles's *Virginius; or The Liberation of Rome* (C.G., 1820), *Marino Faliero* and *The Two Foscari* have a young woman and an elderly patriarch as the butts of a corrupt government.

In both *Marino Faliero* and *The Two Foscari*, Byron's heroes exemplify that notion of self-controlled manliness which emanated from an eighteenth-century interpretation of the classical tradition of Stoicism. This ideology was a feature of the period's neo-classicism particularly adopted by male Jacobins, who often self-consciously compared themselves to heroes like Brutus and Cato of Utica.[2] Like the actual French revolutionaries, Faliero compares his allies to Brutus and Cassius (V, vi. 178), and the plot to the Catiline conspiracy (I, ii. 596–7). The masculine ideal was self-command and even sacrifice of personal sentiment, in order to take authoritative political action. This reflected the contemporary cult of the individual. The virtue—or more properly *virtù*—of a great man guaranteed that public life was free from the corruption of the feminine (the personal and subjective).

In both the Venetian plays, therefore, the sexual temptation of women must be repressed—Faliero's marriage is platonic. Moreover, as female chastity is the measure of masculine authority, then the female equivalent of *virtù* is a narrowly sexual definition of virtue. Marino Faliero's actions are designed to demonstrate the interrelatedness of masculine *virtù* and feminine virtue in the gendered republic. In *The Two Foscari*, the theme is extended: here the patriarch must repress the 'feminine' familial values of sentiment and nurture, for the good of the state. But this seemingly ideal Rousseauistic relationship between the sexes is interrogated in both plays. For neither Faliero nor Foscari is a vigorous or effective statesman, creating or maintaining an ideal republic. Both are helpless octogenarian puppets of a corrupt oligarchy. The republican ideal fostered by the liberal aristocrat's idealization of the classical *polis* has ossified in both Venice and, by implication, Britain. Moreover, it is questionable whether rigorous separation of

[1] See Donohue, *Theatre in the Age of Kean*, p. 141.

[2] Outram, *The Body and the French Revolution*, ch. 5.

the private emotions from the public sphere, by sexual role differentiation, can foster a revival of true republican masculine heroism. Does this ideology of two separate gendered spheres merely facilitate the perpetuation of patriarchal power, creating an oligarchic gerontocracy, impervious to humanitarian concerns?

ANGIOLINA

The republican heroines of the Venetian plays embody the Stoic virtue of dignified endurance of adversity, within a specifically feminine social role. The positive female virtues apotheosized in the plays are chastity, austere classical rectitude, bravery, and loyalty. The heroines of the tales were subjects, and subject to the extreme exercise of tyrannical power over them as female slaves; the women of the Venetian plays are proud, aristocratic republican matrons. In both plays Byron attempts to innovate by giving the heroine a more lofty role than merely the focusing of pity. Angiolina and Marina are articulate, rational, and in control of their emotions. The 'feminine' subjectivity of the heroines of the plays now lies in their capacity for value judgement. They shape the reader's response, by their perceptive analysis or vigorous reactions of outrage to tragic events.

Marchand criticizes the insipid character of Angiolina and suggests that the platonic marriage 'strains credulity'. He does not attempt to account for the link between the political and sexual themes.[3] W. Paul Elledge also fails to elucidate the sexual politics of the play, and he does not find Angiolina's role striking.[4] McGann defines Angiolina as the 'normative ideal of humanity' and 'one of the spiritual poles of human existence'.[5] McGann's view of Angiolina is retained by Farrell, who comments that Faliero's revolution represents a despoiling of Angiolina's finer spirit.[6] Anne Barton takes issue with the interpretation of Angiolina's character as ideal. Seeing her as 'a staunch defender of the political *status quo*', she believes we are meant to judge her as cold and

[3] See Marchand, *Byron's Poetry*, p. 99.

[4] W. P. Elledge, *Byron and The Dynamics of Metaphor* (Nashville, 1968), pp. 100–18.

[5] McGann, *Fiery Dust*, p. 214.

[6] John P. Farrell, *Revolution as Tragedy: The Dilemma of the Moderate from Scott to Arnold* (Ithaca, NY, and London, 1980), pp. 149–62.

complacent.[7] Thomas Ashton is the first critic to draw our attention to the importance of Steno's graffito and the relevance of sexual politics to the themes of the play.[8] Jerome Christensen takes this further, comparing Faliero's marriage proposal with his election as Doge. He sees the graffito as a challenge to the Doge's wish for a zone of privatized freedom: 'This wish for an uncharactered, authentically affective and effective subjectivity can only be inordinate, since the private has no place in a society where every place has already been overwritten by a reticulative discourse.'[9]

However, it will be shown that the Doge's unusual marriage is not only significant as a zone of private subjectivity, but is also central to this political play's concern with patriarchy. In *Marino Faliero* Byron deconstructs the paradox that the Utopian ideal of republicanism is historically associated with patriarchy and male primogeniture.

The platonic union of the Doge with a girl young enough to be his granddaughter, for the disinterested purpose of her chivalric protection, is a typically Byronic exaggeration of the necessity for austere republican masculinity to disregard the temptation of sexuality. It almost falls into self-parody. A variation of the father–daughter relationships in the literature of the period, the platonic marriage also embodies fear of the loss to posterity of the ideals of the patriarch—in this case, the heritage of republicanism transmitted from classical times to the mediaeval Italian city states, to be handed down to the French Revolution and the present. Not only this, but the sterile marriage symbolizes a contemporary fear that the transmission of property and power via male primogeniture seems precarious.

The discontent of the plebeians focuses these fears that a patriarchal aristocratic republican ideal will degenerate through sexual corruption and/or lose its political power. It will be by their revolution that the original ideals of republicanism will be revitalized, if at all, and this will take the form of a direct attack on the patriarchy. By putting himself at the head of the revolt Faliero

[7] Anne Barton, '"A Light to Lesson Ages": Byron's Political Plays', in John Jump (ed.), *Byron: A Symposium* (London, 1975), pp. 138–62.

[8] T. L. Ashton, '*Marino Faliero*: Byron's "Poetry of Politics"', *SiR* 13 (1974), 1–13.

[9] Jerome Christensen, '*Marino Faliero* and the Fault of Byron's Satire', *SiR* 24 (1985), 313–33.

tries both to destroy the corrupt aristocracy and yet to maintain a place for patriarchal rank in the new republic, by his own participation.

The marriage of the Doge is to be taken as a parallel to his relationship with Venice, as Christensen has suggested. The traditional ceremony in which the Doge throws a ring into the sea signifying the marriage of the city with the Adriatic also implies that he is guardian and husband of the Republic and her virtue.

Angiolina, like the plebeians, is without power or political representation. Her father willed it on his death-bed that Angiolina be given to his friend and benefactor. This dynastic exchange of women by the patriarchal rulers facilitates the handing on of government within the oligarchy. Faliero's credentials as husband are the honour, wealth, and protective power of the aristocracy. Angiolina is young, chaste, and nubile, but without property or wealth. The Doge explains her father's purpose to Angiolina in chivalric terms:

> His object was to place your orphan beauty
> In honourable safety from the perils,
> Which, in this scorpion nest of vice, assail
> A lonely and undower'd maid. (II, i. 298–301)

The marriage is Platonic:

> nor was this my age
> Infected with that leprosy of lust
> Which taints the hoariest years of vicious men,
> Making them ransack to the very last
> The dregs of pleasure for their vanished joys; (II, i. 314–18)

Angiolina is made to attribute her ideas and principles to her father (II, i. 76–7); she chooses the Doge's 'patriarchal love' (II, i. 363) instead of a love match. The portrayal of Angiolina as an obedient daughter, who is prepared to defer gratification of her sexuality to marry her father's octogenarian friend, provides a comforting fantasy in a play concerned with a republican society based on primogeniture, that woman will put her generativity at the disposal of the male leaders of society and, in return, may be graciously endowed with property and independence at some time in the unspecified future. For the Doge reassures Angiolina that:

> I knew my days could not disturb you long;
> And then the daughter of my earliest friend,

His worthy daughter, free to choose again,
Wealthier and wiser, in the ripest bloom
Of womanhood, more skilful to select
By passing these probationary years
Inheriting a prince's name and riches . . .
Would choose more fitly in respect of years,
And not less truly in a faithful heart. (II, i. 329–41)

In the Oriental tales patriarchy had been simplistically identified with despotism. But in the Venetian plays, because it is associated with republicanism, it is presented ambivalently. For Angiolina's willing acceptance of an eighty-year-old husband is a dramatic symbol—even more striking on the stage than on the page—that the republic has become a gerontocracy.[10] Faliero is a venerable upholder of the values of republicanism, yet he may also be perceived as a sterile and impotent symbol of patrician rule. Angiolina's marriage to him represents the will of the dead, imposed on the living:

My lord, I look'd but to my father's wishes,
Hallow'd by his last words, and to my heart
For doing all its duties, and replying
With faith to him with whom I was affianced.
Ambitious hopes ne'er crossed my dreams . . . (II, i. 342–6).

However, she is childless, and will remain so, as she decides to enter a nunnery after Faliero's execution. She therefore also focuses the poet's fear that Italy's republican heritage will become extinct.

The hollow shell of a marriage is seen by Faliero as a purely temporary expedient which will protect Angiolina and endow her with a heritage (of property and nobility) after his death when she makes a love match (II, i. 328–41). He takes on the Dogeship in exactly the same chivalric spirit of duty. Later, when he heads the revolt, he also sees this leadership as no more than a temporary expedient. He intends to relinquish his crown afterwards, for his long-term aim is only to ensure that power and liberty is extended to the subjects (III, ii. 209–10; IV, ii. 159–60), in the same way that Angiolina will become his heir. The Doge's marriage thus endows patriarchal rule with the paternal sentiments of love and protection.

[10] See Robert Finlay, *Politics in Renaissance Venice* (London, 1980).

This Burkean belief in patriarchal and patrician stewardship is sincerely held by the old soldier.

Then a young noble, Steno, defiles the ducal chair with a graffito: 'Marin Faliero, dalla bella moglie—altri la gode, ed egli la mantien', which can be translated 'Marino Faliero has a pretty wife: one keeps her while another enjoys her'. If the chivalric motives of the fatherly husband can be thus construed as those of a senile or impotent pander, then it follows that the Doge's guardianship of Venice is seen in a similar light by the *giunta*. This opens up a more general question. Is an aristocrat really a chivalric guardian of traditional liberty, or the prostitutor of the state to private interests?

The graffito finally opens Faliero's eyes to his political impotence as Doge, his inability to protect Venice from being exploited by and for the self-interest of the oligarchy. He realizes that he has been selected because his long history of honourable military service and his liberal principles make him a palatable figurehead—as long as his role is as nominal as that of husband to Angiolina (V, i. 209–17). The play is studded with references to his angry realization that his personal integrity is being cynically manipulated to screen the corruption of his class, that his status as patriarchal protector of the city is as much a joke as his unusual marriage (I, ii. 411; I, ii. 415; III, ii. 161–2; III, ii. 196). What is more, he suspects that his humiliation on account of Steno's light punishment was a calculated insult, designed to show disapproval for his liberal political views (I, ii. 195–6).

His decision to join the plebeian conspiracy is motivated by the desire to prove that chivalry is meaningful, that it is not merely a cloak for privilege, but champions the weak against the strong. The Doge thus finds himself on the wrong side of what is essentially a class battle.[11] Most critics have noted the irony of the feudal nature of his attitude to the plebeians. But, on the other hand, in Faliero's eyes, to decimate the oligarchy would be rightly to destroy those who would sully Venice's virtue as Steno had insulted Angiolina.

Angiolina's feminine virtue is meant symbolically to endorse and guarantee the inner purity of the Doge's masculine republican ideals. Her purity is portrayed as an absolute value, transcending the historical circumstances which have made it open to question.

[11] See Daniel P. Watkins, 'Violence, Class Consciousness, and Ideology in Byron's History Plays', *ELH* 48 (1981), 799–816.

Angiolina herself points this out by her indifference to the graffito and refusal to ask for revenge (II, i. 52–74). This is an attempt by the dramatist to imply endorsement of Faliero's political vision, whilst in no way minimizing the violence of the act he contemplates in realizing it. Angiolina acts as a moral touchstone in condemning the planned decimation of the aristocracy in Act V, but she is not merely affirming the status quo, for she is also scathing in her denunciation of the *giunta*.

The contrasting reactions of the husband and wife to the writing on the chair are symptomatic of their relationship as a whole. The polarization of the sexes into active and passive, public and private, military and moral, political and religious, old and young, is symptomatic of the divorce of the subjectivity of conscience from the power of action. Faliero's speeches and soliloquies show him torn by conflicting class loyalties, rather than the specifically moral issues of revolutionary violence. He is consumed by anger till the last, and it is the heroine's speech in Act V which guides the audience's reactions. On the other hand, Angiolina's abstract virtue is a function of her complete ignorance and separation from the public sphere. She is amazed at her friend's suggestion that the Doge might have suspected the slander to be true (II, i. 39–40), and at the thought that married people might be sexually attracted to acquaintances (II, i. 126–9). She would not presume to discuss public affairs with her husband:

> . . . were it of public import,
> You know I never sought, would never seek
> To win word from you: (II, i. 215–17)

The ethics of the private conscience lead Angiolina, after her husband's death, to withdraw from the corrupt society of Venice altogether and enter a convent. Unlike Shakespeare's Isabella in *Measure For Measure*, she is not herself confronted with the problems posed by a commitment to moral absolutism in an imperfect world. Byron prefers her to remain as a frozen symbol of purity. It is the Doge, not Angiolina, who makes the quixotic attempt to implement his ideals in society.

But Faliero finds he cannot bridge the divide between the private 'feminine' world of conscience and the public 'masculine' domain of power. This is made clear by the dramatization of his inability to discuss his joining the conspiracy with Angiolina. He repudiates the private 'feminine' considerations of sentiment in sanctioning the massacre of the entire ruling class. Men live by and will die in their public roles: 'To me, then, these men have no *private* life' (III, ii. 382). It is impossible to differentiate individuals: 'I cannot pause on individual hate, | In the absorbing, sweeping whole revenge' (III, ii. 418–20). They can scarcely be regarded as human (IV, ii. 163).

High-minded chivalry as a motive for carnage is a shocking Byronic irony, showing the mark of the Terror on the poet.[12] Yet the play also demonstrates the tenacious hold the corrupt aristocracy has on power, by the ease with which the plebian plot is uncovered before a blow is struck. Faliero's project of making Angiolina his heir also fails, as all but 2,000 ducats of his property is confiscated by the court, and, instead of choosing her own sexual destiny, Angiolina has to enter a nunnery.

Byron has Angiolina speak in the Doge's defence at the tribunal, to enact the role of chorus and bring out the contemporary significance of this historical play to the audience. Her virgin chastity is a guarantee that the republican reform for which she speaks encompasses the patriarchal control of female sexuality, and thus of corruption. Because of her rigorous separation from public affairs, she has been established as the voice of independent moral integrity, so her discourse is privileged. Thus, in the trial scene, the enactment of Venetian justice is upstaged by her judgement of all the men present—the rulers of the public domain. Like his female contemporaries, Byron makes woman morally superior, as a condition of her powerlessness, and thus gives Angiolina the privileged discourse of the most lofty character in the play. Contemporary reviewers were less than enthusiastic about the new Byronic heroine. The *British Critic* noted the originality of the character, but remarked condescendingly: 'She is scarcely gentle enough for a woman, and rather too pretty for a philosopher.' Heber, writing in the *Quarterly Review*, thought that Angiolina's

[12] On the political background of the play, see D. V. Erdman, 'Byron and Revolt in England', *Science and Society*, 11 (1947), 234–48, and 'Byron and "the New Force of the People"', *K-SJ* 11 (1962), 47–64; E. D. H. Johnson, 'A Political Interpretation of Byron's *Marino Faliero*', *MLQ* 3 (1942), 417–25. G. W. Spence ('The Moral Ambiguity of *Marino Faliero*', *AUMLA* 41 (1974), 6–17) takes issue with Samuel Chew's identification of Faliero with Byron's own ideals, and sees the play as an honest exposure of the Doge's illusions. For the fullest explication of the political implications of the play, see Kelsall, *Byron's Politics*, pp. 82–118. All quotations are taken from *CPW* v.

speech in Act V was too elevated for a female character and should have been given to Benintende or a male counsel for the defence. He complains that she moralizes 'in a strain of pedantry less natural to a woman than to any other person similarly circumstanced'.[13]

It is Angiolina who pronounces the extent of his guilt to the Doge before the tribunal: 'Thou hast been guilty of a great offence' (V, i. 381). Yet she reserves her scorn for the degenerate oligarchy. After counselling Faliero to die proudly, she turns on Benintende and declaims a fiery speech on virtue which is the climax of the play (and which was cheered by the audience when the play was performed, for its subtextual reference to the Queen Caroline affair). Angiolina repudiates Steno's apology, in terms reminiscent of the Stoics' opposition to the Caesars:

I prefer
My honour to a thousand lives, could such
Be multiplied in mine, but would not have
A single life of others lost for that
Which nothing human can impugn—the sense
Of virtue, looking not to what is called
A good name for reward, but to itself.
(V, i. 412–18)

She compares herself to a rock in her uncompromising moral individualism (V, i. 419–20).

But she acknowledges that republican males aspire not to this higher (but entirely passive) feminine virtue, but to an active *virtù*—like Faliero 'To whom dishonour's shadow is a substance | More terrible than death here and hereafter' (V, i. 423–4). This is an ironic inversion of Burke's lament for the end of the age of chivalry in his *Reflections on The Revolution in France* (1790): 'It is gone, that sensibility of principle, that chastity of honour, which felt a stain like a wound, which inspired courage whilst it mitigated ferocity, which enobled whatever it touched, and under which vice lost half its evil, by losing all its grossness.'[14] Byron appropriates the chivalric call for the republican cause, for in *Marino Faliero* it was the nobility who had insulted the heroine's honour, instead of the Jacobin mob invading the queen's bedroom. The contemporary significance of the speech, for England, was to encourage resistance

[13] Reiman, *Romantics Reviewed*, part B, i. 305–6; v. 2057.
[14] Edmund Burke, *Reflections*, p. 112.

to the government in support of Queen Caroline—the heroine of the Whig *cause célèbre* when George IV put her on trail for adultery that year. In the context of the Queen Caroline affair, the emotional appeal of chivalry could be enlisted in the radical cause.[15]

Angiolina explains, without endorsing, Faliero's *virtù* by reference to the stories of the abduction of Helen, the rape of Lucretia, the seduction of the wife of Arruns of Clusium, and the rape of Florinda. The sexual corruption of oppressive rulers focuses existing reasons for discontent. Once nationalistic, economic, or political causes are endowed with a chivalric rallying-cry, unified armed retaliation to tyranny may be facilitated. Angiolina's discourse is privileged, echoing the poet's own in his preface. She speaks through the play to contemporary Britain, warning that blatant disregard for the conscience of servants of the state or for the discontent of the people creates the opportunity for such a spark as insulting a woman's honour (even that of Caroline) to ignite a rebellion, whose outcome could bring even greater oppression in its wake:

And Steno's lie, couch'd in two worthless lines,
Hath decimated Venice, put in peril
A senate which hath stood eight hundred years,
Discrown'd a prince, cut off his crownless head,
And forged new fetters for a groaning people! (V, i. 443–7)

Faliero goes further. He prophesies that through lack of belief in her republican ideal Venice will degenerate into the courtesan that the nobles had thought Angiolina must be:

She shall be bought
And sold, and be an appanage to those
Who shall despise her!—She shall stoop to be
A province for an empire, petty town

[15] On the relationship between chivalry and the Queen Caroline affair see Thomas W. Lacqueur, 'The Queen Caroline Affair: Politics and Art in the Reign of George IV', *JMH* 14 (1982), 417–66; Mark Girouard, *The Return to Camelot: Chivalry and the English Gentleman* (London, 1981), pp. 67–76; Thomas L. Ashton, 'The Censorship of Byron's *Marino Faliero*', *Huntington Library Quarterly*, 36 (1972–3), 27–45; Kelsall, *Byron's Politics*, pp. 82–118.

In lieu of capital, with slaves for senates,
Beggars for nobles, pandars for a people! (V, iii. 52–7)

Significantly, it is in terms of this imagery of female prostitution that the aristocracies of both contemporary Italy and (by implication) Britain are here castigated for corruption. The patriarchal control of female sexuality, demonstrated by the Doge's marriage, is the guarantee of fitness to rule.

The strategy Byron employed in his republican drama, of using a strong-minded virtuous young woman as the moral measure of the aristocracy, was common in contemporary literature throughout the political spectrum. It was adopted even by a Tory writer like Austen, in making the bourgeois female orphan Fanny Price the moral yardstick of the neglect of his responsibilities by the patriarch of Mansfield Park. Austen was here reflecting a widespread pre–1832 desire for reform of the ruling classes, to pre-empt an English revolution. These stereotypes of perfect feminine virtue, so uncongenial to modern eyes, were particularly popular in the nineteenth century. Even *Blackwood's Edinburgh Magazine*, while considering *Marino Faliero* itself 'a sad damper', asserted: 'Yet nobody could deny that there was great and novel beauty in the conception of one character . . . that of the old Doge's young wife.'[16]

MARINA

In *The Two Foscari* Byron continues to give the heroine a lofty character. Again she speaks for the individual's subjectivity of conscience, arguing in turn with the men who preference civic duty. But Marina is integrated with the action of the second Venetian play in a way that Angiolina was not. Instead of keeping gracefully aloof from male public affairs she intrudes and interrupts. She opposes Loredano, who manipulates Venice's laws for his own purposes; she confronts the Doge, whose mission to guard those laws outweighs humanitarian considerations. She disputes with her husband Jacopo, whose loyalty to the place is stronger than love of life itself. Marina's volubility was harshly criticized by contemporary critics, whether Whig or Tory, as offending against femininity. Jeffrey commented on the venom of her tongue and her vehemence in the *Edinburgh Review*; T. N. Talfourd in the *London Magazine*

[16] Reiman, *Romantics Reviewed*, part B, i. 187.

described her as 'vociferous'; the reviewer of the *Monthly Review* called her 'something of a scold', as did Bishop Heber in the *Quarterly Review*. Perhaps it is significant that the *Lady's Magazine*, on behalf of its female readership, was almost alone in singling out for praise 'The noble spirit . . . and the conjugal affection and fidelity of Marina'.[17]

Instead of keeping silent until asked to speak Marina argues and contradicts. Because of her intrusion into state business, and the constant repudiation of her values by the male leaders of society, she thrusts into view the discrepancy between the theoretical reverencing of women by the chivalrous aristocracy and the reality of contempt for female powerlessness.

The heroine's brave quest to save her husband illustrated the powerlessness of woman, deemed necessarily a private individual, in combating the mechanisms of state power. Like Mary Wollstonecraft, Byron is challenging Rousseau's assertion that the objectivity of republican government can only be maintained by the rigorous separation of reason and sentiment through a policy of rigid differentiation of sexual roles. Wollstonecraft, in *A Vindication*, concentrates on her assertion that women are by nature as rational as men. Byron's Marina, Angiolina, and Myrrha also illustrate this premise. But as a Romantic poet, rather than a proponent of Enlightenment rationalism, Byron strives to demonstrate the indivisibility of reason and passion in both men and women. *The Two Foscari* is an important examination of the artificiality of Rousseau's characterization of republicanism as necessitating Stoic suppression of subjectivity by limiting it to the 'feminine' sphere.

Again Byron uses the vulnerable figures of the venerable patriarch of the republic and his virtuous daughter (in law) to illustrate his fear of the inability of liberal ideals to be transmitted to future ages:

> And the deep agony of his pale wife,
> And the repress'd convulsion of the high
> And princely brow of his old father, . . .
> . . . these moved you not? (I, i. 355–60)

Once more the obscuring of motives and the silencing of words makes the climax of the tragedy not death itself (as this Doge is also over eighty), but lack of communication of the meaning of political

[17] Ibid. ii. 924; iv. 1614; v. 2072; iii. 1127.

events to the people. The subjugation and murder of Foscari after his refusal to submit any further to the oligarchy is obscured by a screen of secrecy and the hypocrisy of a state funeral. Though she is the most vocal and eloquent character in the play, Marina is also the most obviously disregarded. (Her lack of importance is evidenced by the fact that she is allowed to survive.) Marina embodies the tragedy of individual subjectivity: the inability of the powerless either to effect reform even of the grossest tyranny, or to make their words heard in the world at large. A closer examination of the play will show that Marina's words are the privileged discourse of the play, reflecting the frustration of the Romantic poet at the marginalization of his own expression of individual subjectivity, which is considered as effeminately irrelevant to the male world of public affairs.

When Marina enters, her husband has been taken into the secret torture chamber of the state for the third time. In answer to a senator's chivalrous greeting in bidding her command him her wishes, she retorts bitterly—repudiating the hypocritical pretence of female power enshrined in such courtesy: '*I command* !—Alas! my life | Has been one long entreaty, and a vain one' (I, i. 200–1).

When he understands that her wishes involve state business (her husband's interrogation), however, he refuses to answer her. When she retorts that the only permitted form of questioning and answering in Venice is performed with the connivance of the rack, he cuts short her words with a reproof that she is out of her correct domain, both literally and figuratively, and thus has no right to speak: 'High-born dame! bethink thee | Where thou art' (I, i. 204–5).

Marina replies that she is in her 'husband's father's palace', her home and thus her rightful feminine domain. But Memmo corrects her: '*The Duke*'s palace'. His emphasis stresses that public roles have precedence over private. To illustrate the extent to which all subjective feeling has been suppressed or relegated to the separated and powerless 'feminine' sphere of mere private life the groans are now heard which signify the Doge's supervision of the torture of his own son, who is accused of treason. We could compare the tableau enacted in this play with that of Jacques-Louis David's neo-classical painting *The Lictors bringing Brutus the Bodies of his Sons* (1789) (see Plate 2). Here the masculine Republican stoic ability to divorce public from private is celebrated in the polar opposition of the sexes after Brutus' condemnation of his own sons to death for conspiring against the Republic. The division of the composition into heroic male citizens on the left and mourning women on the right is emphasized by the classical column separating stoicism and sentimentalism. Yet, as Ronald Paulson comments: 'The power of the picture lies in its being on a secondary level a psychomachia, an image of divided loyalties . . . deriving from the mixed emotions of the father himself.'[18]

In Byron's play, as the epigraph indicates, the patriarch is not permitted paternal feelings. Marina, as a woman, is sanctioned to express the emotions which have to be suppressed by the ethos of masculine republican stoicism. But she will not retire to weep in the appropriate manner, and hopes her husband will deny the Council of Ten the satisfaction of hearing him cry out under torture, so that a senator questions the extent of her (permitted) feminine 'feeling'. But, refusing to have her responses stereotyped, Marina retorts that she is measuring the extent of Jacopo's heroism by the standards of her own stoic bravery in childbirth:

> We must all bear our tortures. I have not
> Left barren the great house of Foscari,
> Though they sweep both the Doge and son from life;
> I have endured as much in giving life
> To those who will succeed them, as they can
> In leaving it:
>
> (I, i. 239–44)

She again repudiates the passivity of the feminine role when the senator, under the guise of gallantry, tries to usher her away from this place, the inner sanctum of government, as it is presumed that the news that Jacopo has been rendered unconscious will overpower her feminine sensibilities. Brusquely she shrugs him away: 'Off! *I* will tend him' (I, i. 253).

Though the role she claims is the traditionally female one of nurse and comforter, Marina eschews feminine delicacy and modest demeanour, arguing with the senators and rudely barging her way into the 'great arcanum' where not even the senators themselves are allowed:

> They shall not balk my entrance . . .
> Who shall oppose me? . . .

[18] Paulson, *Representations of Revolution*, p. 33.

> . . . Yet I'll pass.
> . . . there is
> That in my heart would make its way through hosts
> With levell'd spears; and think you a few jailors
> Shall put me from my path? Give me, then, way;
> (I, i. 257–70)

Patronizingly, the senators let her pass, confident of her impotence: she will not be admitted, and if she were she would be ignored (I, i. 276–9).

In fact the Council breaks up in disarray when Marina bursts in. She does not have to speak. Just the presence of a woman is an uncomfortable reminder of their repressed subjective feelings, to the officers of the law:

> . . . 'Twas a dreadful sight
> When his distracted wife broke through into
> The hall of our tribunal, and beheld
> What we could scarcely look upon, long used
> To such sights. (I, i. 364–8)

Loredano is incredulous that the appearance of a mere woman could have such an effect:

> And so the Council must break up, and Justice
> Pause in her full career, because a woman
> Breaks in on our deliberations? (I, i. 314–16)

His business is only with the male members of her family: father-in-law, husband, and sons. Jacopo must confess because his reputation must be besmirched. His capacity for transmitting his power or beliefs to a future generation must be eradicated; his children must be disinherited or destroyed. Marina is an irrelevance because she has no such power. As she herself acknowledges, her only form of transcendence is through physical generation: ' . . . my hope was to bring forth | Heroes . . . ' (I, i. 246–7).

Act II opens with an image of the state's bureaucracy: the Doge is signing papers. The peace treaty rewrites the Republic as an Empire. The history of Venice will be passed on in such official records. But there is a discrepancy, dramatized in the play, between the spontaneous words of its citizens and its public written

2. Jacques-Louis David, *The Lictors bringing Brutus the Bodies of his Sons* (1789)
Reproduced by permission of the Musée du Louvre, Paris

documents. Their composure temporarily shattered by the sight of Marina's grief, the Ten had granted her permission to visit her husband in prison. But she finds their spoken words, generated by feeling, are powerless to grant her admittance to the Bridge of Sighs unless confirmed in writing (II, i. 51–62). Catch 22 is that they only reconvene when they resume Jacopo's torture, which he is not expected to survive.

The Doge's acquiescence in this processing of words by eliminating the 'feminine' subjective, and by excluding her personal relationship with Jacopo ('the holiest tie beneath the Heavens', II, i. 68) from consideration, leads to an outburst of Marina's anger against her father-in-law. She repudiates his patriarchal role: 'Call *me* not "child!" | You soon will have no children—you deserve none' (II, i. 70–1). When her husband dies, she will again refuse the appellation 'daughter' from him, contemptuously rejecting his comfort: 'Hold thy peace, old man! | I am no daughter now—thou hast no son' (IV, i. 195–6). Now, when he tells her that the Ten still refuse her request to accompany Jacopo in his exile, she—a fertile young mother—execrates them as a gerontocracy:

> . . . The old human fiends,
> With one foot in the grave, with dim eyes, strange
> To tears save drops of dotage, with long white
> And scanty hairs, and shaking hands, and heads
> As palsied as their hearts are hard, they counsel,
> Cabal, and put men's lives out, as if life
> Were no more than the feelings long extinguish'd
> In their accursed bosoms. (II, i. 108–15)

This hatred and resentment at the rule of old men, which finds expression in seventeenth-century drama like *Venice Preserv'd*, and even more forcibly in the *Sturm und Drang* plays of Schiller and Goethe, expresses impatience with the constraining strait-jacket of authority. As the first Christian republic, Venice could be perceived in two ways: either as a model of constitutional government reverenced throughout the world, perfectly balancing the claims of the aristocracy and the people; or as a former ideal, now corrupted into an oligarchy, and in the process of becoming an imperial power. For Venice, read Britain. Byron's selection of Faliero and Foscari—the only notable representatives of dissent in the history of the Republic—indicate the poet's preoccupation with the decline of the ideal. As venerable patriarchs, they symbolize the precious heritage of republicanism; yet the image of an old man superintending the mangling of his son to the point of death is also one of stultified tradition blighting the future (even more than the January and May marriage dramatized in *Marino Faliero*). Unlike the vigorous and statesmanlike Brutus of David's painting, who has saved the Republic by his heroic action, the frail and feeble octogenarian, Foscari, has merely been the unwitting tool of Loredano's dynastic rivalry.

It is the republican matron, representing the future fertility of the state, who articulates the protest against the rule of old men. As a woman, Marina's speaks on behalf of natural feeling:

> . . . could it be else that
> Men, who have been of women born and suckled—
> Who have loved, or talk'd at least of Love—have given
> Their hands in sacred vows—have danced their babes
> Upon their knees, perhaps have mourn'd above them—
> In pain, in peril, or in death—who are,
> Or were at least in seeming, human, could
> Do as they have done by yours, and you yourself—
> *You*, who abet them?
>
> (II, i. 117–25)

Note the separation of 'men' from the 'human' in her syntax. The pledges of marriage, the events of the life-process are designated effeminate and excluded from importance in the making of history. But by repudiating them, men become less 'human', and women are marginalized. Marina demands in frustration: 'What are a woman's words?' (II, i. 130).

The substitution of the claims of the state for personal commitment is achieved by the displacing of women from public life, and the corresponding imaging of *Venice* as a woman. Venice is personified as a haughty courtly queen shrouded in feminine mystique: '. . . she knows not herself, | In all her mystery' (II, i. 85–6). The Dogeship is a marriage service; Foscari wears the wedding ring, a sign of his overriding commitment until he is forced to relinquish it in Act V:

> . . . every hour has been the country's.
> I am ready to lay down my life for her,

As I have laid down dearer things than life: (V, i. 52–4)

The sons of Venice likewise express their patriotic feeling in terms of mother-love. Jacopo feels like Cain cursed by Eve when exiled: ''tis like a mother's curse | Upon my soul—the mark is set upon me' (III, i. 186–7). Like his father he prizes Venice above life and his real family.

When disputing the superior claims of her rival, Venice, on her menfolk, Marina refuses to be reprimanded for her unpatriotic thoughts (II, i. 276–7). She accuses *Venice* of being dishonoured (II, i. 163–4), and a traitress (II, i. 386–7). Whereas the Doge would give willingly all his sons for the state's service, Marina cries out for individual feeling: 'Accursed be the city where the laws | Would stifle nature's!' (II, i. 418–19). *The Two Foscari* is an important examination of patriarchy as a fundamental principle of government. The distortion of natural relationships it produces in the Foscari family mirrors the stranglehold with which the male oligarchy subjugates all other members of the body politic of Venice.

When Loredano brings the news that the Ten, after another session of torture unproductive of a confession, have decreed Jacopo's banishment, Marina enquires if permission has been granted for her to accompany him, but Loredano is non-committal. The Doge attempts to stem her bitter attack on the villain by advocating the feminine posture of silence and passivity. This leads Marina to make Loredano define her own status: 'well, then, you're a prince, | A princely noble; and what then am I?' (II, i. 292–3). The answer, framed both by Loredano and Marina herself is: 'The offspring of a noble house . . . And wedded | To one as noble' (II, i. 294–5). Her class is defined only in terms of her relationships with men. As a noblewoman, she has outward status but no immanent power. She is therefore in a perfect position to criticize the tyranny of the oligarchy disinterestedly but from the inside. Since the torture chamber has done its worst with her husband, the Ten have no hold on her. Loredano tells her to silence her free thoughts in the presence of representatives of Venetian law. The Doge concurs. She should be deferential to the city's male rulers. Marina contemptuously repudiates such silence and respect:

Keep
Those maxims for your mass of scared mechanics,

> Your merchants, your Dalmatian and Greek slaves,
> Your tributaries, your dumb citizens,
>
> (II, i. 299–302)

Proudly citing her nobility of birth, she refuses to produce the submissive behaviour expected of women. She challenges the oligarchy to punish her insubordination by force, as they did her husband. But, as Loredano drily informs her, her words will never leave the chamber. They are as fruitless as those scrawled on Jacopo's prison wall.

This bitter irony is underlined by Jacopo's plaintive request, when she visits him in prison, that she save him from oblivion by telling his story: 'All then shall speak of me: | The tyranny of silence is not lasting' (III, i. 78–9). He has been refused his request for history books whilst in prison, but finds an alternative record of the past in the graffiti on the cell wall. The building itself is indicative of the process of suppression of dissent: above it is the splendid Doge's palace, with its official tradition of republican freedom commemorated in chronicles and portraits of the city's rulers; below sea level are the dungeons where subversive writing on the wall speaks of past tyranny, read only by those themselves deemed traitors, and then only by dint of the sense of feeling in the total darkness. In *Marino Faliero*, the graffito was an unintentional self-revelation of corruption by the aristocracy themselves. In *The Two Foscari*, the play ends with Loredano's writing on his tablets *his* account of the story, whilst the words on the prison wall remain in obscurity.

Like Wollstonecraft, Byron, in the Venetian plays, portrays the ideal role of woman as a republican matron. In the letter to Talleyrand which prefaces *A Vindication* Wollstonecraft's rhetoric strives to demonstrate that woman's domestic role has a civic purpose: 'If children are to be educated to understand the true principle of patriotism, their mother must be a patriot.'[19] The feminist version of nineteenth-century domestic ideology still saw motherhood as woman's primary vocation, but sought equality for her private sphere, by construing it as the nursery to the state. The portrayal of Marina interrogates this idea. Her marriage is based on friendship between equals, as Wollstonecraft advocated. Jacopo greets Marina as his 'true wife' and 'only friend', while she tells him to 'divide' his sorrow with her (III, i. 215). However, Marina finds

[19] Wollstonecraft, *Vindication*, p. 86.

that family love is not in harmony with her patriotism. As a woman, Byron portrays her as closer to nature than society, and thus an oppositional voice to state authority.

The role of the young woman in rejecting patriarchal control of her fertility is thus a central Byronic concern. Because her role in Venetian society is not immanent, but contingent on her relationships, a woman's loyalty is seen by Byron as purely personal in nature. Marina sees herself as accountable to no one but her husband, and in his defence she can therefore articulate an individualism untrammelled by 'masculine' law. Personal liberty is her first priority: she suggests that they could find happiness abroad. Patriotism is to her a childish clinging to mere 'climes and regions': allegiance to Venice is abrogated now that the republic has become 'an ocean Rome' of imperialism (III, i. 146–54). She wants to forge a new life with Jacopo (III, i. 198–202). Personal loyalty and liberty are not preferences to Marina, but 'duties paramount', to which all other scruples and feelings must be secondary. Jacopo may be compared to Abel, Japhet, and Hugo—Christlike oppressed sons who forgive their stern fathers—who trust that good will eventually ensue from their suffering; who fundamentally believe in the justice of patriarchal authority in spite of the injustice visited on them. When Marina curses Venice, Jacopo points proudly to his silence—his absence of protest.

But Marina, as a woman not permitted to participate in the public sphere, speaks on behalf of all silenced subjects of Venice of

> The blood of myriads reeking up to heaven,
> The groans of slaves in chains, and men in dungeons,
> Mothers, and wives, and sons, and sires, and subjects,
> Held in the bondage of ten bald-heads;
>
> (III, i. 241–4)

Whilst her husband acts with dignified restraint, Marina attacks Loredano as the personification of state tyranny (III, i. 252–5, 263–6, 268–9). When Jacopo tries to silence her, Loredano, like the senators, gives her a chivalrous answer: 'Let the fair dame preserve | Her sex's privilege' (III, i. 268). Loredano now informs Marina he has given permission for her to accompany Foscari only because he is 'One who wars not with women' (III, i. 280). She attempts to repudiate both this patronizing chivalry and his underlying contempt for women by asserting that an individual's quality of nature, like that of a thoroughbred horse, overrides mere categorization by birth (III, i. 289–303). In other words she asserts herself his moral superior, even though a woman. She harangues his degeneration from the ideals of the nobility (in his cowardly and corrupt manipulation of the law for personal vengeance), and triumphs in his discomfiture when the hit strikes home.

Though Marina has proved that she is qualitatively equal to her oppressor by her breed and blood, and morally superior in her unstained honour as wife and mother, she is shown just how hollow is her victory when Loredano insists that her children must remain in Venice as they belong to the state. Previously she had threatened him with her sons' revenge in the future (III, i. 269). Now she is informed: 'They are the state's' (III, i. 387). She now realizes that her maternal rights over them relate only to the menial tasks of breeding and rearing:

> That is
> In all things painful. If they're sick, they will
> Be left to me to tend them; should they die,
> To me to bury and to mourn; but if
> They live, they'll make you soldiers, senators,
> Slaves, exiles—what *you* will; or if they are
> Females with portions, brides and *bribes* for nobles!
> (III, i. 389–94)

Her own metaphor of horse-breeding has rebounded upon her.[20] She discovers that all her nobility and chastity is not in fact valued as *individual* superiority at all, for female virtue is highly prized only to ensure the purity of blood of the male line. Her body is as much at the state's disposal as Jacopo's. A woman's only value in society is in the provision of male heirs to power. A female's inherent worth is so little that daughters are given away as gifts by their fathers, pawns in the power struggle, and even then they must be accompanied with 'portions' or bribes of money to give them value.

When Jacopo dies before they can board the boat that is to take them to exile, and Marina now wishes to join him in death, the Doge reminds her of her duty to live for the sake of the children. She now repudiates what she had previously boasted of—the sanctity of motherhood:

[20] *Vindication* closes by comparing a woman to a horse, in her treatment by man.

My children! true—they live, and I must live
To bring them up to serve the state, and die
As died their father. Oh! what best of blessings
Were barrenness in Venice! Would my mother
Had been so!

(IV, i. 208–12)

Marina's despair is based on her realization of the extent to which the state controls all processes of life. Her simple belief in her aristocratic superiority of 'blood' comes into conflict with the dynastic system of ensuring the perpetuation of power by using and overseeing her biological function as a mother. Her grief at the state's regulation of motherhood is echoed by the Doge's tears—as he, for the first time, mourns Venice's destruction of his benevolent role as loving father (both of his bodily son and of the city in his charge). Before, he had been ashamed of weeping, pretending his eyes were misty from age (II, i. 5–7), and sternly commanding his son to desist from effeminate weakness: 'Boy! no tears' (III, i. 415)

He now acknowledges his own subjectivity to 'feminine' feeling, and paradoxically this gives him the strength to oppose the state's manipulation of his integrity any further. Now he has the dignity to refuse to abdicate when this is demanded. Previously the request to resign the Dogeship had been refused, and he was even constrained to sign an oath that he would not repeat the request. When he is deprived of power, Learlike, he is reunited in sorrow with Marina. He declares to the oligarchy that his allegiance shall henceforth not be restricted to his own class but to a consensus of government: in Rousseau's words, 'the *general* will' (V, i. 56). The discrepancy between the term 'general will' in Chapters I and II of *The Social Contract* (which may be ideally taken to represent all subjects of the State) and the specific exclusion from citizenship of the lower classes and women (in the later section on the Republic of Sparta) constitutes a dilemma which the play leaves unresolved. Wollstonecraft reacted by claiming citizenship for women by denigrating the concept of 'feminine' subjectivity and adopting the 'masculine' criteria of reason for both public and private spheres. But Byron's play cries out against both the silencing of woman and the suppression of masculine emotion in the juxtaposition of Marina and the Doge.

When he is deprived of office, Foscari, as a mere private citizen, like Marina, is urged to leave the precincts of power (V, i. 212–20), and his passionate words (on the subjugation of the Venetian people) are rebuked, as hers had been (V, i. 261). But, as Loredano recognizes, the pathos of the sight of the City's patriarch forced to quit his palace, on the arm of his widowed daughter-in-law, would communicate an unforgettable image to the citizens, which would speak even louder than his silenced words. The Republic should, like Venetian crystal, reveal the presence of corrosive poison within it, by its instant antipathy. But neither stands the test, and the Doge is murdered, his murderer undiscovered, and Foscari's words of dissent obliterated by the 'princely' funeral rites which betoken unbroken allegiance to the status quo.

Like Angiolina Faliero, Marina Foscari is central at the close of the play, her outspoken condemnation of the Council of Ten guiding the audience's response. She sardonically claims as a woman's duty (like the care of the aged) her right to the burial of her dead father-in-law, as well as her husband. Her only legal property—her dowry—will give her the means:

> Though his (the Doge's) possessions have been all consumed
> In the state's service, I still have my dowry,
> Which shall be consecrated to his rites
>
> (V, i. 344–6)

Her request for a private funeral is, of course, refused. Death, like life, is the state's business. Again she is reproved for her impudent excoriation of the male rulers and threatened with punishment, but, in view of the circumstances, reassured that her words will not be written down. The irony of this pronouncement of the futility of Marina's speech is accompanied by Loredano's simultaneous gesture of crossing out words (his grudge against the Foscari family) in his account book. The impotence of the passionate expression in words of individual subjective judgement is the final image of the play. The fact that this is the subject of a poem by Byron makes it a double irony.

MYRRHA

I know that, as a proof of the inferiority of the sex, Rousseau has exultingly exclaimed, How can they leave the nursery for the camp! . . . Yet, if defensive war, the only justifiable war, in the present advanced state of society, where virtue can show its face and ripen amidst the rigours which purify the air on the mountain's top, were alone to be adopted as just and glorious, the true heroism of antiquity might again animate female bosoms.

(Mary Wollstonecraft, *Vindication of the Rights of Woman*)

Byron's decision to reintroduce romantic love into the political dramas of 1821—ostensibly at the behest of his sentimental mistress—was taken in order to create a wholly original, fictional character, Myrrha, to complement his portrait of the historical emperor Sardanapalus. The importance of the introduction of this heroine is that the effeminate emperor and the martial woman together make up a Byronic conundrum on the question of sexual and political power relationships. The complex ironies of their relationship cannot be fully explored by critics, like Marchand, who focus exclusively on Sardanapalus in terms of a Byronic 'self-revelation'. Sardanapalus is perceived by McGann as an idealized character, who 'is the play's chief norm of value' in a reading of the play in which the heroine's exhortations to action merely function to demonstrate her own evil and the hero's moral superiority, 'since he is ahead of her in all these things, and teaches her what integrity, love, and kingship really entail'. John Farrell goes further in extolling the virtues of the king's pacifism, and correspondingly denigrating Myrrha: 'None of the ideologies in the play are compatible with the vision of human purpose that animates Sardanapalus.' These sentiments are echoed by Martyn Corbett in his study of the tragedies. In his commentary on the play in the recently-published volume of Byron's *Complete Poetical Works* McGann still focuses on Sardanapalus as 'an exemplar of peace and forgiveness'.[21]

Such views endorse Sardanapalus' own justification of his hedonism as humanitarian, without recognizing sufficiently its critique within the play. Byron was attempting a problem drama of ideas based on a structural set of ironies, anticipating Shaw at the end of the century. Sardanapalus and Myrrha represent contrasting ideals of the classical past, the Epicurean and the Stoic philosophies. The sybarite emperor sees gender polarities in terms of the two sides of Bacchus: 'feminine' pleasure, represented by wine; and 'masculine' self-aggrandizement, exemplified by his conquest of India (I, ii.

[21] Marchand, *Byron's Poetry*, p. 102. The heroism of Sardanapalus is emphasized by McGann, *Fiery Dust*, p. 228; Farrell, *Revolution as Tragedy*, p. 162; and Martyn Corbett, *Byron and Tragedy* (Oxford, 1988), pp. 114–15. See also McGann's commentary in *CPW* vi. 607–11.

147–52). He learns from Myrrha to complement his rejection of the latter with the adoption of a specifically Stoic masculine ideal.

But, initially, the effeminate Sardanapalus is a figure representing the degeneracy of the aristocracy, in his luxury, self-glorification, and sexual promiscuity. Byron's Orientalism—like that of Montesquieu's *Persian Letters*—focuses strongly on the harem as an image of despotism—making satiric parallels between East and West. So Byron's play, written in the year of the Queen Caroline affair, which begins with the words 'He hath wronged his queen . . . ', and deals with an imperial monarch sapped by luxury, who prefers to amuse himself with his concubines in his newly-built pavilion rather than to concern himself with popular unrest within his realm, is obviously engaged with issues raised by the recent accession of George IV. Since Sardanapalus, as an individual, does not personally oppress anyone, he expects to be popular with his subjects, while none the less enjoying the power conferred by birth. It is his female slave, however, who voices the rival bourgeois values of romantic monogamous love, civic responsibility, and financial rectitude. Myrrha shows the subject's recognition of the need for 'masculine' authoritative rule to defend the realm. Her critique of her master forms the basis both of the comic irony of the play, and of the protagonist's demonstrable unfitness to rule. Of course, his characterization is shot through with Byronic self-referentiality—the poet's own bisexuality and dandyism, and nostalgia for aristocratic values—which render the emperor a sympathetic figure. But even his Wagnerian suicide and final speech are ironized, in the fact that his 'light to lesson ages' is perceived by the post-Enlightenment reader not as endorsing enlightened despotism, as Sardanapalus thinks, but as demonstrating the Godwinian law of Necessity which eventually brings all eras of dynastic imperialism to an end.

The function of Myrrha is also complex. Critics have too easily identified her with the ethos of imperialism, because she advocates the use of force. However, the argument of the play problematizes Sardanapalus' pacifism, discriminating between the force necessary to defend and maintain the realm, and that of imperialist aggrandizement beyond its borders. Myrrha is, after all, a Greek republican—a victim and political opponent of the empire. The irony of her situation is that, to save the life of her lover, she must become a renegade and fight for the empire. So she counsels him how to rule effectively, even though he and his countrymen are her oppressors. This advice is not just pragmatism. Myrrha's discourse articulates the 'masculine' (in Rousseau's terms) political values of authoritative rule based on a social contract between the government and its subjects. Her Whiggish advice to the monarch on the responsibility of rulers to quell reactionary coups and to defend the realm from invasion is put into the mouth of a Greek patriot from a Hellenic city-state. The irony of having this masculine discourse of republican political theory articulated by a woman reinforces the stress on the effeminacy of the male monarch. Of course, this is not to say that the character of Myrrha is staightforwardly endorsed. While the first half of the play is given over to Myrrha's beneficial fostering of masculinity in Sardanapalus, the second half examines the potential danger of her influence, were it to be extended. The emphatic comparison between Myrrha and Semiramis, as images of female usurpation of masculine rule, problematizes the former's justification of the use of force by populism, as an ideology easily leading to empire-building, if not controlled.

Sardanapalus' search, like that of Selim and Manfred, is therefore for an ideal androgyny, one which is essentially masculine, of course, yet which incorporates the 'feminine' values of love and peace. The eventual subordination of 'feminine' virtues within the masculine psyche of the king also empowers him to take rational masculine control of 'feminine' excess passion. Myrrha herself is made to endorse the ironic corollary of her success as counsellor—that the newly authoritative monarch will henceforth reject her inordinate influence. The sentimental idealization of Myrrha's self-sacrifice, not only in her voluntary act of suttee, but in her own acknowledgement of her loss of status, by voicing the claims of the rightful queen, emphasizes the limited parameters of the role of the woman slave—loyal disinterested support of masculine aristocratic dynastic rule.

The necessity for masculinizing Sardanapalus is therefore doubly endorsed by the play, though his personal idealism is given its full weight. The theme corresponds to Byron's intention to 'masculinize' the genre of tragedy, by reviving classical form. Arthur Kahn has documented the strong influence of Seneca, particularly his *Hercules Furens*, and comments on the conventional opening of *Sardanapalus*: 'Sardanapalus is presented as a lax, irresponsible monarch, an incorrigible, effeminate hedonist, unfaithful to his wife and blindly enamored of his paramour. In this first act all the elements necessary for a Senecan tragedy are at hand.'[22] Hercules, of course, was the icon of masculinity adopted by David in 1793 to symbolize the French republic, as the subject both of a colossal statue and of the seal of state. The 'feminine' face of revolutionary freedom, Marianne the goddess of Liberty, was replaced by Hercules, the image of a strongly-established and centralized state. David orchestrated a pageant to celebrate the establishment of the republic, which culminated in the display of the statue: a colossus using his club to smash the hydra of federalism. It is no coincidence that, in the same year, the Jacobins quashed emergent feminism and outlawed women's clubs. The change in iconography reflected the determination of the masters of the republic to take women out of active politics. Their sphere was the personal.[23] In *Sardanapalus* Byron plays with the gendered counters of such republican iconography. Sardanapalus is twice compared to Hercules when he was ridiculed by Omphale, who dressed herself in his armour while he was sitting to spin with her female servants (I, ii. 327–30; III, i. 218–27). Myrrha, the passionate Marianne of republicanism, though 'a Greek, and born a foe to monarchs' (I, ii. 499), is herself made to endorse the necessity for 'masculine' authority, sexually and politically, and to promulgate the monarch's attainment of the conventional martial virtues.

The sexual metaphor on which the play is based derives from Rousseau: that monarchy is an effeminate institution, and only a republic fosters the masculine virtues. It was a commonplace of Enlightenment historicism to point out the sign of ultimate corruption of authority in a regime as the moment when slaves and women begin to wield illicit power. Byron's play therefore opens with a traditional critique of absolutism, in presenting an effeminate Eastern potentate at the end of an imperial era, who irresponsibly lets his female slave decide matters of state. What is innovative about the play is that the problematic relationship of this representative

[22] Arthur D. Kahn, 'Seneca and *Sardanapalus*: Byron, the Don Quixote of Neo-Classicism', *SP 66* (1969), 654–71.

[23] On the replacement of Marianne by Hercules in the iconography of the French Republic, see Lynn Hunt, *Politics, Culture, and Class in the French Revolution* (Berkeley, 1984), pp. 93–119. See also Eric Hobsbawm, 'Man and Woman in Socialist Iconography', *History Workshop Journal* 6 (1978), 121–38; and Vivian Cameron, 'Gender and Power: Images of Women in Late Eighteenth Century France', *History of European Ideas*, 10 (1989), 309–32.

tyrant and slave exposes the way the dualism of the language of sexual stereotyping characterizes the discourse of statecraft. These are, then, the parameters of this political play whose dominant visual imagery is of cross-dressing.

Sardanapalus, effeminately dressed and garlanded with flowers, amongst his women, is a visual symbol of absolute monarchy: he is worshipped as a god (III, i. 24–8). He lives a pagan, purely sensual existence, thinking only of the present. He has forsaken the male aspiration to transcend the physical through imperial aggrandizement, which extends the influence of the individual ruler both geographically and into the future through the dynastic furthering of power. (The latter is evidenced by his abandonment of the queen and his sons.) He prides himself, not on destructive sieges and conquests (symbolized by the sceptre), but on the creative merits (symbolized by the distaff) of having founded two cities whose inscription reads: 'Eat, drink, and love; the rest's not worth a fillip' (I, ii. 252). Wilson Knight states that Sardanapalus' 'scorn of the obvious manly virtues descends from a long series of seventeenth- and eighteenth-century dramas rating love beyond glory and attacking the horrors of war'.[24] Michael Cooke compares Dryden's *All For Love* with *Sardanapalus* in its treatment of the conflict between love and honour.[25] But where Byron differs from Dryden is that, as in Joanna Baillie's plays, it is the heroine herself who shows the king where his duty lies. She functions as an Egeria figure: the nymph who counsels the monarch.

Marilyn Butler correctly points out that Sardanapalus' comment that it would be better to plant vines in India, like Bacchus, than to leave an army's bones bleaching in the sand, like Semiramis, applies pointedly to hawkish contemporary British policy in India.[26] Nevertheless, the main point of the play is to demonstrate that defence of the realm against a reactionary coup is justifiable, and not morally equivalent with empire-building. The differentiation, of course, distinguishes Sardanapalus' original irresponsibility from true liberal pacificism. For Sardanapalus initially plans to desert the

[24] G. Wilson Knight, *The Golden Labyrinth: A Study of British Drama* (London, 1962), p. 237.

[25] Michael G. Cooke, 'The Restoration Ethos of Byron's Classical Plays', *PMLA* 79 (1964), 569–78.

[26] Marilyn Butler, 'Romantic Manichaeism: Shelley's "On the Devil, and Devils" and Byron's Mythological Dramas', in J. B. Bullen (ed.), *The Sun is God: Painting, Literature and Mythology in the Nineteenth Century* (Oxford, 1989), pp. 13–37.

palace, despite the ominous rumblings of revolt in the kingdom, cross the Euphrates, and spend the night carousing in his pavilion with the harem. By the end of Act I, while his male counsellor's arguments, based on reason, go unheeded, he is eventually persuaded to desist in this plan only through his passion for his favourite concubine, Myrrha.

Sardanapalus defends his effeminate rule on humanitarian grounds: 'Till now, no drop from an Assyrian vein | Hath flow'd for me' (I, ii. 408–9). His admirable regard for the sanctity of life distinguishes his civilization of the empire from the blood-lust of his ancestors Nimrod and Semiramis. The difference between his outlook and Myrrha's is illustrated by their contrasting reactions to the entrance of the wounded Pania with news of the rebellion. Sardanapalus is full of concern for the individual soldier's plight, typically offering him a glass of wine. But Myrrha interrogates him in a business-like manner, on the numbers involved, and the morale and extent of the king's army and the necessity for the presence of the king (III, i. 76–98). The ideals of humanism are contrasted with the practicalities of government which necessitate war.

The personal tragedy of the protagonists is that both Sardanapalus and Myrrha are cruelly trapped by the sexual roles delineated by Assyrian society. He, who would prefer a private life, is expected to enter into the bloody business of war and politics. She, who has an aptitude for statecraft equal to any of his aides, is condemned to spend her days frivolously entertaining her master in the harem. The rigid division of the harem from the chamber of state, the private from the public spheres, brings about the tragic constriction of the individual man and woman.

The story of Myrrha, therefore, has a potentially feminist element. A century of British and French Orientalism had fed the Enlightenment debate on the role of woman in society, producing a discourse on the slavery of women utilized by such disparate writers of the 1790s as Meiners and Mary Wollstonecraft. The representation of Myrrha's sexual slavery is not sensationalized by the portrayal of physical force, as in the Oriental tales. Instead, it focuses on a contrast between her outwardly 'feminine' demeanour (she is young, beautiful, modest, obedient, and weeps easily) and her 'masculine' intelligence, practicality, and rigour. Byron does not portray Myrrha's suicide as tragic defiance of her slavery, like that of Montesquieu's Roxana, or Valeria in Joanna Baillie's

Constantine Paleologus, or the Last of the Caesars. Neither does she comically convert her master to feminism, like Bickerstaffe's slave in *The Sultan*. She does not repeat Gulnare's feat of killing her master, though she considers it: '. . . to have stabb'd him on his throne when highest | Would have been noble in my country's creed' (I, ii. 648–9).

Her problem is more complex than Gulnare's or that of Shelley's Beatrice, for Myrrha's degradation lies in the fact that she is in love with her oppressor:

> . . . I love him;
> And that's the heaviest link of the long chain—
> To love whom we esteem not. (I, ii. 643–5)

As McGann has pointed out, Byron read and highly commended Grillparzer's *Sappho* (1819) just before composing *Sardanapalus*.[27] The protagonist of this play is also degraded by her love for Phaon, and her return to self-respect is marked by her resumption of the lyre and the garb which mark her vocation as poet, before she commits suicide. Byron noted the de Staëlian influence on this drama with a feminist theme. In adapting it, he neither makes his heroine the protagonist nor an artist. However, he does have Myrrha explore the Wollstonecraftian subject of a woman's sexual passion for an unworthy man, as constituting the primary means of female oppression:

> Could I save him,
> I should not love *him* better, but myself;
> And I have need of the last, for I have fallen
> In my own thoughts, by loving this soft stranger: (I, ii. 650–3)

Myrrha asserts that the distribution of power cannot be simply discounted by reference to romantic love. She herself therefore pointedly addresses Sardanapalus as 'Great king', 'My sovereign', 'Prince', and 'My Lord' (I, ii. 19; I, ii. 37; I, ii. 437). He protests, but his quasi-democratic talk of equality ill-accords with his unquestioning belief in the Divine Right of Kings, based on a hierarchical hereditary caste system and a belief in nobility by blood:

> Who should rebel? or why? what cause? pretext?
> I am the lawful king, descended from
> A race of kings who knew no predecessors. (I, ii. 202–4)

[27] *CPW* vi. 608–9.

Later, when she has demonstrated her loyalty, it is her enemy Salemenes who comments, 'That slave deserves her freedom' (IV, i. 196), but Sardanapalus never liberates Myrrha. She can never forget the power relationship that exists between them at every level:

> King, I am your subject!
> Master, I am your slave! Man, I have loved you!—
> Loved you, I know not by what fatal weakness.
> (I, ii. 496–8)

Sardanapalus had thought that liberalization could be achieved negatively, by less government (I, ii. 262–6). But he learns that his subjects, like Myrrha, are degraded by the condition of slavery, even under a benevolent monarch. Delegation produces 'ten thousand tyrants' (I, ii. 67–81) in the rule of the satraps; and while the king revels in luxury, his neglected subjects suffer poverty (I, ii. 106–12) and lack of shelter (III, i. 39–44). Like Marina Foscari, Myrrha is no silent and modest model of female propriety, but a sharp critic of the male establishment, who patronizingly comment on her sarcastic wit and 'readiness of speech' (III, i. 60).

However, this potentially feminist theme fades away, since Myrrha's continuing devotion and eventual willing suicide function, in the last analysis, to romanticize and eroticize the ideology of female slavery. In turn, this has the effect of deflecting attention from Sardanapalus' status as polygamous despot of a slave economy. As Susan Wolfson points out: 'The fact of slavery is submitted to the least critical pressure, in no small part because its chief embodiment is Myrrha, who also figures into a sentimental ideology of gender: feminine devotion to a master.'[28] Myrrha's stoic heroism is specifically feminine. Like Ségur's examples of female bravery in the French Revolution, this derives from self-sacrificial personal commitment, not political or patriotic idealism. This biological essentialism is brought out when Myrrha reminds Sardanapalus that woman's love is principally maternal, sexual pleasure being secondary to the impulse to nurture:

> ... The very first
> Of human life must spring from woman's breast,

[28] Susan J. Wolfson, '"A Problem Few Dare Imitate": *Sardanapalus* and "Effeminate Character"', *ELH* 58 (1991), 867–902 (881). I am grateful to Susan Wolfson for letting me read this article in manuscript.

> Your first small words are taught you from her lips,
> Your first tears quench'd by her, and your last sighs
> Too often breathed out in a woman's hearing,
> When men have shrunk from the ignoble care
> Of watching the last hour of him who led them.
>
> (I, ii. 509–15)

On both a sexual and a political level Myrrha asks Sardanapalus to take on the correspondingly masculine role of leadership that was conferred on him by his birth—through gender and class. The case for strong government is, of course, more effective when made by a subject than when put by the leader himself. It is made 'natural' when encoded in terms of a sexual relationship. Myrrha explains the ruler's role as that of an authoritative but benevolent patriarch, controlling the 'feminine' passions of the populace, as a father disciplines his family:

> I speak of civil popular love, *self* love,
> Which means that men are kept in awe and law,
> Yet not oppress'd—at least they must not think so;
> Or, if they think so, deem it necessary,
> To ward off worse oppression, their own passions.
>
> (I, ii. 537–41)

Nevertheless, though the king does become masculinized, adopts military dress, and goes to war, his doubts remain. The ambivalence of the heroism of the Byronic heroes of the tales, the opening of *Don Juan* ('I want a hero'), and the theme of androgyny or sexual role-reversal explored in *The Bride of Abydos*, *Lara*, *Sardanapalus*, and the Turkish and Russian cantos of *Don Juan* are all attempts to explore the validity of the male martial ethos. Sardanapalus' nightmare, as a liberal, is that by taking on the masculine role of warrior to put down the satraps he will make himself the moral equivalent of his bloodthirsty forebears, as his dream in Act IV makes clear. Like Selim, he metamorphoses from an androgynous male to a heroic fighter. But Myrrha, unlike Zuleika, is not horrified at the transformation. Like Gulnare, she is more 'sanguinary' than the hero. Like Sardanapalus' subjects, she loves him all the more for his adoption of force. When he first calls for armour she cries: 'How I do love thee! . . . But now I honour thee . . . Go forth and conquer!' (III, i. 108–9, 173). Whilst the king finds armour and weapons too heavy for his strength, and delays the battle to send for a mirror to check his appearance (III, i. 129–47), Myrrha is impatient to join the fray, and brushing aside the soldier detailed to protect her, plunges into battle herself. Sardanapalus describes her:

> . . . I paused
> To look upon her, and her kindled cheek;
> Her large black eyes, that flash'd through her long hair
> As it stream'd o'er her; her blue veins that rose
> Along her most transparent brow; her nostril
> Dilated from its symmetry; her lips
> Apart; her voice that clove through all the din,
> As a lute's pierceth through the cymbal's clash,
> Jarr'd but not drown'd by the loud brattling; her
> Waved arms, more dazzling with their own born whiteness
> Than the steel her hand held, which she caught up
> From a soldier's grasp;—all these things made
> Her seem unto the troops a prophetess
> Of victory, or Victory herself,
> Come down to hail us hers. (III, i. 386–99)

Plainly we have here the image of Marianne or Nike, common in the visual arts and literature of the Revolutionary and Napoleonic period, deriving from French representations of the Goddess of Liberty. Delacroix's *Liberty leading the people at the barricades* (1830) is a later well-known example. The Marianne of popular revolt was portrayed as a youthful, vehement peasant girl, in the midst of action, with hair floating free and bosom uncovered.[29] We could compare the martial Myrrha with the Maid of Saragoza in *Childe Harold's Pilgrimage* (I, 54–9), Gulnare, and Kaled. Byron's fascination lay in the transformation of woman from the extreme passivity and modesty of 'femininity' to a figure demonically unleashing the most bestial passions. As with the transformation of obedient subjects into a volatile mob, the link between subjection and subjectivity is both exhilarating and disturbing.

So it is now the turn of Myrrha to demonstrate an unsettling sexual role reversal in her love of 'masculine' warfare:

> . . . like the dam
> Of the young lion, femininely raging
> (And femininely meaneth furiously,

[29] Maurice Agulhon, *Marianne into Battle: Republican Imagery and Symbolism in France 1789–1880*, trans. J. Lloyd (Cambridge, 1981), p. 88.

Because all passions in excess are female)
Against the hunter flying with her cub,
She urged on with her voice and gesture, and
Her floating hair and flashing eyes, the soldiers,
In the pursuit.

(III, i. 378–85)

Having inspired her love, Sardanapalus finds out the strength of her protective instinct as she fights to preserve his safety. The ambivalence of the warlike woman, however, lies in her dangerous capacity for action. Once roused, will she be content to return to her former subject state and obedience to the male leader? With both the Maid of Saragoza and Gulnare, Byron devoted several lines to reassuring us of the heroine's return to suitably feminine passivity. In *Sardanapalus*, these fears are encapsulated in the emperor's dream, in which Myrrha, who watches over him, is transformed into his murderous and lustful grandmother Semiramis. In Sardanapalus' dream his attempt at liberalization is imaged in an egalitarian banquet with no host: 'Myself a host that deem'd himself but guest, | Willing to equal all in social freedom' (IV, i. 80–1). But, when he turns to his consort he finds that in Myrrha's chair sits her *alter ego*, Semiramis. Semiramis was another warlike woman:

Semiramis—a woman only—led
These our Assyrians to the solar shores
Of Ganges. (I, ii. 126–8)

Having obtained power through her husband, she disposed of him, as Beleses reminds us: 'No—the queen liked no sharers of the kingdom, | Not even a husband' (II, i. 374–5). The vision of Semiramis is a warning to Sardanapalus of how Myrrha could change from a Marianne of freedom to a Catherine II of imperialism:

In thy own chair—thy own place in the banquet—
I sought thy sweet face in the circle—but
Instead—a gray-hair'd, wither'd, bloody-eyed,
And bloody-handed, ghastly, ghostly thing,
Female in garb, and crown'd upon the brow,
Furrow'd with years, yet sneering with the passion

Of vengeance, leering too with that of lust,
Sate:—my veins curdled.

(IV, i. 102–9)

As Myrrha's youth and feminine beauty had made patriotic martial enthusiasm for the defence of the realm seem an attractive ideal at first, now her antithesis—the insatiable sexuality of an old woman—is Byron's image for the repulsion Sardanapalus feels for the prospect of further warfare:

. . . but the woman,
The female who remain'd, she flew upon me,
And burnt my lips up with her noisome kisses;
And, flinging down the goblets on each hand,
Methought their poisons flow'd around us, till
Each form'd a hideous river.

(IV, i. 148–53)

Here as with Catherine II in *Don Juan*, rampant female sexuality operates in the liberal dilemma over the rightful use of military force, as an image of imperialism. The main weight of the play is behind Myrrha's insistence that the king defend his country and add male heroism to his feminine life-giving values. Similarly it is seen as beneficial that her sexuality is instrumental in fostering in him a more conventionally masculine role. Nevertheless, Sardanapalus' resulting subconscious fear of her is here dramatized and explored. He is afraid that the power she urges him to use, both politically and sexually, will not be subject to his control, once unleashed. Once he has adopted the male role of authoritative ruler which she desires him to take, he needs to be reassured that she (and his subjects fighting to defend the realm) will return to their former subjection. The repellent dream of Semiramis indicates the extent of the reassurance needed. Myrrha must therefore demonstrate an equally extreme abnegation of female will, and this is achieved in her act of suttee: the assertion of a woman that her very identity is contingent on that of the man. Myrrha demonstrates not just her return to femininity, but her triple subjection of sex, race, and class to her master. Her willingness to immolate herself shows her acquiescence in keeping at bay the degeneration, which the 'man-queen' Semiramis represents, both of free female sexuality and the use of military force. Myrrha's youth, beauty, and obedience are forever preserved from the forces of change in self-destruction by fire. Only by her capacity for self-sacrifice can her belief in the use of force to defend the realm be vindicated.

In creating Myrrha, Byron thus found it necessary to make her (like the Oriental heroines) of lowly social status, and also to endow her with the humility of a woman in love, to compensate for her 'masculine' competence in public affairs and battle. Indeed, he succeeded in his aim, for, in contrast to the more queenly Venetian heroines, Myrrha was popular with contemporary critics. The contempt shown her by Salemenes, her own self-disgust as a concubine, her later repudiation by Sardanapalus himself, and lastly the fantasy of male power represented by her (willing) death, all contribute to emphasize her subjection. Heber notes approvingly that:

> [her] energy of expostulation, no less than the natural high tone of her talents, her courage, and her Grecian pride, is *softened* into a *subdued and winning tenderness* by the constant and painful recollection of her *abasement* as a slave in the royal haram; and still more by the *lowliness* of perfect womanly love in the presence of and towards the object of her passion. No character can be drawn more *natural* than her's [*sic*] . . . she is one whom a purer faith would have raised to the level of a Rebecca or a Miriam.[30]

The idealization of Myrrha can only be conditional on her demonstrable subjection to male control, so emphasized by Heber, which finally is summed up as 'natural' to the female character.

In her apotheosis, Byron thus portrays Myrrha as a true feminine ideal, by which to measure Sardanapalus' indolent effeminacy at the opening of the play. The relationship between the sexes which he delineates is one in which the woman is morally the superior, whilst always subject to the authority of the man. The political connotations are that Myrrha's love for Sardanapalus symbolizes the people's patriotic feeling for their country, which inspires the ruler and endows him with authority in a good cause, but which

[30] Reiman, *Romantics Reviewed*, part B, v. 2067 (my italics). Cf. Jeffrey in the *Edinburgh Review*, on Myrrha's submissiveness and her status: 'If the part she takes in the dialogue be sometimes too subdued and submissive for the lofty daring of her character, it is still such as might become a Greek slave—a lovely Ionian girl, in whom the love of liberty and the scorn of death, was tempered by the consciousness of what she regarded as a degrading passion, and an inward sense of fitness and decorum with reference to her condition' (ibid., part B, i. 924).

must always be subservient to enlightened government from above. Her sense of degradation as a female slave has to some extent been palliated by her absolute commitment to him: 'So shalt thou find me ever at thy side, | Here and herafter, if the last may be' (IV, i. 166–7). The woman/subject's role can be safely idealized when her loyalty is irrefutable. However, Sardanapalus is shown to have gone too far, in his gratitude for her help in battle, when he cries: 'That slave deserves to share a throne' (IV, i. 197). For this is the cue for Salemenes to come forward with news of the queen, and within thirty lines Sardanapalus is confronted with the deserted Zarina and his abandoned marriage contract. That the marriage was arranged for reasons of state is stressed (I, ii. 213; IV, i. 250–1), and the passionate love of master and slave is contrasted with the neglected responsibilities of the husband for his wife and children, to whom he should hand on his power. Ironically, once he has been brought to a masculine role by Myrrha, the king wants to ensure that his legitimate heirs rule the empire after his death. The role of the slave has been salutary and redemptory, but it is limited and defined in scope by the introduction of Zarina, the rightful queen. The subject can help to recover, but not share, the throne. The marriage contract, like the social contract, can only be effected between heirs to property and power.

Newly aware of this, Sardanapalus repudiates Myrrha on her next entrance: 'It forms no portion of your duties | To enter here till sought for' (IV, i. 440–1). He now insultingly offers to despatch Myrrha back to Greece with a handsome remuneration. In choosing to stay and share the king's fate the slave re-affirms her disinterested loyalty:

> . . . here I stand or fall. If that you conquer,
> I live to joy in your great triumph: should
> Your lot be different, I'll not weep, but share it. (IV, i. 493–5)

But at the same time she herself has pitied the queen and acknowledged the liaison of king and concubine to be morally wrong:

> Were you the lord of twice ten thousand worlds—
> As you are like to lose the one you sway'd—
> I did abase myself as much in being
> Your paramour, as though you were a peasant—
> Nay, more, if that the peasant were a Greek. (IV, i. 464–8)

This has the effect of preparing us to admire the climactic self-sacrifice of the woman/subject for the king, especially as we bear in mind her own realization of the provisional nature of their relationship.

Reassured that she will not expect a change in status in the case of victory, the king accepts her selfless love with a kiss, and her offer of help in putting down the satraps. Compare his kiss with that of Conrad thanking Gulnare. Now that he controls their relationship with masculine authority, the nightmare of Semiramis fades and he can confidently imagine that his use of force will not necessarily entail a return to imperialism:

> I am content: and, trusting in my cause,
> Think we may yet be victors and return
> To peace—the only victory I covet. (IV, i. 503–5)

Sardanapalus has now reached the correct balance of 'feminine' humanistic values and 'masculine' heroism. To his liberal 'laissez-faire' he has added the Whig doctrine of the necessity for force in resisting tyranny and in defence of the realm. Achieving masculinity has not necessitated adopting a militaristic ideology: 'I am no soldier, but a man' (IV, i. 566).

Ironically, however, his new potency is too late. For nature dictates that the rule of his dynasty is at an end—the flooded river assists the law of Necessity (V, i. 262–3) in ensuring his defeat.

Clearly the closure of the tragedy reassuringly reaffirms the traditional configuration of masculine authority and female dependence. Nevertheless, through role-reversal, Byron's play has interrogated the contemporary ideology of extreme differentiation of sexual role, based on biology. For both male and female rulers evidence self-aggrandizement in lust and conquest, as the comparisons between Semiramis and her grandson, and between Nimrod and the 'man-queen' demonstrate. Both the male and female protagonists are shown to be capable of political and military action. They die an equally heroic death, for the play ends symmetrically with a double suicide: the fitting Stoic response to the humiliation of military defeat, and adopted by many luminaries of the French Revolution.[31] The play concludes with the neat Byronic irony of the sybaritic emperor destroying all the parapher-

[31] See Outram, *The Body and the French Revolution*, p. 90 ff.

nalia of autocracy, while the austere Greek republican brings a libation of wine. Both declare their patriotic love for their respective countries—one a Greek democracy, one an empire. This renders ambiguous Sardanapalus' command that the throne form the core of his funeral pyre (V, i. 362), and his hope that its destruction will be 'a light | To lesson ages, rebel nations, and | Voluptuous princes' (V, i. 440–2).

Though Sardanapalus remains to the end obsessed with the ingratitude of the rebels, his words and actions bear a coded message to the subjects of the new king, George IV. The inevitable end of all dynasties—even 'enlightened' monarchies—is one lesson of the funeral pyre. And, in the last moment of the play, when Myrrha leaps into the flames, it is the self-immolating devotion of woman to man, of the subject to her liberal yet aristocratic master, which is for the poet the condition which makes this vision feasible.

8

'Daughters of Earth': The Divided Self and the Heroines of the Mythological Dramas

In his lyrical dramas, *Manfred*, *Cain*, and *Heaven and Earth*, Byron both used and subverted the Christian genre of the morality play, placing a male everyman protagonist between the forces of evil and good, which contend for his soul. What is shocking about *Manfred* and *Cain* is that, instead of contrasting good and bad angels, Byron has an immortal spirit to represent evil, while using mortal women to embody goodness. But the human-centred ethic of these mythological plays is most iconoclastic in *Heaven and Earth*, where the heroines are most plainly portrayed as morally superior to both the earthly and the heavenly representatives of orthodox Judaeo-Christianity.

As in the political plays, Byron interrogates the dualism of modern Western consciousness: the perceived opposition between reason and sentiment, and the association of the former with masculinity and the latter with femininity. The mythological plays are also particularly concerned with refuting the Judaeo-Christian division of body from soul, the ensuing denigration of materiality, and the traditional misogynistic association of woman with the sins of the flesh.

Gender and the differentiation of sexual role is symptomatic, for Byron, of this fall into dualism. In *Manfred* and *Cain* the hero becomes distanced from those qualities now associated with femininity—closeness to nature, the social virtues, instinctive humanitarianism. As a man, he must intellectualize his situation, assertively challenge the ruling orthodoxy, even become destructive in his will to power. Astarte and Adah are therefore aligned with community values which have to be rejected by the defiant male individualist. In *Heaven and Earth* Byron experiments with heroines who are simultaneously idealized for their capacity for selfless love and yet reviled for their sexual sinfulness. Such feminine stereotypes are common enough. What makes Anah and Aholibamah so interesting is that they are centre-stage of the mythological drama, representing mankind. Throughout these three plays the concepts of masculinity and femininity are constantly interrogated and reassessed.

ASTARTE

More than any other Byronic heroine, Astarte is usually viewed from a biographical perspective.[1] The play was certainly the catharsis of Byron's personal drama of 1816, when his marriage failed and rumours of an incestuous relationship with his half-sister drove him to lifelong self-imposed exile. Here, however, the heroine will be viewed, not as illustrative of Byron's psychological orientation, but solely as a representation of femininity in a literary context. Sandra Gilbert has comprehensively defined the purpose of feminist criticism as '. . . to decode and demystify all the disguised questions and answers that have always shadowed the connections between textuality and sexuality, genre and gender, psychosexual identity and cultural authority'.[2] My examination of the role of Astarte will address some of these issues.

In *Manfred* Byron transformed Gothic elements into a Romantic poetic drama in which states of mind are externalized.[3] The play is best viewed as a psychomachia: the dramatization of the hero's struggle for identity in relation to the material universe.[4] Manfred's

[1] *Manfred* is often seen as a melodramatic therapeutic outpouring after the separation scandal. '*Manfred* is the drama in which Byron symbolically works his way through to mental sanity, to the psychological perspective that made *Don Juan* possible', Edward Bostetter, *The Romantic Ventriloquists* (Seattle, 1963), p. 278. For a psychoanalytical approach to the play see Peter J. Manning, *Byron and his Fictions* (Detroit, 1978), pp. 71–87, who concludes: 'From this complex of originally mother-centred tensions, reactivated by Augusta and Annabella, *Manfred* grows.' For a full account of the biographical implications of the play, see Earl of Lovelace, *Astarte* (New York and London, 1921).

[2] Sandra Gilbert, 'What Do Feminist Critics Want? A Postcard from the Volcano', in Showalter (ed.), *The New Feminist Criticism*, pp. 29–45 (36).

[3] On the influence of Gothic drama, see Bertrand Evans, 'Manfred's Remorse and Dramatic Tradition', *PMLA* 62 (1947), 752–3; on the influence of the Gothic tradition generally, see Thorslev, *The Byronic Hero*, ch. 11. For a summary of other influences on the play consult Joseph, *Byron the Poet*, pp. 103–7.

[4] *Manfred* separates 'the conflicting forces of the poet's own being' and

name indicates less that he is a representative of mankind than that his quest is specifically a masculine one, as he seeks in vain to overcome the dualism of gender and be reunited with the feminine principle, which is in harmony with nature. The apparitions he conjures up represent three ways of perceiving the force of nature. The spirits of the elements of physical nature in Act I are under Manfred's control, but this does not satisfy him. The Witch of the Alps in Act II embodies the spirit of natural beauty, but the proud Manfred refuses to deify it. The destinies, Nemesis and Arimanes, represent the diabolic energies of the organic force of Necessity, which for Byron was a cycle of despair, not Shelleyan progress. Astarte, as Jerome McGann comments, is Manfred's epipsyche, the lost female half of his soul.[5] His search for reconciliation with her is his hopeless attempt to end his alienation from nature. The tragic paradox that the play demonstrates is that only through his separation from the feminine principle does Manfred derive the power to assert his will in confronting Arimanes.

As with Blake's *The Four Zoas*, the notion of making the heroine an emanation of the hero's soul, with whom he must be reconciled for completion, is ultimately derived from Plato. The division of the original ideal hermaphrodite being into two sexes is a fall into dualism. But Blake, in reproducing conventional patriarchal sexual relationships in his portrayal of spectres and emanations, tended—probably unwittingly—to characterize the female emanations as either weak or despicable. Hence, his hermaphrodite ideal partook of more male than female characteristics.[6] But, as Peter Thorslev has pointed out, Shelley and Byron were influenced by Wieland's *Agathon* to use brother-and-sister love to epitomize the relationship between the hero and his psyche.[7] Thorslev rightly notes the subversive and antinomian undercurrents released by a romantic

dramatizes 'what for Byron always was the essential war, the one within man himself' (Gleckner, *Byron and the Ruins of Paradise*, pp. 250–1).

[5] *CPW* iv. 467. See also, W. P. Elledge, *Byron and the Dynamics of Metaphor* (Nashville, 1968), p. 84. Elledge notes that Astarte is an example of Byron's use of counterpart figures: '. . . the motivation behind Manfred's search for "self-oblivion" is not so much guilt over illicit love as it is a more generalized remorse over an unfulfilled potentiality: frustrated attempts to realize within himself the perfectability embodied in the imagined ideal have bred in him paranoiac self-reproach.'

[6] See Alice Ostriker, 'Desire Gratified and Ungratified: William Blake and Sexuality', *Blake: an Illustrated Quarterly*, 16 (1982–3), 156–65; also Anne Mellor, 'Blake's Portrayal of Women', ibid. 148–55.

[7] Thorslev, 'Incest as Romantic Symbol', 41–58.

endorsement of incest, as well as the dangers of narcissism and solipsism to which it is prone.

The equality of the sibling relationship is stressed in Byron's play. Manfred describes Astarte as his intellectual equal and counterpart, as aspiring as he, possessing the same Promethean individualism, yet having the capacity for humanitarian sentiment, which he had not:

> She was like me in lineaments—her eyes,
> Her hair, her features, all, to the very tone
> Even of her voice, they said were like to mine;
> But softened all; and tempered into beauty;
> She had the same lone thoughts and wanderings,
> The quest of hidden knowledge, and a mind
> To comprehend the universe: nor these
> Alone, but with them gentler powers than mine
> Pity, and smiles, and tears—which I had not;
> And tenderness—but that I had for her;
> Humility—and that I never had.
> Her faults were mine—her virtues were her own—
> I loved her, and destroy'd her! (II, ii. 105–17)

However, since Astarte is not dramatized as a separate character in the play, but can only be glimpsed through her recreation via the mind of Manfred, it could be said that the concept of androgyny is rendered here less as an image of wholeness than as the male hero's wish for the appropriation of the feminine quality of sentiment. For, as Alan Richardson has pointed out, his sister is described as a feminized version of himself, which Manfred has assimilated and/or destroyed.[8] Manfred's quest for Astarte expresses his desire to transcend the polarized sexual roles of dominance and submission which makes his life a barren Faustian quest, bereft of humanitarian values now the province of woman. Bram Dijkstra, in his study of the androgyne in nineteenth-century art and literature, suggests that the polarization of sexual stereotypes, which writers like Byron both portrayed and rebelled against, reflects that exaggeration of the nature/culture dichotomy which accompanied and facilitated the rise of industrialized capitalism. The idealized heroine became the repository of certain universal values:

[8] Richardson, 'Romanticism and the Colonization of the Feminine', 13–25.

She was close to nature, close to the intuitive sources of man, and therefore the perfect vehicle for all those passive, unproductive qualities associated with humanist conceptions of moral behaviour. As she became responsible for these qualities, the male could disentangle himself from any embarrassing and inconvenient concern for human values, and pursue his appointed nature within the now validated male–female polarity, by ruthlessly exercising his prerogatives of aggression within the economic realm.[9]

Manfred, as a Faustian individualist, expresses both this defiance of orthodox moral codes by the aspiring male and his sense of spiritual loss caused by sexual dualism. The tragedy which is unfolded reveals how the destruction of the female part of Manfred's nature has elevated his power, yet alienated him from the creative life-force in the universe.

In Manfred's opening soliloquy he refers to 'that all-nameless hour' (I, i. 24) when he and Astarte were separated. Since then his search for knowledge of philosophy and science has been dissociated from humanitarian values. He is cursed with alienation from the animating life-force of nature, and loss of the capacity for sentiment:

> . . . the curse to have no natural fear,
> Nor fluttering throb, that beats with hopes or wishes,
> Or lurking love of something on the earth. (I, i. 25–7)

The Seventh Spirit, which will later choose to manifest itself in the form of Astarte, whose name itself recalls a star, declares:

> The star which rules thy destiny,
> Was ruled, ere earth began, by me:
> It was a world as fresh and fair
> As e'er revolved round sun in air;
> Its course was free and regular,
> Space bosom'd not a lovelier star. (I, i. 110–15)

Manfred's original star, as Manning points out, is described in terms of ideal feminine beauty. Note the words 'fair', 'fresh', 'lovelier', and 'bosom'd'.[10] When the separation of male and female

[9] Bram Dijkstra, 'The Androgyne In Nineteenth-Century Art and Literature', *Comparative Literature*, 26 (1974), 62–73 (64).

[10] Manning, *Byron and his Fictions*, p. 78.

took place, however, Manfred's destiny lost its place in nature: balance and harmony in the individual was replaced by uncontrolled self-aggrandizement. His star is now:

> A wandering mass of shapeless flame,
> A pathless comet, and a curse,
> The menace of the universe;
> Still rolling on with innate force,
> Without a sphere, without a course,
> A bright deformity on high,
> The monster of the upper sky! (I, i. 117–23)

The loss of Astarte destroys the equilibrium and purposeful course of his star; without heart, the light of intellectual curiosity degenerates into the heat of the wanton destruction of a pathless comet.[11] The conjunction of star imagery and the concept of the heroine as guardian of the hero's conscience is common in Byron's poetry (See *The Bride of Abydos*, II, 395).

Peter Manning comments: 'Manfred does not so much seek for Astarte as a separate, independent being as he searches for a state prior to identity'.[12] Our consideration of Act I has shown this to be the case. For Manning, this is not the Platonic hermaphrodite ideal: instead he sees Byron regressing to 'the state in which mother and child form one organic unit'. This view of Astarte as a mother-substitute is not derived from the poem, but imposed upon it. Manning's Freudian diagnosis of both Byron and his heroes leads him to assert that Manfred's sorrows are merely 'private'. It is true that Manfred sees himself as a Gothic villain, replicating the crimes against woman perpetuated by his namesake in Walpole's *The Castle of Otranto*. He hints that he blames himself for Astarte's suicide, through guilt over their incestuous love. (See II, i. 24–8; II, ii. 117–21; II, iv. 121–4.) But Astarte's role as twin source of good and guilt is more significant than either Gothic sensationalism of incest or the poet's possible mother-fixation. She defines the masculinism of Manfred's Romantic quest.

[11] In Zoroastrianism 'comets . . . were regarded as evil influences operating under the direction of Arimanes, since they disturbed the order of the universe'. See Maurice J. Quinlan, 'Byron's *Manfred* and Zoroastrianism', *JEGP* 57 (1958), 726–38 (733). In *Manfred* Byron uses his hero and heroine to illustrate the dualism at war in the universe and the individual. He makes use also of some ideas of Zoroastrianism to illustrate this.

[12] Manning, *Byron and his Fictions*, pp. 78–83.

Ironically, the power he gains from the curse of male individualism does enable him to understand the workings of nature more fully. Byron emphasizes this by having Manfred unsuccessfully attempting to conjure up the spirits by a written charm and then a sign. It is only when he uses a spell originating in the perversion of his own star of destiny that he is successful (see I, i. 42–9). It is masculine aspiring intellectual self-assertion which gives Manfred the power to plumb the secrets of the material world. But the spirits of nature cannot assuage his desire for the oblivion of self. Self-consciousness is the price he has to pay for domination. 'The Tree of Knowledge is not that of Life' (I, i. 12). 'Masculine' knowledge has been separated from 'feminine' unified life.

The play hinges on the dualism created by linking intellectual aspiration with masculinity, and goodness with femininity. This is demonstrated when Manfred asks the 'most powerful' of the spirits of nature to take shape, and it is Manfred's own star which appears. But the form the spirit considers 'most fitting' in which to manifest itself is that of Astarte. Manfred's attempt to embrace Astarte (I, i. 190) is frustrated by her instant disappearance, and he loses consciousness. He is unable to achieve reintegration of full humanity in this life. Like Sardanapalus, until he accepts the burden of guilt which masculinity entails, he cannot face death with defiant dignity.

The 'feminine' virtues, whilst reverenced, must be rejected by the heroes of both plays. This way, the feminine is validated yet also subsumed by heroic masculinity. In this sense, femininity is portrayed ambivalently—by its very idealization. There is, however, little textual justification for Malcolm Kelsall's view that the spirit of Astarte is 'an intensely sinister figure' and an evil succuba, whose name is evocative of that of Ashtaroth, and who later rises from among the demons.[13] He bases this supposition on the fact that Manfred faints on perceiving her, but does not explain why in that case he first tries to embrace her. However, it is not her appearance but her disappearance that causes Manfred's grief-stricken swoon; and the curse spoken over the senseless Manfred is spoken, not by Astarte (who has vanished), but by the star of Manfred's destiny which—it has already been established—has been perverted by the

[13] Malcolm Kelsall, 'Goethe, Byron, Ibsen: The Faustian Idea on Stage', *BJ* 6 (1978), 66–76 (73).

loss of his humanitarian virtues. The curse is therefore essentially self-induced:[14] Like Southey's Ladurlad, in *The Curse of Kehama* (1810), Manfred is alienated from the life-force: the wind, the night, and the sun seem to add to his torment (I, i. 205, 254–5). He is unable to escape self-consciousness by sleep, death, wine, madness, or imagination (II, ii). Kelsall's characterization of Astarte as an evil demon is the product of viewing the play as a version of the Faustian idea. However, the crucial difference between *Manfred* and the various treatments of the Faust legend is that Byron's protagonist does not sell his soul to evil powers, and consequently he does not dread death. It is his inability to relate to physical *life* which becomes Manfred's curse. Hence the importance Byron attached to Manfred's last words: 'Old man! 'tis not so difficult to die' (III, iv. 151)

Astarte was, in fact, the name of a Near-Eastern deity of sexual love, identified with Aphrodite, but accredited with an incestuous nature.[15] Montesquieu took the name of the goddess for the heroine of the story in *Persian Letters*, Letter 67, of a Gheber brother and sister whose sexual love is permitted by their ancient religion, but whose happiness is destroyed when Astarte is made a Muslim and compelled to marry a eunuch.[16] Byron's Astarte is an Eve-figure whose incestuous love for her brother, followed by her death, intensifies the focus on their separation by sexual role. Manfred takes over Eve's overreaching 'thirst of knowledge' (II, ii. 95), whilst Astarte becomes the object of his longing for Prelapsarian harmony between body and soul. The separation of Adam into male and female, and his right to rule Eve, subsequent to the Fall (Genesis 3: 16), is transformed by the Romantic poet into the hero's dissatisfaction with his power of domination over nature, and his

[14] K. McCormick Luke, 'Lord Byron's *Manfred*: A Study of Alienation from Within', *University of Toronto Quarterly*, 40 (1970), 15–26. Luke comments on the curse: 'Viewing the incantation as an aspect of Manfred's own mind will bring the play into focus; recognizing Manfred as his own accuser will reveal an orderly progression of the dramatic structure from cause to effect' (p. 16). See also Stuart M. Sperry, 'Byron and the Meaning of *Manfred*', *Criticism*, 16 (1974), 189–202.

[15] Quinlan, 'Byron's *Manfred* and Zoroastrianism', p. 734. Quinlan does not think it likely that Byron knew that Astarte was the name of a Near-Eastern goddess; however, Byron was probably familiar with Montesquieu's sources, Chardin and Hyde. He possessed a copy of the former.

[16] In a letter to Augusta, written at the time of Byron's journey through the Alps (17 September 1816), he says he wishes they were a nun and monk talking through a grate—obviously recalling the story in *Persian Letters*.

hopeless longing to be reunited with his female counterpart on equal terms.

Yet, as the play progresses, Manfred's reiterated rejections of ways in which he could be reconciled with the 'feminine' virtues emphasize that this separation is the price which he chooses to pay for his powers. As Frederick Shilstone points out, Manfred's guilt over Astarte must be exorcised 'or he will retain a subservience to the societal values that would usurp his right of self-judgment, and so be defeated himself'.[17] Because he lacks Astarte's humility and capacity for human sympathy, Manfred cannot live the Wordsworthian ideal domestic life of 'humble virtues' within a community (see II, i. 64–71), like the chamois hunter. This is fit only for 'brutes of burthen' (II, i. 36). He admits to the Witch of the Alps: 'I had no sympathy with breathing flesh' (II, ii. 57).

Byron follows Rousseau and Wordsworth in associating the beauty of nature with 'feminine' sentiment. In his description of the Witch (II, ii. 13–32) he uses the conventional language of the idealization of the feminine: 'earth's least-mortal daughters', 'virgin snow', 'blush of earth embracing with her heaven', and 'serenity of soul'. The Witch stands beneath the rainbow of the covenant, indicating the role played by the beauty of nature in helping mankind acquire spiritual perception. Yet, ultimately, Manfred prefers to recognize his response to nature as the product of his own mind, rather than to make a god of it in some sort of pantheism (II, ii. 151–9).

When he recounts his life to the Witch, we see that Manfred's guilt at putting his individualistic quest before humanitarian concerns is symbolized by his remorse over his sister's suicide (as we presume it to be from his allusions to her death):

> If I had never lived, that which I love
> Had still been living; had I never loved,
> That which I love would still be beautiful—
> Happy and giving happiness. What is she?
> What is she now?—a sufferer for my sins—
> A thing I dare not think upon—or nothing. (II, ii. 193–8)

Because woman has been made into the repository of all humanitarian virtues, her purity has a redemptive power for her male lover. Yet

[17] Frederick W. Shilstone, *Byron and the Myth of Tradition* (Lincoln, Neb., and London, 1988), p. 164.

by pursuing a forbidden relationship, Byron's heroes experience male sexual guilt for the destruction of this innocence—for ever—through their tainted desires.

Manfred's last test is therefore to confront the spectre of his guilt and call Astarte back from the dead. He stands poised between two extremes. On one side is the feminine phantom of Astarte, who belongs to the powers of good, as Nemesis declares (II, iv. 115–16). On the other side is Arimanes, the male Prince of Darkness. Like Arimanes' attendant Spirits and Destinies, Manfred has shown his domination over the elements; and they themselves compare his sufferings, knowledge, powers, and will to their own (II, iv. 50–72, 159–63). The effect on human society of the cyclical workings of Necessity (which Arimanes represents) has been illustrated by the reimposition of the *ancien régime* in Europe (II, iii. 62–71). It is made clear that Manfred's powers (those of the exceptional individual) are lesser yet not inconsiderable manifestations of the laws of Necessity. Such a man may influence the course of events in history.

Nevertheless, Manfred refuses to worship the mere power for change Arimanes represents. He still reverences goodness (II, iv. 43–8). The first Destiny comments on the hold sentiment has upon him: 'the passions . . . | Have pierced his heart', and he is torn apart by the conflict between desire for masculine individualism, with its Satanic implications, and grief and guilt for his lost 'feminine' virtues, personified by Astarte.

Compare the strife within Manfred with that of Goethe's Faust, who declares:

> Two souls possess, within my breast, a station,
> Each would the other from itself divide;
> One clings, in gross and amorous desire,
> Unto the world with organs steely, never free;
> The other rises from the dust to realms far higher,
> To regions of a noble ancestry. (II, 1112–17)[18]

Faust's dichotomy is clearly between body and spirit in this speech. Goethe's heroine, Gretchen, is correspondingly corrupted through sexuality, and transformed from innocent virgin to child-murderer. Though male sexual guilt is common to both plays, Astarte is not so overtly associated with the virtues of domesticity as is Gretchen,

[18] *Goethe's Tragedy of Faust*, trans. C. F. Coxwell (London, 1932), p. 168.

who is presented as Faust's opposite in every way. Byron makes clear, however (what in Gretchen's case Goethe left to God's judgement), that Astarte belongs to the powers of Good. Arimanes himself is unable to commmand her answer; the fact that she replies to Manfred is indicative of his 'mix'd essence' (I, ii. 41), his capacity for sentiment.

It is in the name of the strength of his passion that Manfred is enabled to question the phantom of Astarte (see II, iv. 135–49), whereas it had been the strength of his will that conjured up the spirits of the elements, and the depth of his love of nature that summoned the Witch of the Alps. He asks that he should die, and only Astarte have eternal life: that he should be punished for both (II, iv. 125–31). His chivalry and monogamous romantic love are, of course, typical of the Byronic hero, as opposed to the Gothic villain, and Astarte is relegated to heaven, leaving the masculine hero to exemplify Romantic defiance alone. This is typical of the way nineteenth-century idealization of woman militates against the association of the heroine with heterodoxy. (Shelley's *The Cenci* and Byron's *Heaven and Earth* are the notable exceptions.) The phantom of Astarte now grants him oblivion: 'Manfred! To-morrow ends thine earthly ills' (II, iv. 152). When Manfred takes on the double burden of guilt, he acknowledges the irrevocable separation of himself and Astarte. 'Feminine' goodness may be granted immortality; 'masculine' individualism is inextricably worldly and defiantly faces extinction at death. The final separation of Manfred and Astarte is indicated by her thrice-repeated 'Farewell!' The fact that she vanishes, not to be recalled, may indicate that she has already entered Heaven. Manfred is convulsed by the torture of the final separation, but when we see him again he is, at last, at peace.

Importantly, the acknowledgement of Astarte's feminine goodness by the higher powers frees Manfred himself from any obligation to fear or conform to the traditional Christian view of the afterlife. The Abbot appears in Act III, Scene i, so that Manfred may now defiantly reject the church as an institution, the concept of eternal punishment, the doctrine of salvation, and social responsibility. In the next scene he addresses, instead, the pagan deities, the sun and moon. The former—'Thou material God!' (III, ii. 14)—represents the life-force and reminds him of the Apocryphal story of the race of giants, who worshipped the sun. They were the product of the union of angels and mortal women whose beauty had lured them down from heaven. He regrets mankind's subsequent decline from this earlier integration of body and spirit with its concomitant power and energy.[19]

Although Manfred rejects the comforts of orthodox religion, as offered by the Abbot, neither does he give himself over to the powers of evil. Either of these would relieve him of moral responsibility for his actions. He dies heroically independent in mind, affirming, even in the face of the extinction of his individuality, the 'mix'd essence' which constitutes his humanity, and refusing to minimize either his dust or his deity.

ADAH

In *Cain* Byron even more plainly places his male protagonist between a bad angel and a good woman, but this time the female counterpart is fully dramatized as a character in her own right. Lucifer embodies the principle of reason, whereas Cain's sister-wife, Adah, expresses socializing human feeling—an inextricable mixture of sexual and fraternal love. Cain's rebelliousness is contextualized more specifically than Manfred's, as an example of the ability of an exceptional individual to challenge a repressive ideology—that of the Judaic consciousness of sin. This endeavour is represented as specifically masculine, resulting from Cain's temporary separation from Adah and her humanitarian values, and it culminates in the murderous violence which constitutes a second Fall. But the reuniting of Cain and Adah at the end of the play demonstrates at least the possibility of the integration of the principles of liberty and fraternity, in an ideal humanism. I use the word 'humanism' here to denote release from ecclesiastical authority, and a faith in mankind's autonomous spiritual and intellectual ability to extend human knowledge of the world and take on ethical problems. It will be shown that the play distinguishes this ideal of humanism from atheism, and also from the Godwinian doctrine of human perfectibility.

Adah is one of Byron's most conventional heroines: a passive, gentle, and nurturing wife and mother. It is therefore often

[19] Cf. *Heaven and Earth*, discussed below, 246–60; see esp. 249.

overlooked that she functions, in the structure of the play, as the antithesis of the evil spirit. Modern readers tend either to ignore the character or censure the sentimentalism of her portrayal. Bernard Blackstone, whilst recognizing that Adah's plea for family life in Act III strives with the disturbing speculations incited by the cosmic journey with Lucifer for the domination of Cain's mind, blames Adah's 'very limited intelligence' for her 'bovine' insistence that humanity is naturally gentle (III, i. 140–7), and concludes that she is a mere 'zombie'.[20] Marchand comments that Adah is 'a typical Byronic heroine, passive and utterly devoted to Cain'.[21] Truman Steffan, too, sees her as a 'devoted and dependent wife, who did not think for or of herself'. However, he then goes on to list several speeches of Adah which express her sense of injustice, remorse, hopelessness, and even aggression. He therefore has to deem them 'uncharacteristic', and suggests that she must have 'absorbed a part of Cain's character'.[22] Robert Gleckner, demonstrating 'Byron's complete rejection of God in a almost fullblown nihilism', mentions Adah only once in passing.[23] Many critics lump Adah together with the rest of Cain's family as all similarly unthinkingly obedient. Wolf Hirst does emphasize the importance in the play of the family's humanity which 'can be emulated by mankind and would have prevented the catastrophe', but he fails to discriminate between Adah's position and Adam's: 'The spokesmen for God's position (Adam, Adah, and Abel) are so much Cain's intellectual inferiors as to provide no match for him.'[24]

Whilst it is true that Adah has a limited role in the play, it is no more limited than that of Lucifer. It is, of course, owing to conventional sexual stereotyping that Byron portrays the intuitive and emotional qualities as female, and the rational as male. The poet obviously intended Adah's 'natural' selflessness and familial love as a counterbalance both to Jehovah's patriarchal severity and Lucifer's alienated rationalism. Leigh Hunt argued for such a

[20] Blackstone, *Byron: A Survey*, p. 249

[21] Marchand, *Byron's Poetry*, p. 90.

[22] T. G. Steffan (ed.), *Lord Byron's* Cain*: Twelve Essays and a Text with Variants and Annotations* (Austin, Texas, 1968), p. 64.

[23] Gleckner, *Byron and the Ruins of Paradise*, pp. 323–8.

[24] Wolf Z. Hirst, 'Byron's Lapse into Orthodoxy: An Unorthodox Reading of *Cain*', *K-SJ* 29 (1980), 151–72. Hirst documents and rightly condemns the one-sidedness of *Cain* criticism in persistently identifying Byron with Lucifer's and Cain's views and not giving him credit for dramatic objectivity. Yet his counter-assertion of the play's orthodoxy is too teleological, and ultimately unconvincing.

reading when, in the *Examiner*, he suggested that hostile contemporary critics were wrong 'to imagine that he [Byron] has no other ideas of the Divine Being than the one which his drama puts in so disadvantageous a light. . . . The noble-mindedness which flashes through the darkest and most mistakable parts of this drama, and the character of Adah alone, who makes a god of her affection, would be sufficient to lead thinking and sensitive minds to higher notions of the Deity . . .'.[25]

A reappraisal of Adah's role will show her to be both the chief spokesman for and the embodiment of human-centred values. As Hunt states, she is therefore essential to the correct balance of the play. Byron himself said *Cain* dealt with 'the politics of paradise',[26] by which he meant the relationship between power and religion. The play is set at the time of the first formulation of ideology. Cain is the first individual to challenge an orthodoxy—that of patriarchy—which forms the basis of the earliest religious beliefs, reflecting familial/social organization. The play dramatizes two contrasting views of the first family: originally a democratic, natural, and benevolent society, it is now in the process of crystallizing into a patriarchal institution based on taboos and fear. Adah's discourse and characterization embody the primeval goodness of mankind, now in the process of being superseded by belief in original sin.

Adah is differentiated from Eve, Adam, Abel, and Zillah right from the opening orisons as they make a dawn sacrifice. The latter stress the necessary division and separation entailed in the creation (I, i. 5–8). (We could compare Blake's Urizen here.) They emphasize Jehovah's power (I, i. 1–4), man's obligations to Him (I, i. 12–13), and their fear of further temptation and punishment after the Fall (I, i. 18–21). Their prayers stress Jehovah's greatness and man's lowliness. The first family image their god as a patriarch and a figure of authority. It is Adah whose prayer redresses the balance, by expecting a parent-god to nurture as well as discipline his children. She praises humanity as the 'best and beauteous' beings of

[25] Extracts from Hunt's essays in the *Examiner* of 2 June and 24 February 1822 are given by Steffan, *Cain*, pp. 316–20.

[26] Byron wrote to Tom Moore: 'The consequence is, that Cain comes back and kills Abel in a fit of dissatisfaction, partly with the politics of Paradise, which has driven them all out of it, and partly because (as it is written in Genesis) Abel's sacrifice was the more acceptable to the Deity' (*L&J* v. 368).

creation, and stresses the necessity of loving them. This forms the basis of humanistic pride in mankind:

> God, the Eternal! Parent of all things!
> Who didst create these best and beauteous beings,
> To be beloved, more than all, save thee,
> Let me love thee and them:—All hail! all hail! (I, i. 14–17)

But because of Byron's reluctance to associate an idealized heroine with heterodoxy, Adah's humanism is uneasily combined with her defence of the status quo. She thus persuades Cain with her tears to join with Abel in sacrificing to Jehovah (I, i. 330–4). However, she does suggest a humane alternative to the ritual killings which appease the god's wrath:

> The fruits of the earth, the early, beautiful
> Blossom and bud, and bloom of flowers and fruits;
> These are a goodly offering to the Lord,
> Given with a gentle and a contrite spirit. (III, i. 105–8)

This is apposite, since Cain and Adah are tillers of the soil, not herdsmen. 'Blossom and bud' and 'the fruits of the earth' also suggest the celebration of generation and fertility, which is predicated on her reverence for the life-force. It is notable that Byron amended the account in Genesis and in Gessner's *The Death of Abel* (1761), to make Cain and his sister parents before their expulsion. This is in order that he can have them express a positive and joyous attitude towards their parenthood (particularly in the words of Adah). This makes a contrast with the patriarchalism of the rest of the family, who emphasize the authority of the father-god, not his love.

Adah urges Cain to love humanity: their parents and children (I, i. 433–7). She defines happiness as necessarily social: 'Who could be happy and alone, or good? | To me my solitude seems sin' (I, i. 473–4). Abel, like Lucifer, is childless, and bases his relationship with Jehovah on the role of supplicant son. When he offers the second sacrifice, in Act III, he prostrates himself before the author of his creation, acknowledges mankind's 'great crimes', accepts the 'justice' of their punishment, and equates Jehovah's omnipotence with a presumption of his benevolence (III, i. 223–44). Likewise, in his relationship with his siblings, he observes his place in the patriarchal family and acts accordingly. He urges Cain to partake of the ceremony, not through love, but because, as elder son, it is Cain's place to act as chief priest:

> Brother, I should ill
> Deserve the name of our great father's son,
> If as my elder I revered thee not,
> And in the worship of our God call'd not
> On thee to join me, and precede me in
> Our priesthood—'tis thy place.
> (III, i. 195–9; see also 220–1)

In the same way, because as a male he is superior in patriarchal status to his elder sister, he peremptorily orders her to leave (III, i. 172). This prefigures the restriction of the priesthood and religious ritual to males in Judaism.

Thus although both Abel and Adah are gentle, obedient, and pious, they are clearly differentiated in the nature of their altruism. Adah would die in order that others might go on living an earthly life (III, i. 79), and reveres the idea of atonement in terms of benefiting mankind (III, i. 85–6). But Abel sacrifices himself through reverence for Jehovah's altar, not for humanity: 'I love God far more | Than life' (III, i. 315–16). Significantly, Abel sets 'God' and 'life' in opposition. Abel's dying words begging God's forgiveness for his murderer anticipate those of Christ (III, i. 318–20). Jesus, it is implied, was also a shepherd willingly sacrificed at the behest of his father-god.[27]

Adah, on the other hand, enacts the altruism of deeds, not martyrdom for faith. She does Cain's work for him, offers hospitality to the strange spirit (I, i. 335–43), and demonstrates empathy in her readiness to weep for his unhappiness (I, i. 517–19). Although Lucifer's questions show her to have accepted unquestioningly her father's anthropomorphic god (I, i. 499–509), she never prostrates herself before an altar like Abel. Unlike the rest of the family, she invests her chance of happiness in earthly human society, rather than fixing her hopes and fears on the hereafter:

> Alone I could not,
> Nor *would* be happy: but with those around us,

[27] Note Byron's comment on the belief in Christ as son of God: 'You degrade the Creator, in the first place, by making Him a begetter of children; and in the next you convert Him into a tyrant over an immaculate and injured Being, who is sent into existence to suffer death for the benefit of some millions of scoundrels, who, after all, seem as likely to be damned as ever' (Letter to Hodgson, 13 September 1811, *L&J* ii. 98).

I think I could be so, despite of death,
Which, as I know it not, I dread not, though
It seems an awful shadow—if I may
Judge from what I have heard. (I, i. 466–71)

Adah's outlook is rooted in the material world, in immanence not transcendence. She accepts the cypress (symbolic of death) shadowing her son's sleep as a natural adjunct, unlike Cain who flinches at the sight. When Cain mourns for the lost Eden, she suggests making another paradise on Earth out of human love:

. . . where'er thou art, I feel not
The want of this so much regretted Eden.
Have I not thee, our boy, our sire, and brother,
And Zillah—our sweet sister, and our Eve,
To whom we owe so much besides our birth? (III, i. 39–43)

Most notably of all, of course, only Adah, like Baillie's Jane de Montfort, shows capacity for forgiveness of sin. She is loyal to Cain despite his murder of their brother, whilst Adam banishes and Eve curses him—reflecting the punitive response to be expected of Jehovah.

The reader can perceive the ironic function of Adah as unconsciously representing the fundamental goodness of human and material life, which her religion seeks to deny. As a feminine stereotype, she obediently aligns herself with the status quo, in countering both Lucifer's and Cain's attack on Jehovah. All heart and no intellect, she mouths the repressive ideology which devalues the material nature of humanity—which she, as a Byronic heroine, particularly embodies.

As a young wife and mother, Adah is a potent image of the claims of sentiment. Lucifer's hostility to her indicates that unmitigated rationalism is unable to take human feeling into account in framing an opposing ideology to that of religious orthodoxy. (We could compare Gretchen and Mephistopheles in Goethe's *Faust* here.) Byron therefore indicates the stages towards the climax of the tragedy in terms of how far Cain moves away from his twin and counterpart in the pursuit of reason. Significantly, it is only when he sends her away, to indulge in private rebellious thoughts, that Lucifer appears to him (I, i. 55–98). When she returns, Lucifer flatly refuses to let her accompany Cain on the cosmic journey.

Rationalism is just as patriarchal as religion, it would seem. Abel again sends her away when the two brothers make the fatal sacrifice that leads to murder (III, i. 172). Afterwards, Cain twice orders her to leave him to his shame (III, i. 459, 526). Adah's final refusal to be separated from her twin indicates the necessary accompaniment of 'masculine' reason, aggression, and defiance by 'feminine' sentiment, forgiveness, and endurance.

Lucifer easily defeats Adah in argument, yet she intuitively discovers his weakness:

> I have heard it said,
> The seraphs *love most*—cherubim *know most*—
> And this should be a cherub—since he loves not. (I, i. 420–2)

When Lucifer challenges Cain to choose between love and knowledge, she begs: 'Oh Cain, choose love' (I, i. 432). Lucifer, however, reveals in his catechism of her that, though she has accepted the religion of Jehovah through unquestioned acceptance of orthodoxy (I, i. 497–509), in fact she portrays the god's attributes in her own image—that of a being whose happiness consists of 'diffusing joy'. The ironic disjunction between her own love for humanity and Jehovah's lack of it is pointed out by Lucifer. But because Cain only sees Lucifer's superior debating skill in attacking Jehovah through proving Adah wrong, he fails to realize the significance of Adah's moral superiority to both Jehovah and Lucifer. He is persuaded to leave her temporarily, and the ensuing lessening of her influence is crucial in bringing about the tragedy.

Adah is unable to combat Cain's sense of the inferiority of the materiality of mankind to pure reason, except through citing Judaic ideology, which itself is predicated on man's sinfulness. Cain is therefore susceptible to Lucifer's dichotomy of body and soul. Lucifer suggests that material beauty is in itself of no value except as a symbol of the spiritual (I, i. 499–502) and that only the distant can be truly beautiful (II, ii. 252–4). Cain counters this Platonism by his earthly love for Adah, which makes him assert that her face is more beautiful to him than anything in either earth or heaven:

> All the stars of heaven,
> The deep blue noon of night, lit by an orb
> Which looks a spirit, or a spirit's world,

The hues of twilight—the sun's gorgeous coming—
His setting indescribable, which fills
My eyes with pleasant tears as I behold
Him sink, and feel my heart float softly with him
Along that western paradise of clouds—
The forest shade—the green bough—the bird's voice—
The vesper bird's, which seems to sing of love
And mingles with the song of cherubim,
As the day closes over Eden's walls—
All these are nothing, to my eyes and heart,
Like Adah's face: I turn from earth and heaven
To gaze on it.

(II, ii. 255–68)

His love for Adah represents his own belief in humanity as the only source of value known to mankind. But to Lucifer such love is merely delusion (II, ii. 269–72). Lucifer reduces Adah to mere matter:

But if that high thought were
Link'd to a servile mass of matter, and,
Knowing such things, aspiring to such things
And science still beyond them, were chain'd down
To the most gross and petty paltry wants,
All foul and fulsome, and the very best
Of thine enjoyments a sweet degradation,
A most enervating and filthy cheat
To lure thee on to the renewal of
Fresh souls and bodies, all foredoom'd to be
As frail, and few so happy— (II, i. 50–9)

Cain asserts that human love is transcendent of self. When Lucifer asks if he loves himself, Cain replies:

Yes, but love more
What makes my feelings more endurable
And is more than myself, because I love it. (II, ii. 320–2)

To Lucifer human love is only appetite, which will perish with Adah's beauty (II, ii. 323–6). Byron uses a tradition of the devil's sterility here to emphasize the opposition between Adah's acceptance of and joy in the material world (shared here by Cain, and whenever he recalls Adah), and the disdain for the merely human evinced by both spiritual principles (see II, ii. 274 and note).

Lucifer's cosmic tour has demonstrated that Jehovah is only an earth-centred god, comparable to Arimanes in *Manfred* or Shelley's Jupiter, who operates by the principle of Necessity, but who is himself subject to the life-force of the universe.[28] Both Jehovah and Lucifer are engaged in eternal combat, and both only use mankind as pawns in the power struggle. The point is that, as in *Manfred*, it is made clear that the play's attack on Jehovah does not either imply sympathy for Lucifer or deny the possible existence of a benevolent divinity greater than both of them.

Cain's initial attempt to assert his independence of Jehovah was based on his recognition of the essential goodness of material nature, and he often uses Adah, or images of generation or fruit, to express this, and to question why power over the material is equated with any ultimately benevolent purpose. The image of the lamb's agony pervades the play: Cain is repelled by the dawn sacrifice, recalls the lamb dying from a snakebite, relieved only to demonstrate the power of its maker (II, ii. 289–304), and, of course, is finally roused to violence by the sight of Abel's altar 'with its blood of lambs and kids, | Which fed on milk, to be destroy'd in blood' (III, i. 292–3). Cain challenges Jehovah on behalf of such lambs—Adah and Enoch, and all victims (including the future Christ (I, i. 163–6)) of a religion which threatens the penalty of everlasting punishment. He is helped by Lucifer, who shows him how to use reason and gives him the perspective of (Enlightenment) relativism with which to perceive the prevailing ideology of his society as oppressive. However, the idealism of Lucifer entails a vision of the material as mere mortal matter, devoid of spiritual good. This engenders its own dissatisfaction with the human condition. Love for humanity plays no part on either side in the dualistic war between Lucifer and Jehovah.

When Cain returns from his cosmic journey, therefore, he feels a double repugnance for material life: 'Well said the spirit, | That I was nothing!' (III, i. 68–9). In his enforcement of guilt and punishment Jehovah shares Lucifer's low opinion of humanity:

> . . . what have we
> Done, that we must be victims for a deed
> Before our birth, or need have victims to
> Atone for this mysterious, nameless sin—
> If it be such sin to seek for knowledge? (III, i. 88–92)

[28] See McGann, *Fiery Dust*, pp. 255–73.

Byron is reluctant to portray a woman condoning iconoclasm, so he has Adah reproving Cain by recourse to mere doctrine: 'Jehovah said not that', and 'Alas! thou sinnest now, my Cain; thy words | Sound impious in mine ears' (III, i. 93–4). Yet when Cain challenges her to leave him her reply is unhesitating: 'Never, | Though thy God left thee' (III, i. 94–5). Though she upholds traditional beliefs, Adah's priorities are ultimately human-centred, and her union with the liberal iconoclast, Cain, will outlast her obedient religious orthodoxy. The heroine, too, will reject her religion—not through use of her own intelligence, but through the specifically 'feminine' heroism of putting love for the defiant hero above all else.

It is a shocking measure of just how far Cain has metaphorically travelled from Adah and her life-affirming values during their separation, that he now wishes Enoch dead or never having been born, rather than engender a race born only to suffer. In vindicating the baby's right to life, Adah (unconsciously) refutes both Jehovah's view of man's original sin, and Lucifer's contempt for his material nature:

> Oh Cain! look on him; see how full of life,
> Of strength, of bloom, of beauty, and of joy,
> How like to me—how like to thee, when gentle,
> For *then* we are *all* alike, is't not so Cain?
> Mother, and sire, and son, our features are
> Reflected in each other; as they are
> In the clear waters when *they* are *gentle*, and
> When *thou* art *gentle*. Love us, then, my Cain!
> And love thyself for our sakes, for we love thee. (III, i. 140–9)

Adah stresses gentleness as the trait originally characterizing the human species, regardless of gender and age. The emphasis on Cain's fundamental gentleness reminds us of his capacity for love of natural beauty and his chivalrous concern for the weak, which he has shown throughout (II, i. 98–117; II, ii. 152–60, 255–68, 289–304; III, i. 10–12). His uncharacteristic murderous violence is produced by a combination of angry resistance to unquestioning faith on the one hand, and a corresponding over-valuation of reason on the other, both of which lead him temporarily to despise human 'gentleness' as weakness, associating it with women and children. Adah intuits that Cain's aggression derives from self-disgust at his own material nature: he must learn to love himself. She asks him to bless his own humanity in blessing Enoch (III, i. 149–56). Her declaration that 'a father's blessing may avert | A reptile's subtlety' (III, i. 158–9) shows that her belief in the power of human love is stronger than her religious guilt. The baby is a powerful symbol of innocence, suggesting Rousseauistic repudiation of original sin.

In returning to the theme of *Manfred*—the tragic separation of sentiment and reason—Byron's literal recreation of Biblical myth demonstrates this dualism emerging in primitive mankind in the form of gender polarities, which produce a fallen masculinity in the form both of patriarchalism and a reactive iconoclasm. As Bostetter has written, 'The politics of Paradise was also the politics of the ruling social order of Byron's day . . . Cain's plea is as much political as religious . . . it is directed against the politics of Paradise and therefore of Western society, against those who rule in the name of God.'[29]

Mere reason leads to self-defeating action, as when the philosophy of the Enlightenment brought about the French Revolution. As John Farrell has observed: 'Savage indignation pierces Cain, clouds his vision, and thwarts the humanistic possibilities of his rebellion. His absolute scorn for God develops into an absolute contempt for man.'[30] With tragic irony, Cain slays his brother in the very name of rebelling against blood sacrifice to Jehovah. The shocking crime is not minimized. Moreover, it implies a pessimistic view of man's capability for human perfectibility. However, the moral touchstone of the play is not divine writ, but Adah's human capacity for forgiveness. Henceforth, the fight for Liberty must be accompanied by true Fraternity, and Adah accompanies her twin into the wilderness. Though the play is deeply tragic, her dream of building an earthly paradise does survive as an ideal for the future.

The relationship of Cain and Adah is comparable to that of Manfred and Astarte in that they are identical twins as well as husband and wife. Byron emphasizes the sibling relationship

[29] Edward Bostetter, 'Byron and the Politics of Paradise', *PMLA* 75 (1960), 571–6 (574).

[30] Farrell, *Revolution as Tragedy*, pp. 174–86. Farrell is one of the few critics to mention the contrast between Cain's intellectual partnership with Lucifer and 'his spiritual and sexual partnership with Adah', who, he suggests, is 'the redemptive possibility in his life'.

throughout, in having them refer to each other constantly as brother and sister. This is in order to bring out their companionship born of a shared upbringing, their equality, and the naturalness of a sexual union developing out of friendship. By having Lucifer refer to the future, when the union of their children will be sinful (I, i. 377–83), Byron draws our attention to the relativism of morals. Adah replies:

> Oh my God!
> Shall they not love and bring forth things that love
> Out of their love? have they not drawn their milk
> Out of this bosom? was not he, their father,
> Born of the same sole womb in the same hour
> With me? did we not love each other? and
> In multiplying our being multiply
> Things which will love each other as we love
> Them?—And as I love thee, my Cain! (I, i. 367–75)

We are also meant to compare favourably the Rousseauistic naturalness of the relationship with modern marriage. Indeed, in his delineation of the first family as a whole, Byron is making use of the new ideas of the Enlightenment in looking at an ancient society to trace the relationship between authoritarian power structures and Judaic ideology, in the same way that he introduces the scientific theories of Cuvier into Act II, to put the Judaic version of the cosmos into historical perspective. *Cain* is Byron's pastoral. He depicts the original family before organized government had evolved, untramelled by laws. (These will come later, according to Lucifer, when consciousness of human sinfulness becomes enshrined in a systematic moral code.) Compare Rousseau's description of the original family in his *Essay On The Origin of Languages*: 'Instinct held the place of passion; habit held the place of preference. They became husband and wife without ceasing to be brother and sister.'[31]

Rousseau suggested that the self-sufficiency of the original family was transcended only by passionate romantic love between those not related by kinship, which fully socialized humanity. He also thought economic development gave rise to private property, the second cause of the politicization of the species. It is interesting, and

[31] See Joel Schwartz, *The Sexual Politics of Jean-Jacques Rousseau* (Chicago and London, 1984), pp. 27–30.

significant, that Byron ignored this latter theme; especially as the interrelationship of ideology, wealth, and class is an important theme of Gessner's *The Death of Abel*, one of his sources. Gessner—a fellow Swiss and contemporary of Rousseau's—has his demon make Cain dream that Abel's descendants become wealthy in their flocks and herds. They become 'sons of luxury' leading an indolent life of pastoral idyll, who plan to capture the descendants of Cain, working in the fields, and make them their female household servants and male field-workers. It is anger at the vision of his decendants becoming 'a tribe of slaves' and 'beasts of burthen' that contributes to Cain's murderous rage. Byron, however, omits Cain's resentment of labour, and rejects Rousseau's socio-economic view that property was the principle which developed a hierarchical human society. He emphasizes instead the role of the exceptional (male) individual—even at the dawn of history—in rebelling against the prevailing orthodoxy on purely intellectual grounds. Cain murders out of rage against patriarchal religious ideology: outlawed by parental authority, he creates the first nuclear family unit. Cain's role may be compared to that of Hegel's 'world-historical individuals'. They have 'no consciousness of the general idea they are unfolding'. Yet they express the dialectic of history, by breaking with the old without scruple: 'Such conduct is indeed morally reprehensible, but so mighty a form must trample down many an innocent flower, and crush to pieces many an object in its path.'[32]

By repeating the mirror-image of brother and sister that he had used to represent the divided consciousness of humanity in *Manfred*, Byron is enabled to valorize such self-assertion, for conventional goodness is both acknowledged as ethically superior and yet separated off into the ineffective feminine sphere, in the idealization of Adah. Her loyalty to the hero at the end of the play, however, also serves to underwrite Cain's access to both masculine and feminine values. While masculine self-assertion may result in murderous violence, feminine humanitarian values are identified with unthinking natural instinct and regressive passivity. The ideology of complementary gender roles united by romantic love is thus utilized in the characterization of the twins, to provide an image of liberal humanism as ideally the marriage of these

[32] J. Bronowski and Bruce Mazlish (eds.), *The Western Intellectual Tradition from Leonardo to Hegel* (London, 1960), p. 489.

masculine and feminine principles, in which Liberty would subsume Fraternity.

Adah had previously expressed her own doubts and grief at the human condition, comparably to Cain. She acknowledged that Lucifer tempted her with her own 'dissatisfied and curious thoughts' (I, i. 403); and her belief was challenged by the suggestion that omnipotence is not necessarily benevolence. Lucifer gives her a glimpse into the future when incest will be a sin, and her certainty of the goodness of human love (I, i. 367–75) convinces her of the relativism of morality to its society (I, i. 380–3). She admits the 'dread and toil and sweat and heaviness' of post-Edenic existence (I, i. 359), and that the human heart cannot be tranquil under the conditions of earthly life imposed by Jehovah (I, i. 483–4). It is, however, her human love, rather than her rationalism, which leads her, when her attempt at conciliation of the two brothers' views has failed and ended in tragedy, to leave the society whose ideology is one of condemnation, punishment, and banishment for the sinner, rather than her own forgiveness.

Adah complements the fiery Cain in temperament: being stoical, patient, and serene, not rebellious. Yet, by the end of the play, she is shown to have cast off unthinking obedience to those in hierarchical authority over her, and has learned the necessity for self-assertion (though always in defence of Cain). She reproves her mother and father for their curse and banishment of their son, argues with the angel for Cain's safe future, in the name of mercy, and refuses to obey Cain's instruction to go ahead alone: 'Let us depart together' (III, i. 528).

The play ends with Adah affirming their complementary sexual roles:

> My office is
> Henceforth to dry up tears and not to shed them;
>
> . . . .
>
> Now, Cain! I will divide thy burden with thee. (III, i. 547–51)
>
> Lead! thou shalt be my guide . . . (III, i. 554)

She will nurture and support him; he will lead. Elledge comments:

> Byron epitomizes in a single image the closest approximation to total identification or unification possible between two human creatures: the physical (or sexual) desire for gratification, the emotional (or spiritual or

fraternal) impulse for correspondence with a kindred spirit, and the intellectual necessity for sympathetic communication (whether that communication be complementary or contradictory) between like minds, are joined and fulfilled in the relationship of Cain and Adah.[33]

Whether or not Cain and Adah have been portrayed as having 'like minds' is debatable. Certainly, Byron has idealized the ideology of complementarity of gender roles here as an image of the possible future achievement of the marriage between rebellion and human values.

ANAH AND AHOLIBAMAH

The voice of the Devil

All Bibles or sacred codes have been the causes of the following Errors:

1. That Man has two real existing principles: Viz: a Body & a Soul.
2. That Energy, call'd Evil, is alone from the Body; & that Reason, call'd Good, is alone from the Soul.
3. That God will torment Man in Eternity for following his Energies.

But the following Contraries to these are True:

1. Man has no Body distinct from his Soul; for that call'd Body is a portion of Soul discern'd by the five Senses, the chief inlets of the Soul in this age.
2. Energy is the only life, and is from the Body; and Reason is the bound or outward circumference of Energy.
3. Energy is Eternal Delight.

(William Blake, *The Marriage of Heaven and Hell*, Plate 4)

SPIRIT. War with yourselves, and hell, and heaven, in vain

. . . .

But the same moral storms
Shall oversweep the future, as the waves
In a few hours the glorious Giants' graves.
(*Heaven and Earth*, I. iii. 209–17)

The marriage of heaven and hell is a prophetic vision of the future for Blake in 1790. From the Byronic perspective of the post-revolutionary and increasingly reactionary post-Napoleonic period, the marriage of heaven and earth is set in a forever-lost Golden Age of antiquity, when the earth was peopled with giants, the progeny

[33] Elledge, *Byron and the Dynamics of Metaphor*, pp. 144–5.

of angels and mortal women. But both poets challenge the Judaic concept of sinfulness by asserting the unity of body and soul.

In *Manfred* a hero representative of mankind was poised between heaven and earth on a mountain peak; 'half dust, half deity', he sought to reconcile his aspiring spirit with his materiality. In *Cain* the hero was fatally separated from his humanitarian female twin by his attempt to challenge Judaic orthodoxy with a rationalist critique that prompted an equally low estimation of humanity. (We could compare Book 4 of *Gulliver's Travels*.) In the next mythological drama, *Heaven and Earth*, Byron takes on the very materiality of humanity and demonstrates that nobility arises as a consequence of it, not despite it. Since women have been traditionally more closely associated by the Church with the sins of the flesh, the poet now abandons the Byronic hero, and takes on the challenge of creating heroines who represent mankind in their own right, and not as counterpart figures. The very notion of portraying female materiality and sexuality as heroic is counter to the prevailing custom of depicting chastity as the main quality of a conventional heroine. Thus, as was shown in Chapter 6, Byron rejects the depiction of such female filial obedience as that of Milman's devoutly religious Miriam. He is not content with dramatizing the victimized virgin's defiance of patriarchal tyranny as enacted by Shelley's Beatrice Cenci. By taking a mythological setting the poet is able to portray his heroines literally—not symbolically—challenging divine authority, in the name of the sanctity of human materiality. Heroines who turn the hierarchical notion of the cosmos upside down, by attracting angels down to earth for their love, are not likely to conform to conventional notions of feminine modesty, submissiveness, and passivity. The outspoken and sceptical Aholibamah is a female character with all the defiance of past Byronic heroes, and contrasts with the more conventionally gentle Anah. The sisters together reflect the dialectic of Heaven and Hell which strives within the human breast. The play celebrates both heroines as equally heroic.

The 'angels', 'men', and 'women' of the Dramatis Personae reflect the moral hierarchy of the Judaic cosmos. All the male mortals are members of the elect, chosen to rule on earth, and awarded a place in heaven; all the women characters are condemned to die. In other words, the sexual division of the human characters corresponds to the Judaic dualism of soul and body in the individual. The religious males believe the two women to be wicked and doomed to death, whilst they themselves will gain immortality.

This polarization of sexual and spiritual role is central to the argument of the play. The poet locates the basis of the Judaic sense of human sinfulness in its association of the sexual with the satanic. Byron cites Genesis 6 as his text:

> And it came to pass . . . that the sons of God saw the daughters of men that they were fair; and they took them wives of all which they chose.

E. H. Coleridge, in his edition of *Byron's Works*, assumed that Byron erred from innocence in sympathetically portraying this profane relationship, when he could so easily have made the play impeccably orthodox by translating 'sons of God' as 'sons of Seth', as did Tom Moore in his poem on the same subject.[34] But it is Coleridge and later critics, who have also taken Byron's protestations of the pious and orthodox nature of the play literally, who are too innocent.[35] As Leslie Marchand comments, *Heaven and Earth* was an even more subversive undertaking than *Cain*, for 'the illicit love with the angels was both immoral and sacrilegious'.[36]

What is at issue here is the Old Testament justification of Jehovah's apparently arbitrary punishment of mankind (with the Flood). Whereas Byron, in many ways, is as scrupulous in following Biblical sources as he protested, the kernel of the play turns out to be based squarely on one of the most contentious texts of the Apocrypha. Byron is fighting Judaeo-Christian tradition from the inside, by focusing on the sexual politics of its mythology, once regarded as divine truth. R. H. Charles defines the object of

[34] *Works*, v. 280–1. Coleridge remarks: 'Nothing is so dangerous as innocence, and a little more of that *empeiria* of which Goethe accused him would have saved Byron from straying from the path of orthodoxy.'

[35] According to Paul West, *Byron and the Spoiler's Art* (London, 1960), p. 102, '*Heaven and Earth* illustrates the folly of brooking divine decree.' Marshall, *The Structure of Byron's Major Poems*, p. 155, thinks that the play cannot be insistently anti-Calvinistic, because Japhet does in the end accede to his father's wishes. Joseph, *Byron the Poet*, p. 124, comments: 'In the main, a traditional theology is accepted without apparent examination.' McGann, *Fiery Dust*, pp. 262–73, however, discusses at length Byron's unorthodox attitudes: his regressive theory of history, yet assertion of the possibility of individual fulfilment. In *CPW* he comments: 'Orthodox views find fuller expression in *Heaven and Earth* than in *Cain* . . . ' (*CPW* vi. 683). All quotations are from this edition.

[36] Marchand, *Byron's Poetry*, p. 91.

apocalyptic literature as 'to solve the difficulties connected with the righteousness of God and the suffering condition of his righteous servants on earth'.[37] This theme fascinated the author of *Cain*. Byron certainly knew 'Concerning the Watchers', a fragment of the Apocryphal Book of Enoch, which was preserved in the *Chronographia* of Georgius Syncellus, published in 1606.[38] It is also significant that Laurence's translation of the whole Book of Enoch was published in 1821, the year Byron wrote his play. The Book of Enoch was regarded as a canonical book until the fourth century, when it was banned. Charles comments that its influence on the New Testament was greater than that of all the other Apocryphal books together.[39]

The Book of Enoch is an attempt first, to explain the origin of evil, and, secondly, to justify God's destructive cleansing of the earth by means of the Flood. It takes the brief account of the descent of the angels in Genesis as its starting point, and elaborates a myth in which female sexuality is the cause of all the evils in the world—which in turn necessitate the Flood. The lust aroused in the angels by the beauty of mortal women leads to unnatural sexual union. The progeny of the daughters of Man and the sons of God are giants who introduce forbidden knowledge such as charms, metal-working, ornaments, cosmetics, astrology, fornication, and flesh-eating. The chaos caused by the giants justifies God in sending the Deluge to purify the earth. Though the giants are destroyed by God, their spirits persist even after the Flood, accounting for the everlasting presence of evil, for they cannot be punished until the final judgement. Thus humanity is forever condemned to a dualistic struggle between body and spirit: man is to be endlessly subject to the temptation of Eve, repeat the Fall, and incur God's wrath.

A straightforward version of this material, in the spirit of the Book of Enoch, would therefore involve characterization of the mortal women as evil temptresses. This is indeed how the theme was often treated by writers of the period. For example, in Southey's *Thalaba the Destroyer* (1801) Thalaba repudiates the trap of sexuality which has endowed the sorcerers in the Domdaniel caverns with their evil power. He meets Haruth and Maruth, two

[37] See *The Book of Enoch: translated from Professor Dillmann's Ethiopic Text*, ed. R. H. Charles (Oxford, 1893), pp. 22–4.

[38] *Works*, v. 281.

[39] *Enoch*, p. 41.

angels who fell through lust for an earthly maiden, and who are eventually purged by prayer and repentance. Southey's poem is based on Arabian myth. Genesis 6: 1–2 derives from a comparable Persian account of how demons corrupted the earth before the coming of Zoroaster.[40] Byron may have been aware of this, having himself used Zoroastrian myth in *Manfred* to illustrate the dualism of the material and the spiritual.[41]

It would have been perfectly possible for Byron to write a play in the spirit of the Book of Enoch, portraying a subversive and satanic sexuality as the cause of almost overwhelming evil, and to have seemed as puritanically orthodox as Southey. On the other hand, had he wished to write amatory yet (almost) respectable verse based on Genesis 6, he might have written a eulogy on marriage like Tom Moore. In his *The Loves of the Angels* (1823) Moore uses a sanitized version of the theme to idealize woman—but only on condition she is humble and submissive. The first woman of the three prefers death to seduction. The second woman is destroyed by the illicit embrace of her angel-lover, rightly punished, firstly for taking the sexual initiative, and secondly for choosing a spirit of knowledge. In contrast with her is the third woman—the heroine Nama—who merely passively accepts her celestial wooer, and her reward is marriage with her angel. Condemnation of woman's forwardness is put into the heroine's mouth:

> Even bliss was humbled by the thought—
> 'What claim have I to be so blest?'
> Still less could maid, so meek, have nursed
> Desire of knowledge—that vain thirst,
> With which the sex hath all been cursed,
> From luckless Eve to her, who near
> The Tabernacle stole to hear
> The secrets of the Angels . . .[42]

Thus, woman, if suitably chaste, meek, and obedient—and circumspect in not voicing her own unseemly desires—may receive her apotheosis through matrimony.

When we turn to Byron's play, we see that his heroines are portrayed neither as the snares of sin, as in Southey, nor

[40] *Enoch*, p. 62.
[41] Quinlan, 'Byron's *Manfred* and Zoroastrianism', 726–38.
[42] *Works*, viii. 98–9.

apotheosized when 'good', as in Moore. In *Don Juan* Byron had already portrayed female sexuality as a force of nature, and the comedy of man's subjection to it. In *Heaven and Earth* he takes two female descendants of Eve, themselves perpetrators of a second Fall (see iii, 706), and vindicates them. It is because he makes sympathetic and heroic characters out of his women, whilst at the same time giving their subversiveness its full weight, that Byron's play was so shocking that Murray would not publish it. By idealizing their love yet acknowledging their sexuality, he makes a serious claim for the indivisibility of the spiritual and the material. The myth of their sexual and profane sin is perceived as the product of shame at being human. But Byron's angels explicitly find mortal love superior to the purely spiritual. Their Fall is portrayed as an enrichment because of the desirability of all knowledge and experience, in spite of its mixed nature. In both *Manfred* and *Cain* Byron refers to the era of the race of giants engendered by the women and angels as a Golden Age, not as a pestilence (*Manfred* III, ii. 3–8; *Cain* II, ii. 44–105). It is Jehovah, not the giants, who causes chaos through imposing the Flood.

The unspoken subtext of *Heaven and Earth* is the representation in classical myth of constant interaction, including the sexual, between mortals and immortals. Classical mythology is thus a pagan endorsement of the holiness of material life. In contrast to the natural humanism of paganism is the Judaic hierarchical cosmos, where body and soul are separate. The Flood is a demonstration of Jehovah's low estimation of the worth of humankind, and also a symbol of the injustice of predestining an élite Elect to immortality and the majority to damnation.

But Anah and Aholibamah are proud to be the descendants of Cain, who was begotten in Paradise (iii. 390–1), whose race is noted for its physical beauty and strength (iii. 421–3), and whose independence they have inherited. Byron uses female characters to express a humanist defiance of moral absolutism: their characterization shows how materiality of body, independence of judgement, and subjectivity of emotion can give rise to the highest ideals of altruism and heroism. As modifications of stereotypical femininity, Anah and Aholibamah emancipate themselves through love not intellect, and without the murderous violence of Cain.

Significantly, as the play stands, the heroines survive and escape Jehovah's vengeance. Though he considered it, Byron did not, after all, choose to write a tragic sequel. Neither could he continue the story on a triumphant note:

> I once thought of conveying the lovers to the moon or one of the planets; but it is not easy for the imagination to make any unknown world more beautiful than this . . . .There was another objection: all the human interest would have been destroyed, which I have even endeavoured to give my angels.[43]

This comment shows Byron's concern to portray the beauty of earth and the value of humanity as the highest good which the imagination can conceive. The heroines of *Heaven and Earth* symbolize such human value, in a play, published in Leigh Hunt's *The Liberal*, and written as a philosophical affirmation of Byron's liberal humanism.

Frederick L. Beaty, in his study of love in Romantic literature, has pointed out the frequency of the metaphor of light from heaven in poetic imagery in the period to portray the endowing of earthly subjects and human feelings with spiritual significance. In contrast with much religious literature, the emphasis is always earth-centred.[44] In *Heaven and Earth* this is the dominant image. Whilst the faithful mourn that they cannot ascend to Paradise, the power of the love of woman is such as to draw the angels down.

Anah and Aholibamah together characterize the way femininity, for Byron, encompassed extremes of submissiveness and passion. McGann points out the etymology of the names 'Anah' as 'one who answers', and 'Aholibamah' as 'my tent is exalted'.[45] In expressing her love, Anah is all humility:

> Oh! think of her who holds thee dear!
>   And though she nothing is to thee,
> Yet think that thou art all to her. (i. 44–6)

Aholibamah is full of pride:

> Though I be formed of clay,
>   And thou of beams
> More bright than those of day
>   On Eden's streams,

[43] Byron anticipated and attempted to forestall criticism of the triumphant escape of the heroines from God's wrath by asserting his intention to write a sequel, possibly with a tragic ending. For Medwin's account, see *CPW* vi. 688–9.

[44] Beaty, *Light from Heaven*, pp. xv–xx.

[45] McGann, *CPW* vi. 684.

Thine immortality can not repay
With love more warm than mine
My love. (i. 97–103)

The love of the mortal women is too generous to encompass sexual jealousy (i. 28–32). They would prefer the finality of death to immortality without the beloved (i. 25–8). However, in human terms, their love is eternal: they will be steadfast even under threat of divine retribution, or if the beloved ceases to reciprocate it (i. 119–33). It is a dangerous love, because it weakens religious faith (i. 12–13), but it produces its own covenant and rainbow (i. 149–52), symbol of the spirituality of human feeling.

The women are constantly identified with the earth itself in the play. McGann has noted this briefly,[46] but the topographical and nature imagery is worth considering in detail. The earth is personified as female, and constantly referred to as young. Her approaching destruction is endowed with the heart-rending pathos of the imminent death of Anah: 'True, earth must die! | Her race, return'd into her womb, must wither' (iii. 559–60). So when Japhet soliloquizes on the approaching doom, his grief is alternately for 'the loveliest of earth's daughters' and for the earth itself:

All beauteous world!
So young, so mark'd out for destruction, I
With a cleft heart look on thee day by day,
And night by night, thy numbered days and nights.
I cannot save thee, cannot save even her
Whose love had made me love thee more; (iii. 47–52)

The world is imaged as a colossal female figure. Japhet's description of its beauty and sublimity is in anthropomorphic terms: its peak is 'exulting', it has a 'tremendous brow'; at evening the sun drops 'behind its head', 'leaving it with a crown of many hues' (iii. 22–32). This is the 'spot | Nearest the stars' where angels alight. But beneath lies a fearful cavern, the womb of this world in human shape:

the cavern, whose
Mouth they say opens from the internal world,
To let the inner spirits of the earth
Forth when they walk its surface. (ii. 41–4)

[46] McGann, *Fiery Dust*, p. 262.

Byron's epigraph from Coleridge's *Kubla Khan* is an acknowledgement of its influence.[47] Compare:

> But oh! that deep romantic chasm which slanted
> Down the green hill athwart a cedarn cover!
> A savage place! as holy and inchanted
> As e'er beneath a waning moon was haunted
> By woman wailing for her demon-lover!

Coleridge's chasm is also womblike: it gives birth to the sacred river of life. It is associated with the savagery of nature and with satanic female sexuality. Byron's male characters enact this dread of the cavern of the irrational forces of nature, and its attendant *femmes fatales*. This is a 'dangerous' place to Irad (ii. 47). Noah, who considers the earth itself evil, associates the cave with the powers of darkness:

> It is an evil spot
> Upon an earth all evil; for things worse
> Than even wicked men resort there; (ii. 91–3)

The depths of this cave, 'which seem'st unfathomable' (iii. 2), are the infernal regions of materiality, which Jehovah seeks to purify:

> and yon cave,
> Which seems to lead into a lower world,
> Shall have its depths search'd by the sweeping wave,
> (iii. 10–12)

Within dwell the anarchic spirits of nature who refuse to worship him, and who laugh to scorn those who do, and whose only reward is extermination. They point out to Japhet that the future history of mankind under Jehovah will be one of degeneration, in comparison with the titanic progeny born out of defiance of his segregation of mortal and immortal.

> Thy new world and new race shall be of woe—
> Less goodly in their aspect, in their years
> Less than the glorious giants, who
> Yet walk the world in pride,
> The Sons of Heaven by many a mortal bride. (iii. 129–33)

47 '*Heaven and Earth* may thus be seen as a commentary on 'Kubla Khan' as much as a sequel to *Cain*' (Blackstone, *Byron: A Survey*, p. 250).

The spirits of the earth throw down a challenge to Japhet not to be 'subdued and tamed' (iii. 138) by 'moral storms' (iii. 215); to be ashamed to survive the rest of humanity, by being selected for immortality; to await death with dignity (like Manfred) rather than be alienated from the rest of his species and nature.

It is near this womblike cavern of infernal materiality that Anah and Aholibamah call down their spirit-lovers, and because they are constantly referred to as 'loving dust' (i. 54), 'formed of clay' (i. 96), and 'Earth's daughters' (iii. 473), they are associated with the materiality of earth itself, and the reproductive force of nature. Though, as we shall see, the representatives of religious orthodoxy, Noah and Raphael, see Anah and Aholibamah as *femmes fatales*, the mixed essence of their love will be vindicated by the play.

The beauty of the sisters is constantly remarked upon, like that of the natural world. Beauty is associated with integrity of being. The race of Cain, because of its independence of Jehovah, has retained more of its original physical vigour. Aholibamah cries proudly:

> Look upon
> Our race; behold their stature and their beauty,
> Their courage, strength, and length of days— (iii. 421–3)

An ironic parallel is being drawn between the evident worth of humanity, with its original capacity to evolve and progress (into a race of giants), and Jehovah's low estimation and crushing of the human spirit. In the same way, Irad despises gold because it comes out of the earth:

> . . . the metal of the sons of Cain—
> The yellow dust they try to barter with us,
> . . . such useless and discoloured trash
> The refuse of the earth, . . . (ii. 32–5)

The women characters, Anah and Aholibamah, unite the beauty of materiality and the pathos of its mutability. The Archangel Raphael describes their fate: 'Born to be plough'd with years, and sown with cares, | And reap'd by Death, lord of the human soil' (iii. 605–6). In addition to their conventional feminine role of beauty and pathos, Anah and Aholibamah are also endowed with qualities usually associated with the masculine Byronic hero: rebellion and passion. The complementary characteristics of Adah and Cain are repeated in the contrasting sisters. Anah is humble, devout, stoical;

Aholibamah is proud, freethinking, rebellious. The pattern of their contrasting speeches is stylized, emphasizing their allegorical function as the altruistic and the heroic poles of humanity. They are always seen together, acting together as counterparts, and any tendency towards undue passivity or aggression is immediately counterbalanced. The reader is therefore forced into a liberal acceptance of the plurality of human goodness: unable exclusively to endorse (as does Moore in his *The Loves of the Angels*) the 'feminine' virtues of obedience and submission by condemning Aholibamah at the expense of her meeker sister, because both take the same course of action, so that both are to blame or neither.

Daniel Watkins characterizes the human society represented in the play as 'a paternalistic, restrictive, and authoritarian order that Noah commands as God's regent; it focuses on submission as the central virtue'.[48] I should like to extend Watkins's argument that the play exposes the interconnections of religion and politics, by drawing attention to Byron's use of sexual politics to challenge this patriarchal ideology. The male characters of the race of Seth, as Watkins has shown, are committed to a hierarchical system of authority, under the father-god and his earthly representative, the patriarch Noah. To Noah, Anah and Aholibamah are 'children of the wicked' (iii. 465), *femmes fatales* whose very presence threatens to doom the righteous Japhet (iii. 467). His sons suffer 'forbidden yearnings' (ii. 100) for these women, but a marriage between Japhet and Anah would be out of the question for Noah (ii. 95–6).

The sisters' love for the angels defies the male authority-figures in the play, who are ranged against them in hierarchical order. First their midnight assignment is secret from the head of their family: the play opens with the words 'Our father sleeps'. Then they are rebuked for walking with spirits at too late an hour, by one of the elect, Japhet (iii. 330–1). He informs them their love is forbidden:

> . . . for unions like to these,
> Between a mortal and immortal, cannot
> Be happy or be hallow'd. (iii. 369–71)

In the exchange which follows, Japhet warns them of their imminent death. He himself is protected by right of birth: 'I am safe, not for my own deserts, but those | Of a well-doing sire'

[48] Daniel P. Watkins, 'Politics and Religion in Byron's *Heaven and Earth*', *BJ* 11 (1983), 30–9.

(iii. 380–1). Though Japhet has wept for earth and her children, he accepts the inevitability of the Deluge, and now only seeks to save Anah. But even in his love for Anah he is made uncomfortable by her heritage of sin, and tries to imagine she is really descended from Abel's 'pure pious race' (iii. 402–7). Aholibamah refuses to be ashamed of the Cainites, even the murderer himself who bravely endured his punishment in his lifetime. Her pride in the human spirit is contrasted with the elect who only glory in the immaterial:

> AHOL. I glory in my brethren and our fathers!
> JAPH. My sire and race but glory in their God, (iii. 425–6)

Anah, too, explains that she would rather not be saved at the expense of her brethren. Human love is the light of her existence. She portrays reality as wholly contingent on human consciousness:

> Thy [Aholibamah's] love— my father's—all the life, and all
> The things which sprung up with me, like the stars,
> Making my dim existence radiant with
> Soft lights which were not mine . . . (iii. 436–9)

Anah will stoically 'endeavour patiently to obey' whatever fate brings (iii. 427–9). In contrast with Anah's philosophical idealism, Aholibamah is a materialist. To her, the earth is palpably real in comparison with notions of the spiritual:

> Who
> Shall shake these solid mountains, this firm earth,
> And bid those clouds and waters take a shape
> Distinct from that which we and all our sires
> Have seen them wear on their eternal way?
> Who shall do this? (iii. 449–54)

Aholibamah refuses to imagine that the creator—a god of love—is the same deity as the Jehovah who would destroy this material world. She rejects the concept of divine punishment (iii. 459–60), and is sceptical at Japhet's view that Jehovah expresses his love for mankind by his sorrow at their wickedness.

When Noah appears, the sisters' profane love for the angels is condemned by the patriarch himself.

> Woe, woe, woe to such communion!
> Has not God made a barrier between earth
> And heaven, and limited each, kind to kind? (iii. 474–6)

He advises Japhet that concern for such sinners may threaten his own future as one of the elect:

> Son! son!
> If that thou would'st avoid their doom, forget
> That they exist: they soon shall cease to be,
> While thou shalt be the sire of a new world,
> And better. (iii. 494–8)

Next the Archangel Raphael himself appears to call the angels to their rightful place in Heaven on pain of losing their eternal life. The archangel, like Noah, portrays the sisters as *femmes fatales* whose sexual attraction is specifically described as diabolic:

> . . . he [Satan] cannot tempt
> The angels, from his further snares exempt:
> But man hath listen'd to his voice,
> And ye to woman's—beautiful she is,
> The serpent's voice less subtle than her kiss,
> The snake but vanquish'd dust; but she will draw
> A second host from heaven, to break heaven's law.
> (iii. 587–93)

Judaic myth is perceived as attributing to female sexuality the source of worldly evil. Yet this view is immediately juxtaposed by the heroic and altruistic speeches of the two sisters as they bid the angels to save themselves. Aholibamah exhibits austere stoic bravery: 'Let us resign even what we have adored, | And meet the wave, as we would meet the sword' (iii. 624–5). Anah's concern is only to avoid inflicting suffering on Azaziel and Samiasa: 'My pangs can be but brief; but thine would be | Eternal, if repulsed from Heaven for me' (iii. 661–2).

This nobility of spirit is specifically human. The capacity for love is linked with the human capacity for suffering (i. 71). The angels cannot weep (iii. 673). Though they are seraphs (angels of love) they should be 'passionless and pure' (iii. 715). Yet they find earthly love preferable, and choose the love of woman (iii. 716–22) in spite of the punishment of alienation from Jehovah. Effectively, they preference human love over divine.

The nobility of the sisters is thrown into relief by Jehovah's implacable wrath. Japhet pleads for the lives of Anah and

Aholibamah to God's earthly and heavenly patriarchal representatives:

> Father! and thou, archangel, thou!
> Surely celestial Mercy lurks below
> That pure severe serenity of brow: (iii. 679–81)

Noah exhorts him to 'Be a man!' (iii. 694). Like Abel he defines goodness as blind filial obedience: 'Do God no wrong! | Live as he wills it—die when he ordains' (iii. 686–7). Japhet, however, like Cain, pleads with God to show paternal love: 'Oh God! be thou a God, and spare | Yet while 'tis time!' (iii. 704–5). God's answer is the first flash of lightning. Noah, the earthly father, refuses to let Anah aboard the ark; and is even prepared to let his son die with her for his blasphemy in doubting God's justice. Raphael rebukes him: 'Patriarch, be still a father!' (iii. 764). But Byron's bitter irony is apparent when the archangel goes on to reassure Noah that Japhet's fit of passion is only a temporary youthful aberration; that he will survive to become 'good as thou'. Whilst the whole of humanity come crying for mercy as the waters rise, Noah and Raphael disclaim responsibility for their fate, citing Jehovah's absolute decree. One boards his ark, the other ascends to Heaven.

It is only the rebellious women and the disobedient angels who show selfless, reciprocal love. Azaziel calls:

> Come, Anah! . . . . . .
> . . . . beneath
> The shelter of these wings thou shalt be safe,
> As was the eagle's nestling once within
> Its mother's. (iii. 813–18)

Eros is not extolled at the expense of *agape* in this play, for sisterly love is shown by Anah and Aholibamah, as well as amorous love for the angels (iii. 439–41). Mercy and compassion are notably lacking amongst the elect, with the exception of Japhet.

The angels fly off with the sisters, defying Jehovah's sentence of death. A chorus of mortals, now they realize their fate—arbitrary death and no immortality—burst out into Cain-like defiance of Jehovah:

> But as we know the worst,
> Why should our hymn be raised, our knees be bent

Before the implacable Omnipotent,
Since we must fall the same? (iii. 858–61)

But one, anticipating Christ, embraces his martyrdom. Like Abel in *Cain*, he uses the imagery of patriarchy to justify blind obedience to his creator: 'He gave me life—he taketh but | The breath which is his own' (iii. 887–8).

Japhet is left alone, with the dialectic of defiance and moral absolutism ringing in his ears and the spectacle of divine tyranny before his eyes. It is, significantly, two women who are now brought in to replace the triumphant absent heroines, facing death as innocent victims, whose last thoughts are for others. The mother, like the woman in Poussin's painting, tries to hold her baby above the waves.

Why was he born?
What hath he done—
My unwean'd son—
To move Jehovah's wrath or scorn? (iii. 835–7)

The reader can only respond to such a plea with Byronic scorn for the injustice of Jehovah's predestination of the elect.

Next a woman whose whole family has been swept away paints a picture of human mutuality as an aspect of nature:

Our valley is no more:
My father and my father's tent,
My brethren and my brethren's herds,
The pleasant trees that o'er our noonday bent,
And sent forth evening songs from sweetest birds,
The little rivulet which freshen'd all
Our pastures green
No more are to be seen. (iii. 912–19)

She would rather die with them than be saved alone. Even in the face of extinction, her human love rejects Jehovah's attempt to divide humanity into a moral caste system based on a dichotomy of body and soul: 'And now they are not!—| Why was I born?' (iii. 921–2). Her complete identification with mankind—despite its materiality and mortality—is echoed by Japhet, who, as she too dies, is the last survivor:

Why, when all perish, why must I remain?

Bibliography

PRIMARY SOURCES

BAILLIE, JOANNA, *The Dramatical and Poetical Works* (London, 1851).

BRUNTON, MARY, *Self-Control* (London, 1811; repr. London, 1986).

BURKE, EDMUND, *Reflections on the French Revolution* (London, 1790).

CAMPBELL, THOMAS, *The Poetical Works* 2 vols. (London, 1837).

COLERIDGE, SAMUEL TAYLOR, *Poems*, ed. E. H. Coleridge (Oxford, 1912).

—— Collected Letters, ed. Earl Leslie Griggs, 6 vols. (Oxford, 1956–71).

—— *The Notebooks*, ed. Kathleen Coburn, 3 double vols. (London, 1957–73).

—— *Collected Works*, 16 vols., gen. ed. Kathleen Coburn; vol. 7 (*Biographia Literaria*), ed. James Engell and W. Jackson Bate (Princeton, 1983).

EDGEWORTH, MARIA, *Belinda* (London, 1801).

ENGELS, FREDERICK, *The Origin of the Family, Private Property, and the State*, ed. Eleanor Burke Leacock (New York, 1972).

The Book of Enoch: translated from Professor Dillman's Ethiopic Text, ed. R. H. Charles (Oxford, 1893).

GESSNER, SALOMON, *The Death of Abel*, trans. Mary Collyer (London, 1761).

GOETHE, JOHANN WOLFGANG, *Poems and Ballads*, trans. W. E. Aytoun and Theodore Martin (Edinburgh and London, 1860).

—— *The Tragedy of Faust*, trans. C. F. Coxwell (London, 1932).

GOUGES, OLYMPE DE, *The Rights of Woman*, trans. Val Stevenson (London, 1989).

HAYS, MARY, *Memoirs of Queens, Illustrious and Celebrated* (London, 1821).

INCHBALD, MRS ELIZABETH, *A Simple Story* and *Nature and Art*, ed. W. B. Scott (London, 1880).

MEINERS, CHRISTOPH, *History of the Female Sex*, trans. F. Shoberl, 4 vols. (London, 1808).

MILMAN, Revd HENRY HART, *The Fall of Jerusalem* (London, 1820).

MONTESQUIEU, CHARLES DE, *Œuvres Complètes*, ed. Roger Caillois (Dijon, 1951).

MOORE, THOMAS, *The Poetical Works* (Edinburgh, 1862).

MORE, HANNAH, *Coelebs in Search of a Wife* (London, 1808).

MUNBY, A. N. L. (ed.), *Sale Catalogues of the Libraries of Eminent Persons*, i. *Poets and Men of Letters* (London, 1971).

MURPHY, ARTHUR, *The Grecian Daughter: A Tragedy in Five Acts*, ed. Mrs Inchbald (London, 1816).

OWENSON, SYDNEY (Lady Morgan), *The Wild Irish Girl* (London, 1806).

—— *Woman, or Ida of Athens* (London, 1809).

REIMAN, DONALD (ed.), *The Romantics Reviewed*, Part B, 5 vols. (New York, 1972).

ROGERS, SAMUEL, *Jacqueline* (London, 1814).

ROUSSEAU, JEAN-JACQUES, *Julie ou La Nouvelle Héloïse*, trans. Judith McDowell (University Park, Pa., and London, 1968).

—— *Émile, or Education*, trans. Barbara Foxley (London, 1972).

—— *The Social Contract*, trans. M. Cranston (London, 1968).

ST PIERRE, BERNARDIN DE, *Paul et Virginie* (Paris, 1787).

SCHILLER, FREDERICK, *The Works: Early Dramas and Romances* (London, 1849).

SCHLEGEL, FRIEDRICH VON, *Friedrich Schlegel's 'Lucinde' and the Fragments*, trans. Peter Firchow (Minneapolis, 1971).

SCOTT, Sir WALTER, *The Poetical Works*, ed. J. Logie Robertson (London, 1908).

—— *The Letters of Sir Walter Scott*, ed. H. J. C. Grierson, 11 vols. (London, 1932).

SÉGUR, VICOMTE JOSEPH ALEXANDRE PIERRE, *Women: Their Condition and Influence in Society*, anonymously translated, 3 vols. (London, 1803).

SHELLEY, PERCY BYSSHE, *Poetry and Prose*, ed. Donald H. Reiman and Sharon B. Powers (New York, 1977).

SOUTHEY, ROBERT, *The Poetical Works*, 10 vols. (London, 1837–8).

STAËL, MADAME DE, *Corinne, or Italy*, trans. Samuel Tipper (London, 1807).

—— *De l'Allemagne*, 3 vols. (Paris, 1810; repr. London, 1813).

SWIFT, JONATHAN, *A Tale of a Tub*, ed. Kathleen Williams (London, 1975).

WOLLSTONECRAFT, MARY, *Vindication of the Rights of Woman*, ed. Miriam Kramnick (London, 1975).

—— *Mary* and *The Wrongs of Woman*, ed. Gary Kelly (Oxford, 1980).

SECONDARY SOURCES

ABRAY, JANE, 'Feminism in the French Revolution', *American Historical Review*, 80 (1975), 43–62.

ADBURGHAM, ALISON, *Women in Print: Writing Women and Women's Magazines fron the Restoration to the Accession of Victoria* (London, 1972).

AGRESS, LYNNE, *The Feminine Irony: Women on Women in Early Nineteenth Century English Literature* (Rutherford, NJ and London, 1978).

AGULHON, MAURICE, *Marianne into Battle: Republican Imagery and Symbolism in France 1789–1880*, trans. J. Lloyd (Cambridge, 1981).

ALEXANDER, J. H., *The Lay of the Last Minstrel: Three Essays* (SSEL: Salzburg, 1978).

—— *'Marmion': Studies in Interpretation and Composition* (SSEL: Salzburg, 1981).

ANDERSON, MICHAEL, *Approaches to the History of the Western Family 1500–1914* (London, 1980).

ASHTON, THOMAS, 'Naming Byron's Aurora Raby', *ELN* 7 (1969), 114–20.

—— 'The Censorship of Byron's *Marino Faliero*', *Huntington Library Quarterly*, 36 (1972–3), 27–45.

—— '*Marino Faliero*: Byron's "Poetry of Politics"', *SiR* 13 (1974), 1–13.

BARRETT, MICHÈLE, *Women's Oppression Today: Problems in Marxist Feminist Analysis* (London, 1980).

—— 'Ideology and the Cultural Production of Gender', in Judith Lowder Newton and Deborah Rosenfelt (eds.), *Feminist Criticism and Social Change* (New York and London, 1985), pp. 65–85.

BARTON, ANNE, '"A Light to Lesson Ages": Byron's Political Plays', in J. D. Jump (ed.), *Byron: A Symposium* (London, 1975), pp. 138–62.

BAUER, N. STEPHEN, 'Romantic Poets and Radical Journalists', *NM* 79 (1978), 266–75.

BEATTY, BERNARD, *Byron's* Don Juan (London, 1985).

—— and NEWEY, VINCENT (eds.), *Byron and the Limits of Fiction* (Liverpool, 1988).

BEATY, FREDERICK L., 'Byron and Francesca da Rimini', *PMLA* 75 (1960), 395–401.

—— 'Byron's Concept of Ideal Love', *K-SJ* 12 (1963), 38–54.

—— 'Harlequin Don Juan', *JEGP* 67 (1968), 395–405.

—— 'Byron on Malthus and the Population Problem', *K-SJ* 18 (1969), 17–26.

—— *Light from Heaven: Love in British Romantic Literature* (Dekalb, Ill., 1971).

—— *Byron the Satirist* (Dekalb, Ill., 1985).

BECK, LOIS, and KEDDIE, NIKKI (eds.), *Women in the Moslem World* (Cambridge, Mass., 1978).

BLACKSTONE, BERNARD, *Byron: A Survey* (London, 1975).

BLOCH, JEAN H., 'Women and the Reform of the Nation', in Eva Jacobs *et al.* (eds.), *Woman and Society in Eighteenth Century France: Essays in Honour of John Stephenson Spink* (London, 1979), pp. 3–18.

BOOTH, MICHAEL R., SOUTHERN, RICHARD, MARKER, FREDERICK and LISE-LONE, and DAVIES, ROBERTSON (eds.), *The Revels History of Drama in English*, vi. 1750–1880 (London, 1975).

BOSTETTER, EDWARD, 'Byron and the Politics of Paradise', *PMLA* 75 (1960), 571–6.

—— *The Romantic Ventriloquists* (Seattle, 1963).

BOYD, ELIZABETH FRENCH, *Byron's* Don Juan (New Brunswick, 1945; repr. New York, 1958).

BROGLIE, GABRIEL DE, *Ségur sans cérémonie 1757–1805 ou la gaieté libertine* (Paris, 1977).

BRONOWSKI, JACOB, and MAZLISH, BRUCE (eds.), *The Western Intellectual Tradition from Leonardo to Hegel* (London, 1960).

BROWN, WALLACE CABLE, 'Byron and English Interest in the Near East', *SP* 34 (1937), 55–64.

BRUNSCHWIG, HENRI, *Enlightenment and Romanticism in Eighteenth Century Prussia*, trans. Frank Jellinek (Chicago and London, 1974).

BUTLER, E. M., *Byron and Goethe* (London, 1956).

BUTLER, MARILYN, *Jane Austen and the War of Ideas* (Oxford, 1975).

—— *Romantics, Rebels, and Reactionaries* (Oxford, 1981).

—— 'The Orientalism of Byron's *Giaour*', in BEATTY and NEWEY (eds.), 78–96.

—— 'Repossessing the Past : The Case for an Open Literary History', in Majorie Levinson *et al.* (eds.), *Rethinking Historicism: Critical Readings in Romantic History* (Oxford, 1989).

—— 'Romantic Manichaeism: Shelley's "On the Devil and Devils" and Byron's Mythological Dramas', in J. B. Bullen (ed.), *The Sun is God: Painting, Literature and Mythology in the Nineteenth Century.* (Oxford, 1989), 13–37.

BUXTON, JOHN, 'Greece in the Imagination of Byron and Shelley', *BJ* 4 (1976), 76–89.

CALDER, JENNI, 'The Hero as Lover: Byron and Women', in Alan Bold (ed.), *Byron: Wrath and Rhyme* (London, 1983), 103–24.

CAMERON, VIVIAN, 'Gender and Power: Images of Women in Late Eighteenth Century France', *History of European Ideas*, 10 (1989), 309–32.

CANOVAN, MARGARET, 'Rousseau's Two Concepts of Citizenship', in Ellen Kennedy and Susan Mendus (eds.), *Women in Western Political Philosophy: Kant to Nietzche* (Brighton, 1987), 78–105.

CARNALL, GEOFFREY, *Robert Southey* (London, 1944).

CAVE, RICHARD, 'Romantic Drama in Performance', in id. (ed.), *The Romantic Theatre: An International Symposium* (Gerrards Cross, 1986), 79–104.

CHRISTENSEN, JEROME, 'Byron's Career: The Speculative Stage', *ELH* 52 (1985), 59–84.

—— '*Marino Faliero* and the Fault of Byron's Satire', *SiR* 24 (1985), 313–33.

CIXOUS, HÉLÈNE, 'Sorties: Out and Out: Attacks/Ways out/Forays', in David Lodge (ed.), *Modern Criticism and Theory: A Reader* (London and New York, 1988), pp. 287–93.

CLANCY, C. J., 'Aurora Raby in *Don Juan*: A Byronic Heroine', *K-SJ* 28 (1979), 28–34.

—— 'Death and Love in Byron's *Sardanapalus*', *BJ* 10 (1982), 56–70.

CLINTON, KATHERINE B., 'Femme et Philosophe: Enlightenment Origins of Feminism', *Eighteenth Century Studies*, 3 (1975), 283–99.

COLEMAN, PATRICK, *Rousseau's Political Imagination: Rule and Representation in the Lettre à d'Alembert* (Geneva, 1984).

CONANT, MARTHA PIKE, *The Oriental Tale in England in the Eighteenth Century* (Columbia, NY, 1908; repr. London, 1966).

COOKE, MICHAEL. G., 'The Restoration Ethos of Byron's Classical Plays', *PMLA* 79 (1964), 569–78.

—— *The Blind Man Traces The Circle: On the Patterns and Philosophy of Byron's Poetry* (Princeton, 1969).

—— 'Byron's *Don Juan*: The Obsession and Self-discipline of Spontaneity', *SiR* 14 (1975), 285–302.

—— *Acts of Inclusion: Studies Bearing on an Elementary Theory of Romanticism* (New Haven, Conn., and London, 1979).

COOLE, DIANA H., *Women and Political Theory from Ancient Misogyny to Contemporary Feminism* (Brighton, 1988).

COTT, NANCY F., 'Passionlessness: An Interpretation of Victorian Sexual Ideology 1790–1850', *Signs*, 2 (1978), 219–36.

CURRAN, STUART, 'Shelleyan Drama', in CAVE (ed.), pp. 61–78

—— 'The I Altered', in MELLOR (ed.), 185–207.

DEEN, LEONARD W., 'Liberty and License in Byron's *Don Juan*', *TSLL* 8 (1968), 345–57.

DENGLER, IAN C., 'Turkish Women in the Ottoman Empire', in BECK and KEDDIE (eds.), 229–44.

DIAKONOVA, NINA, 'The Russian Episode in Byron's *Don Juan*', *Ariel*, 3 (1972), 50–7.

DIJKSTRA, BRAM, 'The Androgyne in Nineteenth-Century Art and Literature', *Comparative Literature*, 26 (1974), 62–73.

DONOHUE, JOSEPH, *Theatre in the Age of Kean* (Oxford, 1975).

DRONKE, PETER, *Medieval Latin and the Rise of the European Love Lyric* (Oxford, 1965).

DUFFY, EDWARD, *Rousseau in England: The Context For Shelley's Critique of the Enlightenment* (Berkeley, 1979).

DUNPHY, JOCELYN, 'Insurrection and Repression: Bligh's 1790 Narrative of the Mutiny on Board H.M. Ship Bounty', in Francis Barker (ed.), *1789: Reading, Writing, Revolution* (Proceedings of the Essex Conference on the Sociology of Literature, July 1981) (University of Essex, 1982) pp. 281–301.

EAGLETON, TERRY, 'Ideology and Scholarship', in MCGANN (ed.), 114–25.

ELLEDGE, W. P., *Byron and the Dynamics of Metaphor* (Nashville, 1968).

—— 'Divorce Italian Style: Byron's *Beppo*', *MLQ* 46 (1985), 29–47.

ELLIS, JAMES, 'A Great Reckoning in a Little Room: English Plays of the Nineteenth Century', *Nineteenth Century Theatre Research*, 5 (1977), 27–42.

ELSHTAIN, JEAN BETHKE (ed.), *The Family in Political Thought* (Brighton, 1982).

ERDMAN, D. V., 'Byron's Stage Fright: The History of his Ambition and Fear of Writing for the Stage', *ELH* 6 (1939), 219–43.

—— 'Byron and Revolt in England', *Science and Society*, 11 (1947), 234–48.

—— ' "Fare thee Well"—Byron's Last Days in England', in K. N. Cameron (ed.), *Romantic Rebels: Essays on Shelley and His Circle* (Cambridge, Mass., 1961), 638–53.

—— 'Byron and "the New Force of the People" ', *K-SJ* 11 (1962), 47–64.

EVANS, BERTRAND, 'Manfred's Remorse and Dramatic Tradition', *PMLA* 62 (1947), 752–3.

—— *Gothic Drama fom Walpole to Shelley* (London, 1947).

EVANS, JUDITH *et al.*, *Feminism and Political Theory* (London, 1986).

FARRELL, JOHN P., *Revolution As Tragedy: The Dilemma of the Moderate from Scott to Arnold* (Ithaca, NY, and London, 1980).

FINLAY, ROBERT, *Politics in Renaissance Venice* (London, 1980).

FLECK, PAUL, 'Romance in Byron's *The Island*', in JUMP (ed.), 163–83.

—— 'Romance in *Don Juan*', *University of Toronto Quarterly*, 45 (1976), 93–108.

FLEENOR, JULIANN E. (ed.), *The Female Gothic* (London, 1983).

FOUCAULT, MICHEL, *The History of Sexuality*, Vol. 1: An Introduction trans. R. Hurley (London, 1976).

FOWLER, ALASTAIR, *Kinds of Literature: An Introduction to the Theory of Genres and Modes* (Oxford, 1982).

FRANKLIN, CAROLINE, 'The Influence of Madame de Staël's Account of Goethe's *Die Braut von Korinth* in *De l'Allemagne* on the Heroine of Byron's *The Siege of Corinth*', *N&Q* NS 35, no.3 (Sept. 1988), 307–10.

FRIEDRICHSMEYER, SARA, 'Romanticism and the Dream of Androgynous Perfection', in Theodore G. Gish and Sandra G. Frieden (eds.), *English and German Romanticism: Cross-currents and Controversy* (Papers from the University of Houston Third Symposium on Literature and the Arts) *Houston German Studies*, 5 (1984), 67–75.

GARBER, FREDERICK, *Self, Text, and Romantic Irony: The Example of Byron* (Princeton, 1988).

GATENS, MOIRA, 'Rousseau and Wollstonecraft: Nature vs. Reason', *Australian Journal of Philosophy*, supplement to vol. 64 (1986), 1–15.

—— ' "The Oppressed State of My Sex": Wollstonecraft on Reason, Feeling, and Equality', in SHANLEY and PATEMAN (eds.), 112–28.

GERIN, WINIFRED, 'Byron's Influence on the Brontës', *K-SMB* 17 (1966), 1– 19.

GILBERT, SANDRA, 'What Do Feminist Critics Want? A Postcard from the Volcano', in SHOWALTER (ed.), 29–45.

—— and GUBAR, SUSAN, *The Madwoman in the Attic: The Woman Writer in the 19th Century* (New Haven, Conn., 1979).

GIROUARD, MARK, *The Return to Camelot: Chivalry and the English Gentleman* (New Haven, Conn., and London, 1981).

GLECKNER, ROBERT F., *Byron and the Ruins of Paradise* (Baltimore, 1967).

GOLDBERG, LEONARD, 'Center and Circumference in Byron's *Lara*', *SEL* 26 (1986), 655–73.

GOSLEE, NANCY MOORE, 'Women in Scott's Narrative Poetry', in MELLOR (ed.), 115–38.

GRAHAM, PETER W., 'A "Polished Horde": The Great World in *Don Juan*', [*Byron and the Regency:* 1] *Bulletin of Research in the Humanities*, 86:3 (1983–5), 255–68.

—— Don Juan *and Regency England* (Charlottesville, Va., and London, 1990).

GREENE, GAYLE, and KAHN, COPPÉLIA (eds.), *Making a Difference: Feminist Literary Criticism* (London, 1985).

HAGELMAN, CHARLES H., and BARNES, ROBERT J., *A Concordance to Byron's* Don Juan (New York, 1967).

HELMICK, E. T., 'Hellenism in Byron and Keats', *K-SMB* 22 (1971), 18–27.

HIGHET, GILBERT, *The Classical Tradition: Greek and Roman Influences on Western Literature* (Oxford, 1949).

HIRST, WOLF Z., 'Byron's Lapse into Orthodoxy: An Unorthodox Reading of *Cain*', *K-SJ* 29 (1980), 151–72.

HOFKOSH, SONIA, 'The Writer's Ravishment: Women and the Romantic Author—The Example of Byron', in MELLOR (ed.), 93–114.

HORN, ANDRÁS, *Byron's* Don Juan *and the Eighteenth Century Novel* (Winterthur, 1962; repr. 1969).

HOBSBAWM, ERIC, 'Man and Woman in Socialist Iconography', *History Workshop Journal*, 6 (1978), 121–38.

HOLMES, RICHARD, *Coleridge: Early Visions* (London, 1989).

HOWARTH, DAVID, *Tahiti: A Paradise Lost* (London, 1983).

HULL, GLORIA T., 'The Byronic Heroine and Byron's *The Corsair*', *Ariel*, 9 (1978), 71–83.

—— 'Women in Byron's Poetry: A Biographical and Critical Study' (unpublished Ph.D. thesis. Purdue University, 1972).

HUME, ROBERT D., '*The Island* and the Evolution of Byron's Tales', in W. Paul Elledge and Richard L. Hoffman (eds.), *Romantic and Victorian Studies in Memory of W. H. Marshall* (Rutherford, NJ, 1971).

HUNT, LYNN, 'Engraving the Republic: Prints and Propaganda in the French Revolution', *History Today*, 30 (1980), 11–17.

—— *Politics, Culture, and Class in the French Revolution* (Berkeley, 1984).

JAMESON, FREDRIC, *The Political Unconscious: Narrative as a Socially Symbolic Act* (London, 1981).

JOHNSON, EDGAR, *Sir Walter Scott, The Great Unknown*, 2 vols. (London, 1970).

JOHNSON, E. D. H., 'A Political Interpretation of Byron's *Marino Faliero*', *MLQ* 3 (1942), 417–25.

JOSEPH, M. K., *Byron the Poet* (London, 1964).

JUMP, JOHN D. (ed.), *Byron: A Symposium* (London, 1975).

KAHN, ARTHUR D., 'Seneca and *Sardanapalus*: Byron, the Don Quixote of Neo-Classicism', *SP* 66 (1969), 654–71.

KAPLAN, CORA, 'Pandora's Box: Subjectivity, Class, and Sexuality in Socialist Feminist Criticism', in GREENE and KAHN (eds.), 146–76.

KELLY, LINDA, *Women of the French Revolution* (London, 1987).

KELSALL, MALCOLM, 'Goethe, Byron, Ibsen: The Faustian Idea on Stage', *BJ* 6 (1978), 66–76.

—— *Byron's Politics* (Brighton, 1987).

KERNAN, ALVIN, *The Plot of Satire* (New York, 1965).

KERNBERGER, KATHERINE, 'Power and Sex: The Implications of Role Reversal in Catherine's Russia', *BJ* 10 (1982), 42–9.

KNIGHT, G. WILSON, *The Golden Labyrinth: A Study of British Drama* (London, 1962).

KROEBER, KARL, *Romantic Narrative Art* (Madison, Wis., 1960).

LACQUEUR, THOMAS W., 'The Queen Caroline Affair: Politics and Art in the Reign of George IV', *JMH* 14 (1982), 417–66.

—— 'Orgasm, Generation, and the Politics of Reproductive Biology', *Representations*, 14 (1986), 1–41.

LANDES, JOAN B., *Women and the Public Sphere in the Age of the French Revolution* (Ithaca, NY, and London, 1988).

LEGATES, MARLENE, 'The Cult of Womanhood in Eighteenth Century Thought', *Eighteenth Century Studies*, 10 (1976), 21–39.

LUKÁCS, GEORG, *Goethe and His Age*, trans. Robert Anchor (London, 1968).

LUKE, HUGH J., Jr., 'The Publishing of Byron's *Don Juan*,' *PMLA* 80 (1965), 199–209.

LUKE, K. MCCORMICK, 'Lord Byron's *Manfred*: A Study of Alienation from Within', *University of Toronto Quarterly*, 40 (1970), 15–26.

MCDONALD, SHEILA J., 'The Impact of Libertinism on Byron's *Don Juan*', *[Byron and the Regency: 3] Bulletin of Research in the Humanities*, 86: 3 (1983–5), 291–317.

MCGANN, JEROME J., *Fiery Dust: Byron's Poetic Development* (Chicago, 1968).

—— Don Juan *in Context* (Chicago, 1976).

—— (ed.), *Historical Studies and Literary Criticism* (Madison, Wis., 1985).

—— *The Beauty of Inflections: Literary Investigations in Historical Method and Theory* (Oxford, 1988).

MANNING, PETER J., 'Edmund Kean and Byron's Plays' *K-SJ*, 21 (1973), 188–206.

—— *Byron and his Fictions* (Detroit, 1978).

MARCHAND, LESLIE A., *Byron: A Biography*, 3 vols. (New York, 1957).

—— 'Byron's Hellenic Muse', *BJ* 3 (1975), 66–76.

—— *Byron's Poetry: A Critical Introduction* (Boston, 1965).

MARSHALL, W. H., 'The Accretive Structure of Byron's *The Giaour*', *MLN* 76 (1961), 502–9.

—— *The Structure of Byron's Major Poems* (Philadelphia, 1962).

—— 'The Catalogues for Sale of Lord Byron's Books', *Library Chronicle*, 34 (1968), 24–50.

MARTIN, PHILIP W., *Byron, a Poet Before his Public* (Cambridge, 1982).

MEACHEN, EDWARD, 'History and Transcendence in Robert Southey's Epic Poems', *SEL* 19 (1979), 589–608.

MELLOR, ANNE K., 'Blake's Portrayal of Women', *Blake: An Illustrated Quarterly*, 16: 3 (1982–3), 148–55.

—— (ed.), *Romanticism and Feminism* (Bloomington, Ill., and Indianapolis, 1988).

MILLETT, KATE, *Sexual Politics* (London, 1969; repr. 1981).

MITCHELL, HANNAH, 'Art and the French Revolution: An Exhibition at the Musée Carnavalet', *History Workshop Journal*, 5 (1978), 123–45.

MOERS, ELLEN, *Literary Women: The Great Writers* (New York, 1977).

MORPHOPOULOS, PANOS, 'Byron's Translation and Use of Modern Greek Writings', *MLN* 54 (1938), 317–26.

MYERS, MITZI, 'Reform or Ruin: "A Revolution in Female Manners"', *Studies in the Eighteenth Century*, 11 (1982), 199–216.

NICOLSON, HAROLD, *The Age of Reason (1700–1789)* (London, 1960).

OFFREN, KAREN, 'The New Sexual Politics of French Revolutionary Historiography', *French Historical Studies*, 16 (1990), 909–22.

OGLE, ROBERT B., 'The Metamorphosis of Selim: Ovidian Myth in *The Bride of Abydos II*', *SiR* 20 (1981), 21–31.

OKIN, SUSAN M., *Women in Western Political Thought* (Princeton, 1979).

ORTNER, SHERRY B., 'Is Female to Male as Nature is to Culture?', in Michelle Z. Rosaldo and Louise Lamphere (eds.), *Woman, Culture, and Society* (Stanford, 1974), pp. 67–88.

OSTRIKER, A., 'Desire Gratified and Ungratified: William Blake and Sexuality', *Blake: An Illustrated Quarterly*, 16 (1982–3), 156–65.

OUTRAM, DORINDA, *The Body and the French Revolution: Sex, Class, and Political Culture* (New Haven, Conn., and London, 1989).

PAULSON, RONALD, *Representations of Revolution (1789–1820)* (New Haven, Conn., and London, 1983).

PICKERING, SAM, 'Hannah More's *Coelebs in Search of a Wife* and the Respectability of the Novel in the Nineteenth Century', *NM* 78 (1977), 78–85.

PIKOULIS, JOHN, 'Scott and "Marmion": The Discovery of Identity', *MLR* 66 (1971), 738–50.

PRANDI, JULIE D., *Spirited Women Heroes: Major Female Characters in the Dramas of Goethe, Schiller, and Kleist* (Berne, Frankfurt-on-Main, and New York, 1983).

QUINLAN, MAURICE, 'Byron's *Manfred* and Zoroastrianism', *JEGP* 57 (1958), 726–38.

RABINE, LESLEY, *Reading the Romantic Heroine: Text, History, Ideology* (Ann Arbor, Mich., 1985).

RAPF, JOANNA, E., 'The Byronic Heroine: Incest and the Creative Process', *SEL* 21 (1981), 637–45.

REA, THOMAS, *Schiller's Dramas and Poems in England* (London, 1906).

RENDALL, JANE, *The Origins of Modern Feminism: Women in Britain, France, and the United States, 1780–1860* (London, 1985).

RICHARDSON, ALAN, 'The Dangers of Sympathy: Sibling Incest in English Romantic Poetry', *SEL* 25 (1985), 737–54.

—— 'Romanticism and the Colonization of the Feminine', in MELLOR (ed.), 13–25.

RIDENOUR, GEORGE, *The Style of* Don Juan (New Haven, Conn., 1960).

RILEY, DENISE, *'Am I That Name?': Feminism and the Category of 'Women' in History* (Minneapolis, 1988).

ROBERTSON, MICHAEL, 'The Byron of *Don Juan* as Whig Aristocrat', *TSLL* 16 (1976), 709–24.

—— 'Aristocratic Individualism in Byron's *Don Juan*', *SEL* 17 (1977), 636–55.

ROGERS, KATHARINE M., *Feminism in Eighteenth Century England* (Brighton, 1982).

—— 'Subversion of Patriarchy in *Les Lettres Persanes*', *PQ* 65 (1986), 61–78.

ROSS, MARLON B., 'Scott's Chivalric Pose: The Function of Metrical Romance in the Romantic Period', *Genre*, 18 (1986), 267–97.

ROSS, MARLON B., *The Contours of Masculine Desire: Romanticism and the Rise of Women's Poetry* (Oxford, 1989).

ROUGEMONT, DENIS DE, *The Myths of Love*, trans. Richard Howard (London, 1963).

RUTHERFORD, ANDREW, *Byron: A Critical Study* (Edinburgh, 1962).

SAID, EDWARD W., *Orientalism* (London, 1978).

ST. CLAIR, WILLIAM, *That Greece Might Still Be Free* (Oxford, 1972).

SCHENK, H. G., *The Mind of the European Romantics: An Essay in Cutural History* (London, 1966; repr. Oxford, 1979).

SCHIEBINGER, LONDA, *The Mind Has No Sex?: Women in the Origins of Modern Science* (Cambridge, Mass., and London, 1989).

SCHWARTZ, JOEL, *The Sexual Politics of Jean-Jacques Rousseau* (Chicago and London, 1984).

SEED, DAVID, '"Disjointed Fragments": Concealment and Revelation in *The Giaour*', *BJ* 18 (1990), 14–27.

SHAFFER, E. S., *'Kubla Khan' and* The Fall of Jerusalem*: The Mythological School in Biblical Criticism and Secular Literature 1770–1880* (Cambridge, 1975).

SHANLEY, MARY, 'Marriage Contract and Social Contract in Seventeenth Century English Political Thought', in ELSHTAIN (ed.), 80–95.

—— and PATEMAN, CAROLE (eds.), *Feminist Interpretations and Political Theory* (Cambridge, 1991).

SHERBO, ARTHUR, *English Sentimental Drama* (East Lansing, Mich., 1957).

SHILSTONE, FREDERICK W., *Byron and the Myth of Tradition* (Lincoln, Nebr., and London, 1988).

SHOWALTER, ELAINE (ed). *The New Feminist Criticism* (London, 1986).

SMITH, BERNARD, *European Vision and the South Pacific, 1768–1850: A Study of the History of Art and Ideas* (Oxford, 1960).

SOLOMOU, KIRIAKOULA, 'The Influence of Greek Poetry on Byron', *BJ* 10 (1982), 4–19.

SPENCE, GORDON, 'The Moral Ambiguity of *Marino Faliero*', *AUMLA* 41 (1974), 6–17.

—— 'Moral and Sexual Ambivalence in *Sardanapalus*', *BJ* (1984), 59–69.

SPENCER, JANE, *The Rise of the Woman Novelist* (Oxford, 1986).

SPENDER, DALE, *Mothers of the Novel: 100 Good Women Writers Before Jane Austen* (London, 1986).

SPERRY, STUART M., 'Byron and the Meaning of *Manfred*', *Criticism*, 16 (1974), 189–202.

STEFFAN, TRUMAN GUY (ed.), *Lord Byron's* Cain: Twelve Essays and a Text with Variants and Annotations (Austin, Texas, 1968).

—— 'The Rank of Lord Henry and Lady Adeline', *N&Q* 218 (August 1973), 290–1.

STONE, LAWRENCE, *The Family, Sex, and Marriage in England 1500–1800* (London, 1977).

SUNDELL, MICHAEL G., 'The Development of *The Giaour*', *SEL* 9 (1969), 587–99.

TAYLER, IRENE and LURIA, GINA, 'Gender and Genre: Women in British Romantic Literature', in Marlene Springer (ed.), *What Manner of Woman: Essays on English and American Life and Literature* (Oxford, 1978), pp. 98–124.

TAYLOR, BARBARA, *Eve and the New Jerusalem: Socialism and Feminism in the Nineteenth Century* (London, 1983).

THORSLEV, PETER L., *The Byronic Hero: Types and Prototypes* (Minneapolis, 1962).

—— 'Incest as Romantic Symbol', *Comparative Literature Studies*, 2 (1965), 41–58.

TOMASELLI, SYLVANA, 'The Enlightenment Debate on Women', *History Workshop Journal*, 20 (1985), 100–24.

TRUDGILL, ERIC, *Madonnas and Magdalens: The Origins and Development of Victorian Sexual Attitudes* (London, 1976).

VASSALLO, PETER, *Byron: The Italian Literary Influence* (London, 1984).

VITAL, ANTHONY, 'Lord Byron's Embarrassment: Poesy and the Feminine', [*Byron and the Regency:* 2] *Bulletin of Research in the Humanities*, 86: 3 (1983–5), 269–90.

VITALE, MARINA, 'The Domesticated Heroine in Byron's *The Corsair* and William Hone's Prose Adaptation', *Literature and History*, 10 (1984), 72–94.

VOGEL, URSULA, 'Rationalism and Romanticism: Two Strategies for Women's Liberation', in EVANS, Judith *et al.* (eds.), 17–46.

WATKINS, DANIEL P., 'Violence, Class Consciousness, and Ideology in Byron's History Plays', *ELH* 48 (1981), 799–816.

—— 'Politics and Religion in Byron's *Heaven and Earth*', *BJ* 11 (1983), 30–9.

—— *Social Relations in Byron's Eastern Tales* (London and Toronto, 1987).

WEST, PAUL, *Byron and the Spoiler's Art* (London, 1960).

WIENER, HAROLD, 'Byron and the East: Literary Sources of the "Turkish Tales"', in Herbert Davis, W. C. de Vane, and R. C. Bald (eds.), *Nineteenth Century Studies Dedicated to C. S. Northup* (New York, 1940), pp. 89–129.

WILKIE, BRIAN, *Romantic Poets and Epic Tradition* (Milwaukee, 1965).

WILLIAMS, DAVID, 'The Fate of French Feminism: Boudier de Villemert's "Ami des Femmes"', *Eighteenth Century Studies*, 14 (1980), 37–55.

WOLFSON, SUSAN J., '"Their She Condition": Cross-Dressing and the Politics of Gender in *Don Juan*', *ELH* 54 (1987), 585–617.

—— 'Couplets, Self and *The Corsair*', *SiR* 27 (1988), 491–513.

—— '"A Problem Few Dare Imitate": *Sardanapalus* and "Effeminate Character"', *ELH* 58 (1991), 867–902.

WOOD, GERALD, 'The Metaphor of the Climates and *Don Juan*', *BJ* 6 (1978), 16–25.

WOODRING, CARL, *Politics in English Romantic Poetry* (Cambridge, Mass., 1970).

Index